THEMES AND EPISODES

Igor Stravinsky and Robert Craft

THEMES
AND
EPISODES

Alfred·A·Knopf: New York

1966

A portion of "Contingencies" originally appeared as "Speculations" in Show, *February 1964.*

"Three Sacred Choruses," "Jeu de Cartes," "Dumbarton Oaks Concerto," "Symphony in C," appeared as "Programme Notes" in The London Magazine, *February 1966.*

"Elegy for JFK" originally appeared as "Dialogue about JFK" in The New York Times, *December 6, 1964. © 1964 by The New York Times Company. Reprinted by permission.*

"Variations" and "Introitus" originally appeared in the Chicago Symphony Orchestra program book, April 17, 1965.

"Abraham and Isaac" originally appeared in The Festival of Israel program book, August 1964.

The following appear as program notes on Columbia Records: "Eight Miniatures," "Four Etudes for Orchestra," "Jeu de Cartes," "Dumbarton Oaks Concerto," "Symphony in C," "Orpheus," "Greeting Prelude," "The Rake's Progress" © 1964 by Columbia Records.

The first letter in "Letters to a Cousin in Moscow" appeared under the title "Stravinsky at Home" in Musical America, *January 1963.*

The first letter in "Concerning a Music Journalist in Los Angeles" originally appeared as a letter to the Los Angeles Times *on January 28, 1962.*

"Some Observations on V. D." originally appeared as a letter to the editor of Listen, *September–October 1964. © 1964 by The AGR Publishing Corp.*

"In the Name of Jean-Jacques!" originally appeared as "Music: A Dialogue" in Show, *April 1964.*

"A Talk With Stravinsky" originally appeared in The New York Review of Books, *May 27, 1965.*

"A Perfect Total" originally appeared in Seventeen, *August 1966.*

"A Decade Later" originally appeared as the preface to the book Anton von Webern: Perspectives *compiled by Hans Moldenhauer, edited by Demar Irvine, published 1966 by the University of Washington Press.*

"Some Table Talk of T. S. Eliot" originally appeared as "Memories of T. S. Eliot" in Esquire, *August 1965.*

"Schoenberg's Letters" originally appeared as "Schoenberg Speaks His Mind" in The Observer, *October 18, 1964.*

"On Conductors and Conducting" originally appeared in Show, *August 1964.*

The portion from Robert Craft's diaries on Aldous Huxley originally appeared as "Huxley and Stravinsky" in Encounter, *November 1965.*

The portion from the diaries on Warsaw originally appeared as "With Stravinsky in Warsaw" in Harper's Magazine, *February 1966.*

The portion from the diaries on Brazil originally appeared as "In Brazil" in Vogue, *October 1, 1964.*

THIS IS A BORZOI BOOK
PUBLISHED BY ALFRED A. KNOPF, INC.

FIRST EDITION

To

Eugene Berman

CONTENTS

PART I

Miscellanea

1 CONTINGENCIES   3
   (With Some Notes on "Twentieth-Century Mannerism")

   Words   3
   Current Enemies of Art   4
   Art and Money   4
   The Rising Cost of Art   4
   An Imperfect Science   5
   Education by Automation   6
   Talent and the Population Explosion   8
   Provincialism   9
   Form and Function   10
   New Music: Five Examples   11
   Conspiracy of Silence   17
   Longevity   19
   The New Terminology   20
   By Any Other Name?   21

Individuality   22
Change of Life   23
Eye Music   24
Envoi   25

2 PROGRAM NOTES   27
Pribaoutki   27
Symphonies of Wind Instruments   29
Eight Instrumental Miniatures   30
Three Sacred Choruses   31
Four Etudes for Orchestra   32
Jeu de Cartes   34
Dumbarton Oaks Concerto   39
Symphony in C   40
Danses concertantes   45
Orpheus   46
The Rake's Progress   48
The Rake's Progress: "La Prima Assoluta"   51
Greeting Prelude   54
Abraham and Isaac   55
Elegy for J.F.K.   56
Variations   60
Introitus: T. S. Eliot in Memoriam   62

3 LETTERS AND RIPOSTES (*Billets Doux*)   64
Letters to a Cousin in Moscow (*from Vera Stravinsky*)   64
Concerning a Music Journalist in Los Angeles   82
Concerning Edgard Varèse   87
Some Observations on V.D.   89

4 INTERVIEWS   *96*
   Transcript of BBC Television Interview   *96*
   In the Name of Jean-Jacques!   *97*
   A Talk with Stravinsky   *101*
   A Perfect Total   *108*
   A Decade Later   *115*

5 OBITUARY   *124*
   Some Table Talk of T. S. Eliot   *124*

6 BOOK REVIEWS   *132*
   Schoenberg's Letters   *132*
   Wagner's Prose   *138*

7 ON CONDUCTORS AND CONDUCTING   *145*

PART II

From the Diaries of Robert Craft, 1949–1966

1949   *159*
1950   *166*
1951   *169*
1952   *177*
1955   *182*
1956   *186*

1957   *195*

1958   *197*

1961   *200*

1962   *219*

1963   *232*

1964   *305*

1965   *313*

1966   *348*

INDEX I   following page   *352*

INDEX II: *Compositions by Stravinsky mentioned in the text*   *366*

PART I

Miscellanea

CONTINGENCIES

With Some Notes on
"Twentieth-Century Mannerism"

Words

I expect half of today's crop—an estimate from past averages—to embarrass me tomorrow, and I know that a far higher percentage will not survive my better judgment for as long as a month. Moreover, the relatively weatherable leftovers are certain to be concerned with what is of most negligible consequence. Worse still, following the bad-penny principle, the most obvious howlers—"Beethoven did not possess the gift of melody," "*Falstaff* is corrupted by Wagnerism"—are the most difficult to lose. Why bother, then?

Because the failures and embarrassments are nothing compared with the accident of truth (provisional and hypothetical as it will be) that could occur. Silence will save me from being wrong (and foolish), but it will also deprive me of the possibility of being right.

Current Enemies of Art

1o Improvisers. 2. "Indeterminists" (the quotation marks are necessary because waterproof parallels do not exist between the sciences dealing with sub-molecular magnitudes and the "free combination" scores of so-called indeterminist composers). What I demand of any author is that which he has finally determined. I ask him for his choice, his preference, not that of his intermediary or collaborator—who, incidentally, if he were a member of one of our symphony orchestras, would be limited in his improvisatory field to a hash of late last-century ideas. But, then, a post-composer period is already upon us, and concerts of sub-music and of musical blindman's buff are major tourist attractions.

Art and Money

The purchase of a Renoir at Sotheby's not long ago for $170,800 is to me an example of a flagrant lack of respect for money.

The Rising Cost of Art

At a recent concert featuring one of Bell Laboratory's IBM computers (an unusually buxom soloist), I learned that the instrument costs more than $100 an hour to rent and a

great deal more than that to operate. If I were to compose
even a small work with it, therefore, the technical overhead
might tally as high as a million dollars—though I could be
in error, I admit, as my own computer apparatus is now a
rusty eighty-four years old. The concert was also an inci-
dental demonstration, and a convincing one, that this new
means of communication has nothing as yet to communicate.

An Imperfect Science

An accident, in fact. Yet, before acoustics became a
major concern to science because of its importance to industry, Europe possessed many good concert halls. The greater
size of newer halls is often advanced as a reason for acoustical
disaster, and we have already been warned that in the new
and enlarged "Met" the singers will have to wear portable
microphones if they are to be heard by the denizens of the
crows' nests (who are also promised a view of the stage about
the size of Astrovision). But this argument is refuted, locally,
by Carnegie Hall, which is larger than that acoustical corpse,
Philharmonic Hall. The architect of the New York State
Theater, Mr. Philip Johnson, has claimed in its defense that
the acoustics should not be judged by the presentation of
plays. The theater (in which, incidentally, the loges look like
cowboys' diamond-studded belts) has "the perfect reverberation time for music, 1.7," he has said, "which is not fitted for
the human voice." But surely "music" includes the human
voice, and the concert repertory contains a body of works—
my *Persephone* is one—with spoken texts. And is the 1.7 the
resonating volume of the empty hall or of the hall with what
average loss by audience absorption? In either case it seems

to be, like most modern halls, about .2 or .3 too dry and too short.

Acoustics is not a very certain branch of architecture, it would seem, but an occupation of repairmen whose tools—in our day frequency filters, Helmholz resonators, electronic resonance supporters; in ancient Greece and Rome, the bronze resonating jars of the odeums (according to Vitruvius)— are used to *re-create* sound. Sometimes the re-creation is noticeable, sometimes not, but it is always good propaganda for the stay-home stereo-recording buff. For what my experience as a conductor is worth, the most satisfactory halls acoustically are the Gewandhaus, the Franz Liszt Hall in the Budapest Conservatory, the Teatro San Carlo in Naples, the Teatro Colón in Buenos Aires. All of them are wood-paneled and all are very, very "live"—more, I am sure, than 1.7.[1]

Education by Automation

*"Technology is the knack of so arranging the world
that we don't have to experience it."*—MAX FRISCH.

The wisdom of the world on tape (the knowledge explosion), complete with dial systems and portable units (the Cornberg carrel), and pocket computers with plugs in the

---

[1] I have lately been introduced to Dr. C. A. Volf of Copenhagen and his Reflex Theory of acoustic therapy by which he claims ability to detect cancer and schizophrenia. According to Dr. Volf, sound waves directed to various nodules of the body with a vibrating C–128 tuning fork will travel immediately to a cancerous area; and in the case of schizophrenia they will not travel at all but leave the body directly through the fingers and toes. Dr. Volf has dispatched the *1812* Overture through my bones on his resonator, but with what therapeutic effect I cannot say; and you will probably not be able to discover in a similar experiment on yourself, for the instrument has been banned not only by the AMA, but also by the A. F. of M.

universal computer grid: these, for me, are the latest visions of Purgatory. (So is the recurrent dream in which a berserk clerk punches new holes in my magazine subscription card,[2] thus causing the automaton to send me *Die Reihe* instead of *Mad*.) Easier access to more information is not the point, and no matter that the information may be the best that has been thought and said. Education, in its earlier stages at any rate, is a trial-and-error process supervised by beings, preferably humanid,[3] more experienced and instructed than oneself. As one grows older, other stages of one's own changing self are substituted for the supervisor. Speaking from my own experience, I know that I have learned throughout my life as a composer chiefly through my mistakes and pursuits of false assumptions, not by my exposures to founts of wisdom and knowledge. In the matter of learning artistic skills, I am, moreover, a pious Aristotelian: imitation is the beginning of art. For illustration I recommend a visit to one of Balanchine's dance classes. There the learning processes are scenes from "natural history"; Balanchine is like a mother bird with a flock of baby (girl) birds flapping their wings behind him.

The revolution in research techniques effected by automation is another matter, of course, and the value of computers to all "serious scholars" (as they like to call themselves, implying that large numbers of extremely frivolous scholars are flitting about) is obvious. These more versatile adding machines are clearly the salvation of Ph.D. candidates, most of whose theses are mere counting exercises to begin with ("The Use of the Penis through the Ages," for example, and "How to Tell the Difference between Englishmen and Homosexuals") and footnotes listing agreements or disagreements with

[2] In Ottawa recently a government computer went haywire as a result of being fed confusing data, and sent one and a half million dollars in bonuses to students in Quebec Province.

[3] Though in other fields—think of some of the hands now within reach of the hot wire—I definitely prefer the "passionless" machine.

earlier statisticians. Consider the field of philology, where
researchers in textual analyses have calculated that a single
day with a computer can be the equivalent of a year's manual
labor. Progress has been claimed not only in computation,
however, but also in a so-called Parametric Artificial Talking
device, or speech "synthesizer" said to be "a resonance ana-
logue of human speech organs"; and we are also promised
mechanical translation soon, by conversion of "input" and
"output" languages to "correlational structures of thought."
But stylistic analysis by computer, as exemplified in the so-
called concordances of poets, is to me one of the most depressing results of the machine. To be informed as the result of
its work that Shakespeare averaged 61 "ands" every two
thousand words as against Bacon's average of 80 is no test of
Shakespeare or Bacon. Which Shakespeare? Were *Titus* and
Lear counted together? Is there no differential between
Shakespeare's poetry and Bacon's prose?

Talent and the Population Explosion

"O Divine Average"—WHITMAN

Creative talent certainly seems to be spreading thinner,
in any case, if only to support the hypothesis that diffusion is
necessarily followed by corresponding loss of density. And
creation itself hardly seems to exist—when put by the side
of explanation—which is why census estimates of fifth-century
Athens, fifteenth-century Florence, or the other fallen towers,
seem so disparately small compared to the concentrations of
creative talent. More recent and reliable figures for, say,
Bach's Weimar, a hamlet of a few hundred souls, point to
the same conclusion; and whatever its population, was the

London of 1600 very much larger than a modern township in the matter of literacy? That London could boast a hundred poets, though, and two or three immortal ones, whereas the present megalopolis includes not a single poet of comparable stature but only several thousand reviewers. And the Art Centers? Are they not merely the newest expression of quantitative ideals? I have no answers, of course, but I will not endorse the now popular formula that the larger the Art Center, the smaller the creative art. After all, the appearance of even one new creative talent of some size—and in music we are all over-ready for him, or, more likely, her—could disprove it.

Provincialism

Sir Kenneth Clark's new lecture under this title is addressed primarily to connoisseurs of English painting, but the generalities of his discussion are equally relevant to music. The history of European art, he says, is "the history of a series of centers from each of which radiated a style." Provincialism is at first "simply a matter of distance from a center, where standards of skill are higher and patrons more exacting."[4] The art of the center fails, Sir Kenneth says, because of overrefinements of style, whereas the failure of provincial art is its lack of style. He goes on to observe that the provincial artist will attack the metropolitan style when he considers its sophistication and elaboration moribund, or when he thinks "human

---

[4] *Cf.* the argument in Harold Rosenberg's *The Anxious Object*, that "only in the creative centers, if there were any, does the artist have a chance to get away from the ideas of the center. In the provinces he is swamped by the latest."

values" have been neglected for "formal" ones. The rebellion of the provincial is therefore launched in the name of "individual judgment," "common sense," "wholesomeness," or "truth to nature." And it also follows that the ingenue genius from the perimeter is as suspicious of the foreign as he is complacent about the local. Sir Kenneth regards this complacency as provincialism's "worst and commonest feature" (with which I dissent only in order to reserve the distinction for provincial rhetoric, Livy's patavinity).

Transposing the categories to the contemporary musical scene, we find on the one hand *Baby Doe, The Passion of Jonathan Wade, Amelia Goes to the Ball;* and on the other, Darmstadt, with its undoubtedly "higher metropolitan standards of skill" (including, one assumes, professional codebreakers). The rejection of each by the other is complete and justified, but it is time to say *au revoir* to Wahoo.

Form and Function

"Form as an aim is formalism."—MIES VAN DER ROHE

Building means finding a shape for the processes of our life—or so Gropius has said, and I recalled the remark years ago in Boston during a visit to his home, which, like himself, was spare, attractive, quiet, not very cozy. But observe the absence of esthetic considerations (*cf.* Brancusi's "architecture is inhabited sculpture"), and of ideals other than that of the definition itself; and of the way the problem of symbolisms is ignored, though the "processes of our life" still seem to require banks and insurance companies to look solidly rectangular, and the corporate image as a whole to appear reassuringly physiological—consider, for example, the trend to breast-fixation (Fuller's "Geodesic" domes) and intestinal (the Guggenheim Museum)[5] styles. But how does this purely functional approach compare with the approach of the composer? I must begin by confessing a prejudice. Pure functionalism has always seemed to me a Protestant conception, and for this reason it is foreign to my natural cultural soil. Even apart from that, though, and insofar as exteriors and interiors can be compared, my case is the other way around. I build with what the architect seeks to avoid. My processes are determined by esthetic accidents—though accidents are not accidents, of course, until we recognize and designate them as such, giving the word to those we catch, not to those which escape, so that in this sense our accidents are also determined.[6]

New Music: Five Examples

I

Stockhausen's *Carrée* has never failed to interest me when I have followed it with the score, but the same music seems to me dull and timeless in the wrong sense when, instead of watching, I merely listen. This is equally true of the same composer's ideogram percussion scores. My interest in them is sustained primarily by the novelties of the notation, which

[5] It is the viewer who is digested through this *art nouveau* crumpet, rather than the paintings in the viewer, unless, of course, his legs happen to be of unequal length. I am not so constructed, however, and I am too frightened to use a wheel chair. The gradient appears to be gentle, but it has been estimated that a wheel chair which had been lost control of on the highest level would be traveling 125 miles per hour at the bottom.

[6] Which reminds me of Theodor Lessing's description of history as putting accidents in order—*Die Geschichte als Sinngebung des Sinnlosen*, history as sense-giving to the senseless (or to the amorphous).

is not the composer's intention, I think, as it is with the so-called graphic composers whose scores claim to be and—some of them look so like Rorschach tests—must be designed for the eye only. I admire *Carrée*, nevertheless, though it will no doubt be discovered that my admiration extends only to superficialities.

First of all, Stockhausen's orchestral uses are attractive; and the non-uses, too, the absence of those exoticisms (except for the *accelerando-ritardando* Kabuki drums at [39]) that drench-perfume so much of the music of this mid-far-out school. I am especially fond of the *glissandi* at [67]; and of the role of the piano, both solo and in combination; and I am even more attracted by the variety and range of choral uses; the whispering and muttering (a whole winter of discontent at one place), the distortion—by electronic means—of these and other effects, and the stereophonic distancing by which one hears voices somewhat in the manner, I imagine, of Joan of Arc or William Blake.

When I first met Stockhausen, at a rehearsal of his *Gruppen* now almost a decade ago, he introduced himself with: "Please tell me what you *don't* like." Very well. *Carrée* depends too heavily on pedal points, or whatever one is to call the D at [69X], the C at [80] (though the instrumental combination is very good here), the E-flat at the beginning and at [76] (which, for a bad moment, makes one think that a recording of *Das Rheingold* may have been put on by mistake), and the open fifth at [74], a drone bass which lasts so long that a latecomer entering the hall at this point could suspect a last-minute change of program in favor of a modish orchestration of Perotin. Stockhausen is most interesting when he is busiest (as in the section after [82X]). A comparison of *Carrée* with the older *Gruppen* puts the newer work a good length ahead, I think, though it also underlines some now characteristic lapses—at [63X], for instance, the 2/4 march with all four orchestras synchronized to a 120 Sousa beat. *Carrée* shares another fault with nearly all of its kind of music, the monotony of the too-regular run from dense to simple, from movement to stasis, from loud to soft, from high to low, from *tutti* to *solo;* and the equally regular return trips. Berg is the father of these ideas, though he used them only as building elements in his very personal forms; and, of course, Berg was too great an artist to show his hand. But enough of what I don't like. There is, in *Carrée*, much more of what I do.

2

The tide of applause virtually packaged along with the *War Requiem* is so loud and the Battle-of-Britten sentiment is so thick that these phenomena, and the national inferiority feelings in music they expose, are at least as absorbing a subject of investigation as the music. Behold the critics as they vie in abasement before the wonder of native-born genius. (Not all the critics, though, for one of the great Chams of the weeklies —sufficient unto the Sunday edition should be the music column thereof—proclaimed himself too moved even to take his nib in hand.) Here is *The Times*, in actual, Churchillian quotes: "Few recordings can ever have been awaited so eagerly and by so many people as that of Benjamin Britten's *War Requiem*" . . . and ". . . practically everyone who has heard it has instantly acknowledged it as a masterpiece . . ." Farther along, after a stirring description of the "grief-laden unison melody of the opening" and of the "doom-laden funeral march," *The Times* declares that "the grandeur and intensity of [Mme. V.'s] phrasing exorcise all conventional notions of angelic insipidness," which means, I take it, that unconventional notions have the field. (In fact, Mme. V.'s singing is often harsh and badly out of tune.) G. B. Shaw— though I should clear the air before mentioning him in such a context—was greatly mistaken in his day about one Herman

Goetz. "Schubert, Mendelssohn, and Goetz," he wrote, and many readers must have taken the last name as a misprint for "Goethe," until they went on to learn that the Symphony in F Major and *The Taming of the Shrew* overture are "masterpieces which place Goetz above all other German composers of the last hundred years save only Mozart and Beethoven." The claim sounds odd nowadays. I wonder how some of the eulogies. . . .

Kleenex at the ready, then, and feeling as though one had failed to stand up for "God Save the Queen," one goes from the critics to the music, to find: (a) a Honegger-type cinemascope epic in an idiom derived in part from Boulanger-period Stravinsky (the "shifting" major-minor thirds at [96], the "shifting" accents of the 9/8 rhythm in the "Offertorium"); (b) patterns rather than inventions (the timpani figure at [49], for example, is a good invention but a poor pattern); (c) one very effective dramatic idea, that of casting the chorus in Latin and the male soloists in English; (d) an absence of real counterpoint; (e) a bounteous presence of literalisms ("The drums of Time," sings the baritone, and "boom, boom, boom" go the obedient timpani); of cinema music (the fanfares before [111], and the strings-and-drum music at [95]; and of organ-point (the sedative in C at [74]).

So, in short, and in spite of "practically everyone," the composer laureate's certified masterpiece has turned out, for this well-disposed listener, at least, to be rather a soft bomb. An "overwhelming success," the panegyrists continue to say; but then, nothing fails like success.

3

Messiaen's *Turangalila* is another example of *plus d'embarras que de richesses*. But perhaps I should confess my disqualifications as a judge: I am not an ornithologist; I do not know the supposedly better later music of this composer and hence cannot see the direction of the earlier; and I am hampered by a strong barrier of taste against what so often seems to me a mixture of gamelans and Lehár. Like the *War Requiem*, it contains passages of superior film music ("Charlie Chan in Indochina") as well as traces of yesteryears of oneself (some counterfeit *"Petrushka"* at [9] and [17], and in measures 6–9 of the piano cadenza beginning at [11], to choose unornamented examples; I am flattered by this attention, of course, but I would prefer to receive royalties). A fundamental and more regrettable similarity is in the attempt to stretch small and inelastic patterns into large ones. At first contact the quality of Messiaen's ideas, especially rhythmic, is more arresting, but attention rapidly dissipates in the crude routine of the continuing procedure: repetition *con crescendo*, with an ever-wider spread of octaves, though there is already a plague of octaves throughout. These attentuating episodes expose a naïveté that the first statements often successfully conceal; or perhaps I should say that the initiating measures contain false promise of a comparatively high degree of sophistication. What *Turangalila* needed, however, was a very cold *douche* of the most intensive self-consciousness. It is not easy to imagine anything more inane than the *"Joie du Sang des Étoiles,"* with its stage directions to the conductor, *"dans un délire de passion";* or to imagine a more vapid melody than the one for *ondes Martenot* (which instrument invades me as unpleasantly as a colonic irrigation) in the *"Chant d'Amour II,"* compared with which Godard's *Berceuse* is noble. Little more can be needed to write such things than a large supply of ink.

4

And what is a masterpiece? I can only answer by example. Ives's *Decoration Day* is a very small example. Why is it? Not because of genuineness of feeling—innumerable nonmasterpieces have been genuinely felt—or even because it is feeling of a high order (*ditto*); and also not because its range of rhythmic and harmonic imagination (the harmony at [D], for instance) outstrips other contemporaries (to "outstrip" is nothing in itself, and Ives's "anticipations" have been given too much importance and the sooner we get over that and the romanticizing-of-the-life phase the better; what, then, of Alkan's anticipations of Ives?—those piano pieces in two simultaneous tempi and those rhythmic groups of thirteen, fourteen, and fifteen in the time of twelve, all dating back to the 1850's!); and not even because it eschews hand-me-down devices and replaces them with such astonishing originalities as the chord with trombones and bassoons two measures before [C]; the dissonant clarinet notes at [H] and at three measures before [H]; the string shimmy before [I] and the two-flute obligato at [I] and at the end of the eleventh measure of [I]; the trombones five measures before [M] (the town sports razzing it up); the settings of "Nearer, my God, to Thee," *Taps, Adeste Fidelis,* and the Second Regiment March (though let it be admitted that tune-detection is a dull sport); and the surprise ending (albeit a surprise well prepared for by, among other means, a "shadow violin," as Ives calls the marginal fiddle playing in major sevenths with the others), which is the loneliest and one of the most touching I know of.

But I have come far enough to see that I cannot answer my question. I only know that *Decoration Day* is a masterpiece, one of Ives's greatest.[7]

5

Boulez's *Éclat* for piano and chamber ensemble is another small masterpiece, and one which introduces a new technique

[7] For I am a discriminating admirer; so far as I am concerned *The Unanswered Question* can also be the unplayed; and I am doubtful of the universal appeal even of this *Decoration Day;* I mean, that these American holiday parade tunes will have much effect on Bulgarians.

of time control. The score does not list the conductor's part along with those for the other performers, yet it is composed just as any of the instrumental parts are composed, and is, in fact, the most interesting part of all, so much so that for the moment one fails to see any conductor being able to perform it half so well as Maître Boulez himself. Indeed, to watch him conduct it, as I did recently, is an experience inseparable from the music itself. What a sense of timing he has! The score contains only verbal directions for tempo (*"tres vif," "plus modéré," "très longtemps,"* etc.) and is therefore at the opposite pole to mechanically geared pieces such as my *Variations*. Every event is controlled by cue, ordinal in most cases, but aleatoric in others. The aleatoric idea is not new—each player stands by cocked and ready to play his group of notes, his turn determined by the flick of Maître Boulez's fingers —but the effect is attractive. I do not wish to overlook the sonorous beauties of the work—like all of Boulez's music the sound is very femininely subtle—but I consider the greater achievement to be in the domain of time control. *Éclat* is not only creative music, but creative conducting as well, which is unique.

Conspiracy of Silence

Or, "Heard melodies are sweet, but those unheard are sweeter"

"Why is there anything at all rather than nothing?"—HEIDEGGER

Weh and *miserere*! Old-style festivals of modern music are doomed; and only now do we realize our debt, which is that thanks to them fashionable noises became unfashionable more quickly, that "in the swim" tricks were sooner dried out, and that mere decorators of in-vogue ideas were more rapidly unmasked (which is an important service to an old man who does not believe in movements but only in talented individuals—not in "Cubism" but in Picasso and Braque and Gris). Remember the programs of *das neue Werk* and the others, back in the fifties, with all those enticing events listed in Bauhaus print—sober sans serifs, no caps, and the letters tumbling about the page *à la* Mallarmé? Remember the always promising bouquets by Anis Fuleihan and Fartein Valen (mysteriously described as "traditional composers")? And the Mittel-Europa serial shriners and 12-tone fundamentalists? And the microtonalist sects? And old Bo Nilsson, who seemed to have been born at a later date each year and to have come from an ice floe farther north? And each year's crop of new Japanese and Polish geniuses with half-minute pieces for several hundred percussion instruments and featuring the fallopian tubes? And Karlheinz and Luciano, steam-rolling old masters in full boom then, tycoons of the lecture circuit and mainstay BMI classics now? And the mathematical hocus-pocus of the compositions written principally for analysis in *Die Reihe*? And the noble, never-ending Soviet symphonies in 4/4 time dedicated to female cosmonauts? And the English? Let us not forget the tingling anticipation of another *Umbrage for Eleven Instruments* by Humphrey Searle, or the welling up of keen emotion at the thought of a new *Pandemonium X* by Cornelius Cardew. And remember the coteries with their slogans, platforms, proclamations?—"Henze is the Fortner of the fifties," "Stockhausen for Wirtschaft Minister of Electricity," etc. And the props, like Stuckenschmidt? Sad, one is, to see it all pass.

Because the sixties are the Aleatoric Age. And the nature of aleatoric amusements allows for the possibility that selected parts[8] or even all of them will not be performed. Add to this

---

[8] To ensure that each performance is different, which solves the impresario's problem of how to have a world premiere every time.

the fact that in these do-it-yourself days very few composers actually bother to write their music out, or, for that matter, to compose it,[9] which may be what Walter Lippmann means by "masterly inactivity." And now that Mr. Cage's most successful opus is undoubtedly the delectable silent piece *4′33″*, we may expect his example to be followed by more and more silent pieces by younger composers who, in rapid escalation, will produce their silences with more and more varied and beguiling combinations. (I myself can hardly wait to hear Thorkell Sigurdjörnsson's silent *Fluctuations*, or Señor Kagel's toneless *Evaporations* and imaginary *Oblongs*, or Mr. Ligeti's unwritten orchestral *Happenings*, and I only hope they turn out to be works of major length.) Soon, though, we will settle down in an academicism of silence, with silent concerts and silent ISCM festivals as well. Oh, sad, I say, sad.[1]

Longevity

Experiments at Ann Arbor indicate that rat life-expectancy increases with a diet of ecstasy.[2] Raffish rats live as long as eight years, the tests show, while puritan rats, on love-free and otherwise grubby diets, succumb at five. The auto-

[9] A celebrated recent example of non-composed music is the imposture called *Arco* (in fact, a single *pizzicato* note), which after its Palermitan première provoked a battle of critics half of whom rated it an exiguous effort and half a squandering of talents.

[1] A suggestion for the next phase after this laissez-faire school, and after the playlet composers, the Op maniacs, the beats, the "sick," the hoked-up, and the quietist schools: a helium atmosphere can extend the range of human and other voices by more than an octave. Soon, via the Collins Helium Cryostat, we shall have *Herzgewächse* yet an octave higher.

[2] See Vitus Dröscher's *Mysterious Senses*, a study of competitiveness in rat society. No rat can relax.

biographical parallel is tempting, but though "love" is said to be a good metabolizer, and though bacchanals have been recommended for the circulatory system, for me to say whether my fourscore and four years have been sustained in any measure by a steady devotion to both, or whether I am still here in despite of that, would be only a lay opinion—and a "philosophy of life." The facts are the rats'.[3]

The New Terminology

I do not doubt that the computer prose (written by computers for computers) of present musical analysis contains a necessary set of tools for the exploration of new music. I merely regret that a graybeard like myself is left so many leagues behind, in a vocabulary composed entirely of hang-over expressions from earlier traditions, expressions which now

[3] See, however, Wynne-Edwards's *Animal Dispersion in Relation to Social Behaviour*, with its theory of the "glossy rat" (chap. 21). According to Professor Wynne-Edwards, the three classes of males in rodent social organization can be described as, first, the "large, glossy-furred, unscarred individuals who roam with impunity all over the enclosure"; second, the slightly smaller individuals with tattered fur and a tendency to slouch; third, the small, emaciated, unaggressive, lackluster individuals. All status resides with the glossy rats, of course, and these company-president types get all of the girls, so that the recessive rats, the beatnik and the neurotic, the deviate and the solitary diner, do not even breed. (A principal argument of the book, dealing with what might be called rat Malthusianism, is that the animals have a built-in social instinct by which they control their own population, and that human animals have lost this instinct.) Not all people can be compared with rats, of course, and Professor Wynne-Edwards does not indulge in facile parallels, but the reader can hardly resist doing just that. "Now let's see," he thinks, "who are the musical melanochroi, the masters of podium realpolitik, the slick-back rats of the concert hall?" Everyone will have his own answer to that, to be sure, but we can all agree in identifying the small, tattered rats. They are the contemporary composer.

require quotation marks and other qualifiers such as "so-called" (so-called "melody," so-called "electronic music," etc.) as warning flags for word-inflation. I had no idea what the "ontological structure" boys were talking about in the music journals of the thirties, and I do not see why the young Turks of today fancy such neologisms as "dyads" (the genitalia?—i.e., gonads?), "simultaneities" (yclept "chords" in days of yore; imagine asking an orchestra to "play that final simultaneity a little more simultaneously"), and "pitch priorities" ("and now you will hear the 'Beethoven in D-priority' ").

By Any Other Name?

In Russian "Stravinsky" is an adjectival, not a nominative form; I am not Stravinsk[4] but Stravinsk-y(an). I have wondered about the consequences of this fact in my music, which is often characterized as adjectival in the sense of belonging to a descriptive mode (Stravinsky, the adjective, transubstantiating Pergolesi, Tchaikovsky, Bach). In any case I believe that language questions of this sort are involved in our most active roots of culture (as, for example, in Sommerfelt's celebrated example that China could not have developed an Aristotelian logic because Chinese lacks the constraining subject-predicate proposition). I suggest, also, that a proper (computer) study of myself would include a differential analysis, with English and French, of the operations of my Russian thought-language, which lacks such items as the pluperfect

---

[4] I once told a reviewer who asked what had become of the final "y" in *Agon*, that it was silent like the "y" in Stravinsk.

tense, the definite article, and the Latin copula (we say "I happy," not "I am happy"). Such a study is at least as important as the catalogue of physical and psycho-physical statistics[5] (blood group, cortisone curve, etc.).

Individuality

Some biologists say that the organism at its formation "is not equipped with a unique label of individuality,"[6] and some philosophers have proclaimed the doctrine of separate individuals to be a myth. An end to one's mystical beliefs in one's "self," then, and an end to "inexplicable." The "I," in the tenements of my brain, is a chemico-electrical system, a homeostat of nerve cells,[7] and a change in my chemistry, in the ribonucleic acid content of my "memory molecules" (a fascinating idea, that the experience of the eye is encoded in the structure of molecules!), can alter my "thought." But whether the fact that my chemical system is producing more blood now than a decade ago, whether this affects my "cerebration" I am unqualified to say, and though I think that my music is more sanguine now, "sanguine" is only a metaphor. Oh arrogant Abraham, would you be so certain today of

---

[5] When psycho-physiological measurement becomes a part of the future state's Vocational Guidance for Economy Program, only very lean ectomorphs will be allowed to perform my music. May these Kretschmer-type ideas go no farther, however. One already foresees a time when sociopsychogeneticists will be determining such questions as the most suitable environments for all vocational pursuits (so that the biochemistry of sperm will be studied in Las Vegas, for instance).

[6] But, see P. B. Medawar's *The Uniqueness of the Individual*. London, 1957.

[7] See J. Z. Young's *A Model of the Brain*. Oxford, 1964.

your "I am I" (or as Shakespeare put it, "Richard loves
Richard"), and if you were, how would you know that
you knew?

Change of Life

I have had to survive two crises as a composer, though as I
continued to move from work to work I was not aware of
either of them as such, or, indeed, of any momentous change.
The first—the loss of Russia and its language of words as well
as of music—affected every circumstance of my personal no
less than my artistic life, which made recovery more difficult.
Only after a decade of samplings, experiments, amalgamations
did I find the path to *Oedipus Rex* and the *Symphony of
Psalms*. Crisis number two was brought on by the natural
outgrowing of the special incubator in which I wrote *The
Rake's Progress* (which is why I did not use Auden's beautiful
Delia libretto; I could not continue in the same strain, could
not compose a sequel to *The Rake*, as I would have had to
do). The period of adjustment was only half as long this time,
but as I look back on it I am surprised at how long I continued
to straddle my "styles." Was it because one has to unlearn as
well as to learn, and at seventy the unlearning is more difficult? However that may be, the slow climb through the
1950's eventually brought me to the *Movements*, which I now
see as the cornerstone of my later work. And the future? I
know only that in the *coronat opus* of my later years, the
Princeton Requiem (I say that now because I am working
on it), I continue to believe in my taste buds and to follow
the logic of my ear, quaint expressions which will seem even

quainter when I add that I require as much hearing at the
piano as ever before; and this, I am certain, is not because of
age, is not a sign of dotage.[8] I know, too, that I will never
cross the gulf from well-tempered pitches to "sounds" and
"noises," and will never abdicate the rule of my ears. But pre-
dictions are dangerous. *Basta!*

Eye Music

To see Balanchine's choreography of the *Movements* is to
hear the music with one's eyes; and this visual hearing has
been a greater revelation to me, I think, than to anyone else.
The choreography emphasizes relationships of which I had
hardly been aware—in the same way—and the performance
was like a tour of a building for which I had drawn the plans
but never explored the result. Balanchine approached the music
by identifying some of the more familiar marks of my style,
and as I heard him fastening on my tiniest repeated rhythm or
sustaining group, I knew he had joined the work to the corpus
of my music, at the same time probably reducing the time lag
of its general acceptability by as much as a decade. I owe
him even more for another aspect of the revelation: his discovery of the music's essential lyricism. I gather that his dra-

---

[8] Pitch and interval relationships are for me the primary dimension,
whereas for such younger colleagues as the Stockhausen followers (call
them the *eau de Cologne*) the pitches may be less important than the shape
of the room or the direction of the sound. I understand this switch of
emphasis, however; after all, a new composer must win his spurs in new
territory. What I cannot understand is the mind which chooses to leave the
completion of its work to the megrims of performers; that and the manic-
depressive fluctuations of a fashion that swings from total control to no
control, from the serialization of all elements to chance.

matic point is a love parable—in which ballet is it not?—but the coda had a suggestion of myth that reminded me of the ending of *Apollo*.

The ballet, which might also have been called *Electric Currents*, is a double concerto for male and female solo dancers, both identified with the piano solo. The choric group is spare —none of Balanchine's usual attendant caryatids this time but only a hexachord of those beelike little girls (big thighs, nipped-in waists, pin-heads) who seem to be bred to the eminent choreographer's specifications. The full dancing sextet is identified as a unit only in the Interludes,[9] an idea which projects the shape of the entire piece with great clarity.

I should add that I have heard Balanchine's choreography only once, and then at a rehearsal. (At that time I found a Japanese-type head movement, presumably a holdover from *Bugaku*, too obtrusive, but perhaps it has disappeared by now.) At one point Balanchine asked the dancers to repeat a section without the music, and to my amazement they were able to count it by themselves, which is rather better than many orchestras. But are the *Movements* ballet music? Barbarous locution to a Balanchine! What he needs is not a *pas de deux* but a motor impulse.

Envoi

And what do they come to, these half-formed or truncated thoughts from the mental wastebasket—aside from showing that away from my work table I am, intellectually

---

[9] Which are introductions rather than codas; the conductor should pause *before* them. I like these caesuras, incidentally, and I want the seams and sutures in my music to show.

speaking, a low-category consumer statistic? Do they show that if "youth" is a pretext for a great deal of rubbish, so is age (and as we are living in the Age of Old Age we will have to struggle with the point of view of the very old)? And do they show, for example, that because of my inability to adjust my mental habits to probability as a property of the mental world (never having learned Newtonian calculus), I have become a self-righteous old man behaving like a dog in the manger about the future? The computer would undoubtedly answer: "insignificant variables." And what are the *in*variables? A talent with natural traction mated to a mind with too little conception; a mind divided in the attempt to hold up the shattered wall of religious beliefs on the one hand and the scientific analysis wall on the other; and a mind now complicated by the tendency (an old man's defense) to fall into solipsism—not "fall," though, for if that is where I am I have been brought there under force (frog-marched, in fact). I am sure of but one thing: that I am able to tend only the very few sprouts that grow in my own garden—which, by the way, I must go and water.

PROGRAM NOTES

Pribaoutki

After *The Nightingale*, my sketchbooks began to fill with melodic-rhythmic and chordal ideas, any one of which might have become part of *Renard*, *Les Noces*, or even *Histoire du soldat*, almost equally well;[1] or so it would appear at a glance, though a composer soon separates his materials or, rather, fits them together when he begins to work. The profusion was so great in the summer and fall of 1914 that a considerable number of sketches were left over from this time and finally never fashioned at all; this little tune, for instance, which also illustrates my point of the commonality with any of four or five works:

[1] I still possess seven pages of an early version of *Les Noces* scored for 3 violins, 2 violas, 2 cellos, 1 bass, cymbalom, 1 clarinet, 2 flutes, oboe and English horn, 2 bassoons, 2 horns, timpani: in other words, approximately the orchestra of *Renard*.

I had hardly begun *Renard*, with the notations for the cello accompaniment to the cock's aria, and the figure

when I set it aside to compose the *Pribaoutki*. As I have stated elsewhere, I wished to explore certain functions of words in music, and my *Pribaoutki* notebooks are full of texts from Afanasiev (especially from Vol. III of his collected work, beginning at page 548), which I have covered with my prosody marks.

One of the *Pribaoutki* melody fragments, the second part of the first song

(*sic*, in that octave) came to me in London in July 1914 (before *Renard*!); next to it in my sketchbook are three variant notations of the bells of St. Paul, all, in my irregular barring, looking remarkably "Russian." I note that the "*Colonel*" was finished on August 29, but that the last two measures were different in the original writing:

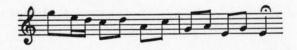

The last song gave me the most trouble. The original manuscript score of it was a half step lower in pitch, and what is now the bassoon solo, in the middle section, was a clarinet solo at first, in a higher octave. This is also the only song of the group I have ever tampered with again; I rewrote a rhythmic figure in it as recently as October 1964. Many listeners profess to hear my Russian "homesickness" in this music, incidentally. Not being a musical pathologist I cannot identify feelings of that sort for certainty, but I do know that during the composition, which was at the beginning of the "great" war, they were in me. If the *Pribaoutki* are sung by a woman, incidentally, the voice must be very strong—like the tomcat I require in *Berceuses du chat*.

Symphonies of Wind Instruments

The chorale which concludes the *Symphonies* was composed June 20, 1920, in Carantec, a fishing village in Finistère; I had rented a cottage there for the summer, but had to have a piano carted in from a neighboring town. The complete work was composed by July 2, though I returned to it a few days later to add the two adumbrative bits of chorale in the body of the piece. My sketch score contains few indications of instrumentation, but that is because I was certain of the sound and knew I would remember its components; I had merely to copy my sketch score into full-score form. One curiosity in the sketch score, incidentally, is the absence of metrical lines in many places (as in my *Piano Rag Music* and solo clarinet pieces). Another is in the strikingly different phrasing from either of the published scores (1921 and 1947) though the latter are also so different from each other (*cf.* the horns and trumpets at the return of the first motive after the first flute-clarinet duet) that I suppose both versions will continue to be played as two different pieces; or, as at present, not to be played.

Eight Instrumental Miniatures

The originals of the *Miniatures*, the *Cinq Doigts*—or, to borrow a better title from T. S. Eliot, the "Five-Finger Exercises"—were composed in 1920–21 in Garches, near Versailles, in the house of Mme Gabrielle Chanel. (Mme Chanel was one of my closest friends during this period, and she was also one of Diaghilev's most generous supporters, for which reason balletomanes should always hold her name in the best odor.) Unlike the *Easy Pieces* for piano duet, these studies were intended not for my children but for any piano debutant. My idea was to confine each finger of the right hand to a single note and thus to limit myself to a five-note row (an idea repeated in the *Gigue* in my *Septet*). I orchestrated the pieces a few years ago, one by one for different occasions, at the suggestion of Robert Craft. The *Tango*, which I call the "*Tijuana Blues*," was performed, though with an alternate (a wind-octet) instrumentation, at a concert in Mexico City, in December 1961; the first four were transcribed with the frail budget of the Monday Evening Concerts of Los Angeles in mind, and the other three for the more affluent Canadian Broadcasting Company in Toronto. The instrumental versions are dedicated to Lawrence Morton, the rugged Minnesota musicologist and formidable music director of the above-mentioned Monday concerts, which have been generally from five to ten years in advance of any similar New York group in the presentation of "new" music, and which are unique in the United States in the high standards of selecting "old" music.

Three Sacred Choruses

My *Pater Noster, Credo,* and *Ave Maria* were inspired in antipathy, I might almost say, to the bad music and worse singing in the Russian Church in Nice. I became a communicant there in 1925, about a year before the composition of the *Pater Noster,* and the sentimental expression and harmonic and melodic banalities of the musical services eventually provoked me into composing something of my own. I knew nothing of the traditions of Russian Church music at that time (or now), but instinctively I sought older roots than Bortniansky, our classic composer in the genre, who, after his long stay with Galuppi in Venice had been wholly converted to the Italian style. But what *was* the true Russian manner, and do my choruses recapture anything of it? I can only say that my pieces probably fuse early memories of church music in Kiev and Poltava with the conscious aim to adhere to a simple and severe harmonic style, a "classical" style but with pre-classical cadences. I should add that apparently all traditions of Russian church singing are decrepit nowadays, for which reason I rewrote the *Credo* in June 1964, spelling out the rhythm of the *faux bourdon.*

The *Credo* and *Pater Noster* were intended for actual use in the Russian liturgy. The *Ave Maria* occurs in several services, too, and it is characteristically repeated three times. I no longer recall when I first heard a performance of it, but I do remember hearing the *Pater Noster* sung by the Afonsky Choir in the Alexander Nevsky Church in Paris, during the Requiem service (forty days after death, according to Russian custom) for my sister-in-law Ludmilla Beliankin in 1937.

One day I shall compile my memories of this church in the

rue Daru. Built in the time and style of Alexander II, it was an island of Russian color in the drab Parisian quarter; and not one island only, but a whole archipelago of Russian shops, bookstores, restaurants, cafés, *bijouteries*, *antiquaires*. During feast days the hubbub and the *décors* were like an oriental fair. I remember, as no doubt so do the elders of the Russian colony, the wedding of an American heiress and a disinherited Russian prince (Miss Hutton and Mr. Mdivani), for which event the sidewalks of the neighborhood were strewn with flowers. When I first went to Paris the church and the cafés and restaurants of the neighborhood were the foci of social life for all Russians in Paris, believers and nonbelievers. Then, in the mid-thirties many of the habitués decided to recognize the Metropolitan in Moscow instead of his opposite number abroad. After this fissure, dissenting churches sprouted up all over Paris, some of them portable and pocket-sized, housed in apartments or studios. One of these, in the rue d'Odessa, was located over a nightclub, and I remember when money had to be raised to buy a half hour of quiet during the Saturday night Easter service and until midnight when, as soon as the priest had cried *"Christos Voskreseh,"* business resumed below with a bam, boom, and crash. At this time the Nevsky Church, to which I remained an adherent, became the center of the anti-Soviet church-in-exile. Its place in my life in the nineteen-thirties was very important.

Four Etudes for Orchestra

Though the *Four Etudes* were not performed until 1930, the orchestrations of the first three of them date back to 1917. The fourth piece, originally the *Etude for Pianola* (1917), was orchestrated in 1928 or 1929, at which time I gave it the name *Madrid* and added titles to the other pieces as well. The first is a *Danse* for the woodwinds. They repeat a four-note chant over and over—"The *Four* Fingers" one could call it— but at varying rhythmic distances. The second, *Excentrique*, was inspired, as I have said before, by the eccentric movements and postures of the great clown, Little Tich. The third is called *Cantique* or *Canticle* because the music is choral and religious in character, but *Hymne* would have been as good a title.

I composed the *Danse*—the original string-quartet piece, that is—in June 1914, though it was conceived two months earlier, just after the completion of *The Nightingale*, in Leysin. The quartet original of *Excentrique* was written in Salvan in a single day, July 2, 1914. I began with the figure

and worked from this first sketch toward the beginning. My notebooks contain a number of sketches for the cello motive

including this merry tune which might have been a solo for *cornet à pistons*:

The quartet original of the *Cantique* was composed in Salvan on July 25–26, by much trial and error. Several pages of my notebook were covered before I found the right harmony, and the melody in its first form looked like this:

Jeu de Cartes

More than a decade prior to the composition of *Jeu de Cartes*, I became aware of an idea for a ballet in which dancers, dressed as playing cards, would perform against a gaming-table backdrop of green baize. I have always been interested in card games (and in cartomancy, too), and I have been a cardplayer all my life, since I first played *durachki* as a child. While composing *Jeu de Cartes*, poker was a favorite pastime in the rest periods between composition, but the origins of the ballet, in the sense of the attraction of the subject, antedate my knowledge of card games. They are probably to be traced back to childhood holidays at German spas; my first impression of a German casino, at any rate—the long rows of tables at which people played baccarat or bezique, roulca or faro, as now in the bowels of ocean liners they play bingo—is still a vivid memory. I remember now, too, and remembered when I composed the music, the "trombone" voice with which the master of ceremonies at one of these spas would announce a new game. "Ein neues Spiel, ein neues Glück," he would say, and the rhythm and instrumentation of the theme with which each of the three "Deals" of my ballet begins are an echo or imitation of the tempo, timbre, and indeed the whole character of that invitation.

It will have to be admitted also that *Jeu de Cartes* is in many ways the most "German" of my works. Its period and setting, if I had chosen to identify them, would have been a Baden-Baden of the Romantic Age, and it is as part of that picture that the tunes by Rossini, Messager, Johann Strauss, and from number [66] in the first movement of my own Symphony in E-flat, are to be imagined floating in from the Municipal Opera or from the concert by the Kursaal Band. But *Jeu de Cartes* might also be described as "German" by virtue of its march rhythms and now somewhat painful (though never uproarious) humor. I cannot say to what extent I may have been aware of this at the time, or to what degree (unconscious, in any case) the music may have been designed for German tastes and German audiences. (The score was nearly completed before I received the commission from the American Ballet Company.) If spirit of place exerted any influence, the spirit of the music would have been Parisian. With the exception of a small segment[2] that was, in fact, written on German territory (aboard the *Kap Arcona,* on which I sailed from Boulogne to Buenos Aires in 1936), the score was composed entirely in my rue Faubourg St. Honoré apartment. I do know, however, that the greatest success of the music was in Germany. It was performed there in all the larger cities and by all the most eminent conductors, in 1937, 1938, and even in 1939. In 1938, after a great stage success in Dresden, Telefunken invited me to record it, which I did later that year in Berlin.

The fortunes of my music in the Third Reich, incidentally, were unaccountable. One of the most curious documents is an interview that Richard Strauss gave to the *Fränkischer Kurier* (November 28, 1934), defending me against the charge of cultural Bolshevism, but entirely for the wrong rea-

[2] The section from [189] to [192], which is also one of the rare examples in my music of a passage not composed at the piano.

sons. In May 1938, Schoenberg, Berg, Hindemith, Weill, and myself were the chief butts of a scurrilous exhibition entitled *Entartete Musik* (Degenerate Music). Several rooms in a Düsseldorf hall were opened for a display of "decadent," "Jewish," and "cultural Bolshevist" music, and a recording of *Pierrot lunaire,* described on a poster as *"Hexensabbat"* music filled the spectators' ears as they regarded photographs and documents of a viciously defamatory character. A reproduction of one of J.-E. Blanche's portraits of me was hung on the largest wall with, subjoined to it, a placard saying, "Judge from this whether or not Stravinsky is a Jew." When photographs of the show and clippings from the German newspapers reached me in Paris, I lodged a protest with the French ambassador in Berlin, M. François-Ponçet, but nothing came of it. In spite of this, my music was performed in Germany up to and even during the war, and in 1942 the Nazis actually organized a gala performance of *Le Sacre du printemps* at the Paris Conservatoire.

I informed Cocteau of my plan to compose a ballet with a card-game plot and invited him to concoct a "book" for me, thinking that as he was then in his period of bicephalous eagles, bleeding bards, and so forth, he might spawn some idea for a novel approach. When nothing came of this, I set to work with my own notions, using the Joker as the principal dancer. The ballet must have three parts, I thought, each with a deal of poker as its argument. In the first deal, one of three players is beaten while the other two remain with even "straights." In the second deal, the Joker is victorious because he makes the fourth Ace, which defeats four Queens. In the third deal, the Joker is beaten by three flushes. I no longer remember the details of ballet action that I must have had in mind as I composed, but I did not supply Balanchine with an explicit program because I felt that the character of the dance episodes was unmistakable in the music.

Playing cards are ideal material for a ballet if only because of the rich possibilities in combining and grouping the four suits with the solo-dancer royalty. The latter divide into sexes, too, which is important; male and female are to a ballet composer what *forte* and *piano* were to an eighteenth-century *concerto grosso* composer. As a bonus, the Joker provided an element of chance and an escape from these very combinations. My first thoughts for him were that each of his appearances should interrupt not only the stage situation but also the music; and that he should win all the battles but lose the war. The contest resulting in his defeat begins at number [152] in the score, at which point he enters at the head of a sequence of spades, and ends at number [160]. He reappears at the end, though, and this is represented by the final seventh-chord, which, together with the return of the master-of-ceremonies music, suggests that the game is perpetual, as all games are.

The curtain cue is at number [6], after an orchestral introduction developing the master-of-ceremonies theme, and the dancing begins at number [7] with a solo ballerina, though of which suit I no longer remember. At number [12] the lady dances a variation of [7], until, at [16], she is joined by her consort, at which point a new episode begins. Number [21] is the cue for the Joker, whose dance determines the action until number [34]. He disappears at this point, leaving the queen alone for the waltz-coda which is a return, *mutatis mutandis*, to number [7]. I composed the march in the Second Deal (number [43] and the returns) as a dance for the hearts and spades, with the Joker interrupting at number [55]. The Variations were intended as solo dances for the queens, in the order hearts, diamonds, spades, clubs; the fifth variation is a *pas de quatre* of their highnesses together. The Coda was conceived as an ensemble piece for the whole company, until the Joker interrupts at number [92]. Of the Third Deal, however, I recall only that the *corps de ballet* was busier than in the other two.

I did not give even this sketchy program to Balanchine with

whom, indeed, I hardly discussed the choreography. I sent him the piano score from Paris, rehearsed tempi with him on my arrival in New York two months before the performance, and departed for a concert tour leaving him to his own devices. In fact, my only participation at that time was to criticize the costume designs. These were inspired by some beautiful Tarot and medieval playing cards, but they seemed to demand a sumptuous period-piece score rather than my "brittle" and "heartless" music. I insisted that the artist copy some contemporary and very ordinary playing cards from the corner drugstore.

Jeu de Cartes was my first commission from Lincoln Kirstein, who is now known as a gifted poet and a learned and intelligent ballet critic, and who has recently had a whole center in New York named for him. Kirstein was a young giant then, who wore a fierce expression and who matched it with a bellicose dedication to the beautiful and a contempt for the sham. At that time his career as a patron had only begun, but too few people are aware even now that to Lincoln Kirstein, as much as to Balanchine, we owe the existence of the finest ballet company and ballet school in the world today.

I remember only three others associated with the performance, the rehearsal pianist Leo Smit, the music copyist William Schuman ("to err is Schuman," people were saying about his first compositions) and the Joker-dancer William Dollar (it is clear why I remember him). Of the ballet itself, however, I have no recollection, probably because I was conducting and my nose was in the score.

A few days after the première I received news of the death of Ludmilla Beliankin, my wife's sister and one of my closest friends since childhood; I returned to Europe with a heavy heart. The Paris premiere of *Jeu de Cartes* occurred at the time of another sad event, the death of Ravel, and it was also associated with an unhappy departure, being the last work I conducted in Europe—during a concert in La Scala, in May 1939—before the war.

I read La Fontaine regularly during the composition and in him I found my sermon as well as what struck me as a good sermon for the times:

> *Qu'il faut faire aux méchants guerre continuelle.*
> *La paix est fort bonne de soi,*
> *J'en conviens; mais de quoi sert-elle*
> *Avec des ennemis sans foi?*

Dumbarton Oaks Concerto

The name of my Concerto in E-flat is that of the District of Columbia estate of the late Robert Woods Bliss, who commissioned the music and sponsored its first performance there in 1938. The composition was begun immediately on my return to Europe after *Jeu de Cartes*, or in other words, in the spring of 1937. I had moved from Paris to the Château de Montoux, near Annemasse in the Haute Savoie, to be near my daughter Mika, who was confined to a sanitarium in the neighborhood. Mika had recently married Yuri Mandelstam, a Russian-Jewish poet who worked for the emigré newspaper *Sovremenniya Zapiski* in Paris, and who was financially unable to stay with her. (All I can remember of Yuri Mandelstam now is that he laughed a great deal but had no sense of humor. I did not see him after Mika's death because he had soon remarried. He was deported to Germany shortly after the occupation of Paris, and was never heard from again.) Annemasse is not far distant from Geneva, and Charles-Albert

Cingria, my closest friend in that city, was a helpful visitor at this most difficult time of my life. I studied and played Bach regularly during the composition, and I was greatly attracted to the Brandenburg Concertos, especially the third, which I have also conducted. The first theme of my Concerto is, of course, very like Bach's in that work, and so is my instrumentation—the three violins and three violas, both frequently *divisi a tré*, though not chordally as in Bach. I do not think, however, that Bach would have begrudged me the loan of these ideas and materials, as borrowing in this way was something he liked to do himself.

Symphony in C

Even after twenty-five years the *Symphony in C* continues to remind me of the unhappiest period of my life. I was in poor health when I accepted the commission (from Mrs. Robert Woods Bliss), and I did so only out of necessity: the burden of my own, my wife's, and my daughter's medical expenses. Shortly after the premiere of *Jeu de Cartes*, a New York doctor discovered a lesion in my left lung and clusters of staphylococci in my sputum. The family malady had struck me, too, and it was already in an active form. On my return to France I was ordered to the sanitarium in which my wife, Catherine, and my daughters, Mika and Milena, had preceded me with the same disease.

I did not go, however, but cured myself, or at least, forgot about myself by composing the *Dumbarton Oaks Concerto* and the *Symphony in C*. The first movement of the *Symphony* was completed in my rue St. Honoré apartment in

the fall of 1938, though I was obliged to interrupt the composition in November and, for financial reasons, embark on
a round of concerts through Italy. At the end of the stay
in Rome, a telephone call from my elder son informed me
that Mika's condition had suddenly become grave, and the
next day, November 30, calling Paris myself from the Turin
railway station, I received the news of her death. I think it
is no exaggeration to say that in the following weeks I myself
survived only through my work on the *Symphony in C*—
though I hasten to add that I did not seek to overcome my
personal grief by "expressing" or "portraying" it "in" music,
and the listener in search of that kind of exploitation will
search in vain, not only here but everywhere in my art.

Three months later, March 2, 1939, a hemorrhage, long
predicted by the doctors, ended Catherine's fifty-year struggle
with the disease. After that, because I could no longer bear
to live in the apartment (which, in any case, had to be dis-
infected along with all of my wife's effects) and because I
had been warned again about my own condition, I moved to
the sanitarium at Sancellemoz where Catherine and Mika had
lived and where Milena, after pneumothorax treatment and
surgery on the phrenic nerve, was to spend the next six years.
There, on this not at all "magic" mountain in the Haute Savoie,
I remained for the next five months as an out-patient. One
of my infrequent absences was necessitated by the death of
my mother on June 7. For the third time in half a year I
endured the long Russian requiem service for one of my own
family, walked through a field to the cemetery of Sainte
Geneviève des Bois (in Mont Léris, on the road to Orléans),
and dropped a handful of dirt in an open grave; and for the
third time I was able to live only through my composition—
though no more than before were the sections of the *Symphony* written in these dark days an attempt to free myself
from my feelings. The second movement, begun at Sancel-

lemoz toward the end of March, was completed there in August.

Among those who visited me in Sancellemoz were Pierre Suvchinsky and Roland-Manuel. (Suvchinsky is my oldest living friend. He knew me more closely than anyone else in my later Paris years, and he has been my closest confidant, by correspondence, again in the last decade. He has always fed books to me, and I remember that at Sancellemoz he brought me a novel by the most discussed new writer of the moment, Jean-Paul Sartre's *La Nausée*.) Having agreed to deliver the Norton lectures at Harvard in the winter, I sought the assistance of these men. Suvchinsky helped me to draft the lectures in Russian and at a later date Roland-Manuel assisted in revising, improving, and otherwise polishing the French text. Suvchinsky reported in Paris that he had seen the score of Tchaikovsky's First Symphony on my piano. This information, together with the discovery of a similarity in our first themes, is responsible for the rumor of relationship between my Symphony and Tchaikovsky's which was soon claiming model status for the latter. In fact, there probably is a rapport between the two works, in Russian sentiment if in nothing else—the E-flat-minor episode in my first movement and the introduction to my last movement—but Tchaikovskyan antecedents have been or will be discovered elsewhere as well, "my" eighteenth century and "Tchaikovsky's" sharing a Russian family-likeness, as critics of *The Rake's Progress* have noted. And I did relish this score of the young Tchaikovsky, which I had last heard in St. Petersburg forty years before, but as *music*, not as a *symphony*. What, however, if Suvchinsky had told of the Haydn and Beethoven scores on my desk? No one would have paid him any attention, yet those two celestial powers stand behind the first, and even the pastoral second, movement far more significantly than my lonely, self-pitying compatriot.

To return to the chronicle and composition of the later movements, the world events of 1939–40, though happily not tragic in their bearing on my personal life, did disrupt the tenor of the Symphony. The third movement, composed in Boston, and the fourth movement, stapled together in California (I had gone to the Southwest for concerts, but I was also fleeing Boston, whose only seasons, or so it seemed to a Mediterraneanized European, were winter and the Fourth of July) are very different in spirit and design from the "European" movements,[3] and they have seemed to many to divide the Symphony down the middle. This schism is especially marked, of course, in the domain of rhythm. The metrical and tempo changes in the third movement are the most extreme in the whole inventory of my work, and they follow a second movement with a steady *ductus* and a first movement with no variation of meter at all.

The public life of the Symphony began in Chicago, November 7, 1940, on which date I conducted the Chicago Symphony Orchestra in the first performance. But in fact, the public career of the work has not been conspicuous. Conductors of the older generation are afraid of the difficult third movement, and the younger conductors avoid the work because of the unfashionable apple called neo-classicism: for many years the only performances were my own. Nor was the streak of ill-fated personal associations at an end. Conducting it in Berlin, October 2, 1956, I was overcome, near the end of the first movement, by a paralyzing pain in my right side. I remember only an eclipsing blackness, but after the concert, orchestra members said that I failed to beat the

---

[3] The two measures before number [104] would not have come to my ears in Europe, I think, and the passage beginning at number [145]—which, incidentally, is perfect movie music for a Hollywood traffic scene—would not have occurred to me before I had known the neon glitter of the California boulevards from a speeding automobile.

final chords of the movement and that I began the second movement only after a long pause. I *did* continue, however, and somehow brought the Symphony to the end, though in my dressing room afterward I was unable to write my name and did not have full use of my speech. The next night, in Munich, a doctor in the Red Cross hospital to which I had been taken told me that I had suffered a cerebral thrombosis.

But enough of autobiography! And enough of musical biography, too—for what can one say about a score that is so unmysterious and so easy to follow at all levels and in all of its relationships? The answer is that critics (who must also earn their livelihood) will find a great deal of nothing to say, finding factitious comparisons with other music, then drawing attention to the severity of the diatonicism while tracing the development of the motive in the first movement and accusing me, in it, of consistency (which I dislike because only mediocre composers are consistent, as only good ones are capable of being very bad). They will also uncover my supposed use of Italianate song-and-accompaniment in the second movement, and of *fugato* in the last two movements,[4] and discover the existence of a suite-of-dances in the third movement and of flirtations with ballet in other movements, but anyone who had failed to notice this much would require a different sort of commentary in any case.

How would I evaluate the Symphony today? I cannot answer, for it is so far from my present work that I am unable to judge it at all, and I will not apply the obvious criticisms from my present position, namely, the episodic effect of the many *ostinati*, the heavy emphasizing of key centers; this, as I say, is my point of view today, not that of the Symphony.

---

[4] To answer one of their comparison questions in advance, the *fugato* in the *finale*, abandoned there like a very hot *pomme de terre*, may well have been in my mind when I began the Symphony in Three Movements, but I do not remember.

Like the *Symphony of Psalms*, the manuscript score is inscribed "*à la gloire de Dieu.*"

Danses concertantes

In spite of choreographic titles such as *Pas d'action* and *Pas de deux*, the *Danses concertantes* were not intended for ballet performance or composed with dance action in mind. They may be compared in this respect with the waltzes of Chopin or Schumann's *Carnaval* which, in my opinion, are also unsuited to the theater. This is not to say that the *Danses* are unacceptable as ballet music, but only that I do not like or think of them as such; and I must confess that though I liked the *décors*, by Eugene Berman, the ballet is not among my Balanchine favorites.

Many listeners professed to hear an American note in the *Danses*, and even, to narrow the geography a bit, a Broadway note. I have also been told that the theme of the third movement "sounds like Copland" (now people are saying that Nielsen's *Fifth* "sounds like Copland"). I am not a competent judge of Mr. Copland's influence on me, but what I do know and what does seem obvious is the influence (almost everywhere, but literally in the little march at [159]) of *Jeu de Cartes*. I am not a believer in *ex nihilo* explanations of art, and in my own case I know positively that reactivated springs from my past work have continually nourished the present— which is one reason why I think my work deserves to be considered as a whole.

The newest music in *Danses concertantes* is contained in the passages from [79] to [83], I think, but it is difficult for

me to criticize my music of that time—whereas I am confident
and detached in my evaluations of fifty years ago. The *Danses
concertantes* instrumental ensemble is similar to that of my
arrangement, the year before, of excerpts from the *Sleeping
Beauty* for a wartime ballet orchestra. About half of the music
was composed before I received the commission from Mr.
Werner Janssen.

Orpheus

A so-called plaintive quality was remarked for the first
time in my music with *Orpheus*, but the quality I believe to
be meant is, in fact, already present in my String Concerto—
for example, in the phrase:

But how different are my time scales, today and in 1947!
I could never compose such a motionless measure now as the
one before number [4]; or allow the flutes and clarinets to
run on at such dilatory length at [100], or the strings, *ditto*,
in the measure after [98]. And the whole of the *Pas d'action*
seems spread out and repetitious now, compared even with
the *Ebony Concerto*, which does not say the same thing quite
so many times, and which comes to mind because of its similar
two-note motive. And the time scale is the vital question. It
must work for every age. Miscalculation is death.

Orpheus, the subject, was George Balanchine's idea, com-
municated to me in 1946 only shortly before he went to

Hollywood to help me construct a plot. Following Ovid and a classical dictionary, we divided the action into three scenes and a dozen dance episodes, aiming at a work of approximately a half hour's length. The titles are partly mine, partly the dictionary's. The contributions of the latter—"*L'Ange de la mort et sa danse*," for example—might have done for Messiaen, if they had been a little less definite.

I had not thought about the *décors*, nor had Balanchine, and it was Lincoln Kirstein's happy idea to invite the Japanese master Isamu Noguchi, who at least saved us from cliché "Greek," the chlamys, Doric backdrops, and so on. Noguchi's maquettes promised a bleakly attractive landscaping of the stage, but at the performance his greatest success was the transparent curtain which fell over the scene during the Interludes like a fog. He had also designed beautiful though somewhat ethnographic masks, but unfortunately they interfered with the dancers' view of the floor and consequently with their timing. Orpheus looked like a baseball catcher in his mask except for the hair that flowed down his back like a horse's mane. There were uptilting projections from the wings, too, hobgoblin-like and at the same time, as people quaintly said back in the forties, "Freudian." These constructions are as dated now, in any case, as my cadences with added sixths, sevenths, or ninths, or Balanchine's rather corny choreography for the Furies.

The ballet was an immediate success, largely because it was brilliantly danced, especially by some of Balanchine's present and future wives. Balanchine offered a kind of preview of the "*Pas de deux*," incidentally, in a dance-duetto *entr'acte* to my *Elegy* for viola solo.[5] This slow-motion study of amor-

[5] Composed at the request of the violist Germain Prévost, in memory of Alphonse Onnou, founder of the Pro Arte Quartet. I arranged it for solo violin subsequently, at the suggestion of Mr. Sol Babitz, who played it *scordatura*, with the strings at F-C-G-D, to give what he deemed a more violistic color.

ously intercising limbs was a masterpiece, though many people thought the dancers too much like lobsters in a restaurant window, and though the music was divided, ruinously in my opinion, between two players.

It is in the string music of the *Pas de deux*, I may add, that I now find the most delectable pages of the *Orpheus* score; there, and in numbers [41]–[46] of the first Interlude, where a developing harmonic movement and an active bass line relieve the long successions of *ostinati*. The question of influences, incidentally, cannot be broached at all. They do not exist—not Monteverdi in the end movements, not Czerny in the arpeggio passages before [146] and [148], not Ives in the tantara which almost spells "Taps" at [38]. What I *can* say is that because so much of *Orpheus* is mimed song,[6] it seemed inevitable that my next work would be an opera.

The Rake's Progress

Rather than seek musical forms symbolically expressive of the dramatic content (as in the Daedalian examples of Alban Berg), I chose to cast *The Rake* in the mold of an eighteenth-century "number" opera, one in which the dramatic progress depends on the succession of separate pieces—recitatives and arias, duets, trios, choruses, instrumental interludes. In the earlier scenes the mold is to some extent pre-Gluck in that it tends to crowd the story into the *secco* recitatives, reserving the arias for the reflective poetry, but then, as the

---

[6] In Orpheus' oboe aria the harp accompaniment should sound as dry and choked as a not very resonant guitar, and in Orpheus' violin aria the violin solo should be played as silkily as possible, though the desired effect is also calculated by the choice of the technically awkward key.

opera warms up, the story is told, enacted, contained almost entirely in song—as distinguished from so-called speech-song, and Wagnerian continuous melody, which consists, in effect, of orchestral commentary enveloping continuous recitative.

* * *

Having chosen a period-piece subject, I decided—naturally, as it seemed to me—to assume the conventions of the period as well. *The Rake's Progress* is a conventional opera, therefore, but with the difference that these particular conventions were adjudged by all respectable (i.e., progressive) circles to be long since dead. My plan of revival did not include updating or modernizing, however—which would have been self-contradictory, in any case—and it follows that I had no ambitions as a reformer, at least not in the line of a Gluck, a Wagner, or a Berg. In fact, these great progressivists sought to abolish or transform the very clichés I had tried to re-establish, though my restitutions were by no means intended to supersede their now conventionalized reforms (i.e., the leitmotif systems of Wagner and Berg).

* * *

Can a composer re-use the past and at the same time move in a forward direction? Regardless of the answer (which is "yes"), this academic question did not trouble me during the composition, nor will I argue it now, though the supposed backward step of *The Rake* has taken on a radically forward-looking complexion when I have compared it with some more recent progressive operas. Instead, I ask the listener to suspend the question as I did while composing, and, difficult as the request may be, to try to discover the opera's own qualities. For a long time *The Rake* seemed to have been created for no

other purpose than journalistic debates concerning: (a) the
historical validity of the approach; and (b) the question of
pastiche. If the opera contains imitations, however—especially
of Mozart, as has been said—I will gladly allow the charge
if I may thereby release people from the argument and bring
them to the music.

※ ※ ※

The Rake's Progress is simple to perform musically, but difficult to realize on the stage. I contend, however, that the
chief obstacles to a convincing visual conception are no more
than the result of an incapacity to accept the work for what
it is. True, Tom's machine-baked bread may be hard to swallow, but even *it* will go down, I think (with a lot of butter
and more than a few grains of salt) if the stage director has not
lost sight of the opera's "moral fable" proposition by over-
playing the realism of "the Rakewell story." As Dr. Johnson
said, "Opera is an exotic and irrational art."

※ ※ ※

It is easy to find faults of this sort in the *Rake*, to be sure,
though, alas, it offers nothing quite so foolish as the concealed-
identity scene in *Un Ballo in Maschera*, or the post-stabbing
coloratura concert in *Rigoletto*, to name two far greater
operas which, like my own, I love beyond the point where
criticism can make a difference. Having perfect 20-20 hind-
sight, like most people, I am now able to see that Shadow is
a preacher as well as a Devil; that the Epilogue is much too
"nifty" (as Americans say); that the *ostinato* accompaniment
style could do with an occasional contrast of polyphony, the
dramatic opportunity for which might have been found in
an extra ensemble or two during which the minor characters

might also have been given more development and connection. But though such things matter, they are not fatal. And in any case, I am not concerned with the future of my opera. I ask for it only a measure of present justice.

I.S.

Paris 8/16/64

The Rake's Progress: "La Prima Assoluta"
by Vera Stravinsky

Venice, *September 11, 1951.* A night of stifling heat and a sirocco that blows like a bellows. The alleys near the theater have been roped off to keep the Fourth Estate at bay during the arrival procession, though the Higher Estates come not as pedestrians but are deposited by gondolas and motor launches directly at the theater door from a strongly redolent canal. Our own (pedestrian) party includes Nadia Boulanger (who carries Igor's valises), Wystan Auden and Chester Kallman (both nervous in spite of liquid fortifications—a moat of martinis, in fact), Stephen Spender (shy, deferential), and Louis MacNeice (handsome, arrogantly silent, but perhaps pickled).

A familiar unfamiliar face veers toward me as I enter the foyer, but no sooner have I identified it as Maxim Gorky's adopted son, Zinovy Peshkov (last seen in the Caucasus during the Revolution), than others crowding around me crowd General Peshkov out. The list of old friends who have come to criticize and otherwise "assist" at the performance is too copious to be continued.

La Fenice, the most beautiful theater in the world, has never glittered as it does tonight in honor of the debut, and as an extra garnishing, bouquets of roses, like debutantes' corsages, have been pinned to each loge. Unfortunately, the beauty of these stalls on the inside is even less than "skin deep." The plush seems to have had chicken—or rather, moth —pox, and it and everything else is badly in need of deodorants. Another discomfort is that the seats are like European railroad compartments. The occupants on the side nearer the stage (i.e., the men) face in the wrong direction as if their ears were encased in their legs and abdomens, like grasshoppers.

The audience glitters, too; everyone, that is, except a New York newspaperman who has no doubt already prepared a jobbery on the event consistent with his apparel and life-long devotion to the commonplace. (*Note:* Air travel was not yet the rule at that time and therefore neither were blue denims and Beethoven sweaters.)

In Italy nothing respectable begins on time. During tonight's long delay my thoughts drift back through the weeks of preparation, to the first conferences with stage directors and music coaches, which took place in Naples. I spent the mornings in the Naples aquarium then, drawing an old *joli laide* crustacean, a "liquid prisoner pent in walls of glass" (Shakespeare). But I also think, during the wait, about echoes in the opera of Igor's so-called private life—of how, for example, the card game stemmed from his own fondness for cards; to me, Shadow's harpsichord arpeggio is an imitation of Igor's way of shuffling cards, as the *staccato* of that instrument recalls the way he snaps playing cards on a table. Perhaps Auden had actually observed Igor playing solitaire and heard him utter Russian *gros mots* when the wrong card appeared, which may have given him the idea for "the Deuce!" I think, too, of how the *Epilogue*, and the idea of pointing to the audience—

"you and you"—was inspired by Walter Houston in *The Devil and Daniel Webster*, a film Igor admired.

At 21:35, a prompt thirty-five minutes late, Igor enters the pit and bows to the audience which, though ultra *mondaine*, applauds him with (it seems to me) a core of genuine appreciation. He then turns quickly to the orchestra so that we can see only his extraordinary occipital bumps and small, vital beat. The singers are Robert Rounseville, who has only recently emerged, or not quite fully emerged, from a film career and manner, but who is aptly cast as Tom Rakewell; Elizabeth Schwarzkopf, who is a cool and perfect Anne; Hugues Cuénod, a subtle, mysterious, and believable Sellem; and Jennie Tourel, who as the diva, Baba, could swagger through her grand exit on an elephant without risking a snigger from the audience. At first-act intermission we drink *caffè espresso* in the Campo San Fantin, mercifully rescued from impertinent judgments by the unforgettable effect on everyone of Frl. Schwarzkopf's high C.

Igor claims no more for the music than that it is conventional, but what beautiful *inventions* are in it, too. I would mention, for a preliminary list, the chord progressions at the end of the first half of the Cavatina, the modulation to "O wilful powers" (following Anne's "how evil in the purple prose they seem"), the transformation of the Ballad Tune in the final two scenes, and the double appoggiaturas, those wonderfully style-embalmed representations of Tom's graveyard fear which reappear during his madness. But it seems to me that Igor has saved the finest moments of all for the final scene. These are the music of "Venus, mount thy throne," the duet "In a foolish dream," and—the most touching music Igor ever wrote—Tom's "Where art thou, Venus?"

The "*prima assoluta*" is tentative in many ways, and it shows more "might" as the preterite of "may" than power; at every change of tempo the opera could "fall apart" (as the

Americans say). Nevertheless, it conveys much of the opera's "inner resonance" (as the British say), and all of us except the unglittering New Yorker are deeply moved. The post-mortem party does not break up until the bleary dawn.

Greeting Prelude

Intended as a kind of singing telegram for the eightieth birthday of Pierre Monteux, the *Greeting Prelude* was performed on that occasion, April 4, 1955, by Charles Munch and the Boston Symphony Orchestra. It is unnecessary to say anything about the music, a half-minute primer of canonic writing for very young kiddies and critics, but I will tell the story of my acquaintance with the tune. I gave the down-beat to begin a rehearsal of Tchaikovsky's Second Symphony in Aspen one day in the summer of 1950, when instead of the doleful opening chord out came this ridiculously gay little tune. I was very much surprised, of course, and quite failed to "get it," as Americans say—the "it" being that one of the orchestra players had just become a father. I confess that the shock of the substituted music and the change of emotions piqued me, and that for some time I considered myself the victim of a practical joke. I remembered the tune, though, and a year later, when asked to compose a fanfare for a festival in North Carolina, I set about composing canons on it. Now, when my own birthdays are reaching a frightening total, the *Greeting Prelude* is sometimes sprung on me. Though I hardly recognized it two years ago in Stockholm, and though it took me by surprise in London last year, it will not, I think, catch me anywhere unaware again.

Abraham and Isaac

A*braham and Isaac* is a sacred ballad for high baritone voice (*baryton martin*) and small orchestra composed on the Hebrew (Masoretic) text of Genesis ('reshit) chapter XXII.

The six parts, including one purely orchestral movement, are performed without interruption, but they are distinguished by changes to successively slower pulsations. Nineteen verses are used, and they are comprised in ten musical units. Though the verses are sometimes expressed in dialogue form in the Bible, my setting does not impersonate the protagonists, but tells the whole story through the baritone-narrator. The change of speaker is indicated by, among more interesting devices, changes in dynamics.

No translation of the Hebrew should be attempted, the Hebrew syllables, both as accentuation and timbre, being a principal and a fixed element of the music. I did not try to follow Hebrew cantillation, of course, as that would have imposed crippling restrictions, but the verbal and the musical accentuation *are* identical in this score, which fact I mention because it is rare in my music. Repetitions of words occur— not a rare event with me—but never with exact musical repetitions. "Abraham" is the most often repeated word, and it is sung the first time without instruments. The vocal line is partly melismatic (*bel*-cantor), partly an interval-speech of single syllables.

I do not wish the listener any luck in discovering musical descriptions or illustrations; to my knowledge none was composed, and as I see it the notes themselves are the end of the road. Though I thought long and deeply about the meaning of the text, I am also unaware of symbolisms in my use of

canons, or of expressive rhythmic devices. Anyone who pretends to hear such things in, for example, the passage referring
to Isaac and the two youths, will have made too much, I think,
of what for me is no more than a coincidence. Associative
listening is not a habit of mine and not one I would wish to
cultivate in others. I expect to be told of echoes of the "Pastoral" Symphony in my flute cadenza, nevertheless, and of
Oedipus Rex in my music for *"Vayikra Malakh Adonay."*

A twelve-note series is employed, but hexachordal and
smaller units are stressed rather than full orders. Octaves
occur frequently, fifths and doubled intervals are everywhere,
and I suppose that "key" gravitations will be found to exist.
None of these is in contradiction to the serial basis of the
composition, but the result of concordances from the several
serial forms, or what I call serial verticals.

Of the multiple origins of every work, the most important
is the least easy to describe. I must say, however, that the
initial stimulus came to me with the discovery of Hebrew as
sound. But there was a strong extra-musical motivation, too:
I wished to leave a token of gratitude to the people of Israel,
to whom the score is dedicated, for their generous hospitality
during my tour of their country in 1962.

Elegy for J.F.K.

N EW YORK TIMES: Would you tell us something about
the origins of the composition, Mr. Stravinsky?
STRAVINSKY: The idea came to me in mid-January 1964. I
felt that the events of November were being too quickly forgotten and I wished to protest.

Observing *first* reactions to the events, incidentally, I was struck by resemblances to anthropological accounts of the Divine Kingship (the second such manifestation within a few months, as it happened, the other being the warnings of danger from occultation during the solar eclipse; they sounded exactly like the wrath-of-god stories of tribal medicine men). Immediately after the assassination I thought I could detect vestiges of the atavistic belief in the well-being of the community deriving from the well-being of the King, and therefore of regicide as not only the ultimate sacrilege but as an act of destruction against the tribe as well. I even thought that the tribe seemed to be expecting punishment—no Theban plague, of course, but something in its own line: a Bear Market, for instance. (Naturally, there were other reactions, too, a few people using the shock for some sensationalism of their own—"the President is dead, therefore I must divorce my wife," and that sort of thing.)

But I am wandering. . . .

TIMES: You were saying that you wished to protest. . . .

I.S.: Or to remember, though I am, secularly, a lifelong protestant. But none of this has much to do with the piece itself. It is a very quiet little lyric.

TIMES: How did the collaboration with Mr. Auden come about?

I.S.: At my request. Auden knows my time-scale, and in a touchy affair like this one he can draw the finest of lines. (I say this imagining the albatrosses of "epic" poetry and symphonic sentiment that the event will give rise to and, for a time, excuse.) I gave him some hazy hints, nothing I had really thought about but enough to help him start. And to confine him to the simplest language, I told him I was thinking of a choral rather than a solo piece. But Auden is almost too skillful. He is able to anticipate the uses of music, and he is so ready to subordinate himself to it that sometimes he has to be circumvented so as to be kept far enough upstage. For the *Elegy*, he devised a movable final verse, repeatable anywhere as a refrain (in other words, a poem of adjustable length); in fact, I begin with it. His concern for qualities of sound is shown in his request to me at a slightly later date "to replace *sadness* by *sorrow*: too many s's in the former and the latter is more sonorous."

TIMES: When did you begin to compose?

I.S.: I had the poem in hand at the beginning of March, only a few days before a trip to Cleveland for concerts. Melodic ideas came to me immediately, but the first phrase I was certain would never come unglued was composed in flight between Los Angeles and Cleveland:

the   hea - vens   are   si - lent

This quotation was transposed in the course of composition, but the content, not the ramifications, is the point of interest (if any). The two reiterated notes are a melodic-rhythmic stutter characteristic of my speech from *Les Noces* to the *Concerto in D*, and earlier and later as well—a lifelong affliction, in fact.

TIMES: And the subsequent stages of the composition?

I.S.: I wrote the vocal part first and only later discovered the relationships from which I was able to derive the complementary instrumental counterpoint. Schoenberg composed his *Phantasie* in the same way, incidentally, the violin part first and then the piano.

TIMES: Would you describe the music as "twelve-tone"?

I.S.: *I* wouldn't. The label tells you nothing; we have no

organon any more, and card-carrying twelve-toners are practically extinct. Originally, a series, or row (the horizontal emphasis of that word!) was a gravitational substitute and the consistently exploited basis of a composition, but now it is seldom more than a point of departure. A serial autopsy of the *Elegy* would hardly be worth the undertaking, in any case, and the only light I can throw on the question of method is to say that I had already joined the various melodic fragments before finding the possibilities of serial composition inherent in them, which is why the vocal part could begin with the inverted order and the clarinet with the reverse order—i.e., because the series had been discovered elsewhere in the piece. There is virtually no element of predetermination in such a procedure.

TIMES: What, if any, is the relation between the series and Mr. Auden's verse form?

I.S.: None, I think, except that the whole seventeen "notes" of his haiku are contained in a single statement of the series.

TIMES: Was the haiku form your idea or Mr. Auden's?

I.S.: Auden's; in fact, we had talked about a different meter; but Auden is having a haiku period, you know—like Byron with his discovery of *terza rima*. The *Elegy* is a haiku, however, only by virtue of syllable counting. The *matter* of it belongs more to the parsonage and the manse than to the Mysterious East.

TIMES: Just one more question, Mr. Stravinsky. Was the choice of three clarinets suggested by the *Berceuses du chat*?

I.S.: Oh no, the *Berceuses* are a very different kind of master-puss. . . .

Variations

My Variations were composed on the following pitch series, a succession of notes that came to my mind as a melody:

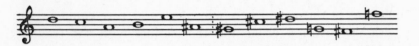

After writing it out, I gradually discovered the possibilities in it as material for variations. The bipartite division is basic, six-note formations being as integral components as the classical four orders. The halves, moreover, are unities as well as fragments, and are therefore divisible in turn, and invertible, reversible, mirror-invertible, mirror-reversible. The vocabulary of the composition (at least) was very abundant.

❊ ❊ ❊

Veränderungen—alterations or mutations, Bach's word for *The "Goldberg" Variations*—could be used to describe my Variations as well, except that I have altered or diversified a series, instead of a theme or subject. In fact, I do not have a theme, in the textbook sense, whereas Bach's theme (for comparison) is a complete aria.

❊ ❊ ❊

Some of us think that the role of rhythm is larger today than ever before, but, however that may be, in the absence of harmonic modulation it must play a considerable part in the delineation of form. And more than ever before, the composer must be certain of building rhythmic unity into variety. In my Variations, tempo is a variable and pulsation a constant.

* * *

The density of the twelve-part variations[7] is the main innovation in the work. One might think of these constructions as musical mobiles, in that the patterns within them will seem to change perspective with repeated hearings. They are relieved and offset by music of a contrasting starkness and even, notably in the first variation, by *Klangfarben* monody—which is also variation.

* * *

The question of length (duration) is inseparable from that of depth and/or height (content). But whether full, partly full, or empty, the musical statements of the Variations are concise, I prefer to think, rather than short. They are, whatever one thinks, a radical contrast to the prolix manner of speech of most of the late last-century music which is the pabulum of our (an editorial "our") regular concert life; and there lies the difficulty, mine with you no less than yours with me.

* * *

I do not know how to guide listeners other than to advise them to listen not once but repeatedly, though for tonight twice will have to do. I may say that I think they should not

---

[7] At the first performances the variation for twelve violins—i.e., in one timbre—pleased me most. It sounded like a sprinkling of very fine broken glass.

look for the boundary lines of the individual variations, but try instead to hear the piece as a whole. And on second thought I *can* recommend one guide, the orchestra itself. The use of families and individuals in contrast is a principal projective element of the form, especially of its symmetries and reversibles. The leading solo roles are those of the flutes, bassoons, and trombones; and perhaps my economy is inconsistent in that the trumpet and horn families have in comparison so little to do, but I needed only a spot of red, and a spot of blue. I might add that the orchestral dramatis personae is unusual in that four rather than the standard five string parts are required (there is only one division of violins) and that all must be of equal weight. Percussion instruments are not used, but their position is occupied by the piano and harp which appear as a couple (married).

The composition was begun at Santa Fe in July 1963 and completed in Los Angeles in October 1964. Although it is remote from the musical tastes of my dear friend, the late Aldous Huxley, I could not refrain from dedicating it to his memory.

March 11, 1965

INTROITUS: T. S. Eliot in Memoriam

In this small parting song for the great poet, tenors and basses intone the Introitus of the Latin Requiem Service to the accompaniment of a group of string and percussion instruments restricted to the male-voice range.

No novelty will be found in the manipulation of the series except, perhaps, in chord structure where, however, it is less a question of seriation than of choice; the choral chant is punctuated by fragments of a chordal dirge. The four melodic versions of the pitch orders are sung as a *cantus firmus* and in the form of a processional, which is a little ritual the poet might have liked. With the fourth phrase, the trapezium shape complete, the two choral parts unite to sing the last sentence in counterpoint. The last phrase, *"et lux perpetua,"* repeats the melody of my setting of Auden's line "The Heavens are silent."

The incidence of the complete series in a group of timpani *coperti* is the only instrumental novelty, and the main function of the viola and string bass is to support and clarify the tuning of these funeral drums.

March 19, 1965

LETTERS & RIPOSTES
(Billets Doux)

Letters to a Cousin in Moscow
from Vera Stravinsky

I

Hollywood, December 10, 1962

Vladimir Ivanovitch Petrov[1]
8 Pokrovsky Boulevard
Moscow

Dear Valodya,

To answer your request for an account of Igor's home life, perhaps I may best begin with a description of the house itself, though as it has but one bedroom and is so small, with low ceilings that might have been designed for Igor's height, probably I should not call it a house at all but a bungalow. Twenty years ago panoramas of the Hollywood valley and Beverly Hills were exposed from the front terrace, but these views are obstructed now by skyscrapers and taller trees. Twenty or even fifteen years ago a feeling of the wildness

---

[1] Son of Mrs. Stravinsky's mother's sister Olga (*née* Malmgren), now a professor of radiology at the University of Moscow. (R.C.)

of the West still existed, too, even here in Hollywood. One summer night an opossum charged through an open door and into Igor's studio, and on another hot night, during a drought, a small wildcat sprang to our roof from the hill behind the house, where we kept chickens during the war, clawing an awning. Such adventures are not only unlikely now but hardly believable. Nowadays the only invasions we can expect are those of autograph hunters, or of the cadastral surveyors Igor perennially fears to find distraining on our door, though we have also been besieged by more than one presumptive composer.

Visitors say that it is a gay house, and it *is* bright and cozy, with light-colored upholstery, pillows, rugs, and a plentiful array of flowers. Even the floppy rubber plants in the dining and living rooms are happy, I think, though hunched by the ceiling. The furniture is recent, American, ordinary; we have none of those dynastic French chairs which seem to offer you their *"sentiments les plus distingués"* before you sit in them. The house is also brightened by a large number of windows and mirrors—like Igor's mind, I might say. But it is heavily crammed, too, for which reason we have recently had to part with one of our three pianos, leaving one in Igor's studio, and one in the library so that the memento-seeking among the piano-playing visitors will not have an excuse to go to his studio.

Our library of ten thousand books spreads to every room. It is classified by author, subject, and language, but art books form the largest category, with books of poetry and *romans policiers* competing for second place. The Shakespeare section is extensive, and so is the collection of old Baedekers, but a catalogue of the other shelves would reflect a heterogeneous curiosity rather than an abiding philosophy. Igor is a steady reader, and though he is inclined to pursue one author or subject to a rut, his interests are varied and unpredictable.

You will be interested to hear that since his Russian reawakening last fall he has been reading Pushkin again, and dipping into Blok, Anna Akhmatova, and younger Russian poets. Did I tell you in my last letter that he also tends to converse in Russian now more than at any time in the last forty years? He talks of orchestrating Moussorgsky's *Sunless*, too, which is of course a result of his Russian visit.

The house bulges with "art." The visitor first sees some posters on the backs of the dining-room doors advertising performances of *Oedipus* and *Persephone* at the Warsaw Opera. He would then probably notice the objects on tables and shelves: atlases; glass obelisks and paperweights from a bygone Murano; "Santos" from New Mexico; squat and (to me) ugly pre-Columbian statuettes (the best of them were smashed a dozen years ago during a *terramoto;* central California is creased by a geologic fault, as you may know, and we have learned to expect terrestrial heart attacks from time to time); a head of Igor in bronze, the work of Dr. Max Edel, his physician and friend for twenty years; Russian cups, spoons, samovars, pyrogravure wooden boxes, Igor's family silverware with his mother's crown-shaped coat of arms; Inca and Copt textiles (Igor's interest in Coptic art is long-standing); Early American antiques (including an attractive pair of eighteenth-century wooden ducks from Long Island); entomological specimens taken from tropical boats that call at Monterey, California (horrible things even when stuffed, mounted, and stored in glass cases, but they fascinate Igor); clumps of coral (one like Bourdelle's Beethoven) and bits of lapis lazuli.

The walls are covered with paintings, Russian and Balkan icons, old maps, old cartoons (Rossini lighting a giant firecracker), new cartoons (an unreadable diploma drawn by Saul Steinberg for Igor and still his only academic credential), photographs of friends and of people Igor admires, such as Lincoln and Pope John. All of our paintings are contemporary except for a Turner pastel, tiny ink drawings supposedly by Watteau and Tiepolo but probably fakes, and a "Monsù Desiderio" which is on a hexagonal marble slab. Nearly everything we have was the gift of the artist, a description that includes a dozen Picassos, among them the well-known full-face line portrait of Igor, several Giacomettis, many Bermans, charming pieces by Klee and Kandinsky (including a Klee drawing given to Igor by Frau Alma Mahler), Jacques Villon, Tanguy, Henry Moore, Miro, Masson, Dufy, Tchelichev, Chagall, Vieira da Silva, Bérard, Léger. In fact, the only pictures we purchase are by young painters we wish to encourage, and this is how we have acquired our gallery of Sartoris, Vedova, Warshaw, Bacci, Bill Congdon, Jimmy Leong, Francis Bott. But for a complete catalogue I would have to mention my own paintings, of which more than a score can be counted about the house.

Igor's day is carefully routined. It begins with a headache which, however, is dispelled or forgotten in the shower. His bathroom, incidentally, looks like a laboratory or a prescription department in a pharmacy. There are blue-and-white porcelain apothecary jars, trays of syringes, and a curiously mammalian display of hot-water bottles. The vials of medicines, counteragents for every ailment, all neatly labeled in Russian by Igor himself, may be counted to the hundreds, and that, as the Americans say, is an underexaggeration. A branch-office drug store has gone into business on his night table, too, but the supponerals, the powders, the unguents and ointments, the drops, the herbs and other materia medica are so mixed up with the sacred medals that I fear he will swallow a Saint Christopher some night instead of a sleeping pill. Igor once told me that he acquired his taste for medicines at the precocious age of five. The family kept a cupboard of such remedies as aconite, belladonna, henbane, calomel, valerian, veronal, feverfew, centaury seeds, senna leaves, and he soon learned to climb up to it and "tranquilize" and "unhinge" himself.

The apparent totality of Igor's belief in medical materialism is the most curious dodge in his character. Every ill, serious or slight, must have a chemical solvent, he pretends to believe, and he will actually clock the action of an aspirin, as though to test the claims of the advertisements. It follows that he is also concerned with the health of people near him. Puff your cheeks in his presence and very likely he will give you a carminative; or cough, from momentary dryness of the throat, and instantly one of his silver pillboxes (favorite objects of virtu) will appear and you will be obliged to swallow a grain of antiplague or other sugar-coated placebo—as I suppose them to be. As for Igor's own coughs, they have long since been forelaid with one of his many brightly colored treacles. No matter how well he may feel, Igor will check his temperature at least once daily, for a half degree rise of the thermometer may spell a forecast of flu to him, and thus warned he can batten down with his medicines and conquer it weeks ahead. It also follows that he will never allow Nature to take its course, or at least not without giving it a good nudge. Every meal is dispatched with two tablets of "concentrated saliva," a Japanese confection said to stimulate digestion.

Speaking for myself, I find it odd that a man of such wide medical experience has never developed any suspicion of doctors, but he is always ready to rub out the whole of his medical history, and to transfer his faith *in toto* to the newest and most transient practitioner. One result of these peremptory transfers is that he sometimes finds himself on a chastening diet—boiled groats and turnip juice, say—younger diagnosticians being appalled at the intake of alcohol. He will observe these regimens with Mohammedan strictness, too, until after a few days, when he is *really* ill, a new and whisky-approving doctor is called to the rescue. In 1951 a physician friend of Igor's in Geneva concocted the perfect formula of one pill to excite and one to calm, and for years Igor swallowed this Swiss neutrality thirty minutes before every concert, with excellent effect. (Need I tell you that I am not *frileuse* myself, that I abhor all medicines and am unsympathetic to invalids, and that I would be the world's worst nurse?)

Igor's breakfast, which is later than mine, coincides with the arrival of the post and by that time I try to be out of the house. In the game we used to play in Paris of choosing apt substitute occupations for our friends, "postman" was always chosen for Igor, next to "pharmacist." (Other choices were "carpenter," "frame-maker," "bookbinder"; Igor likes to work with his hands.) He is so keen to receive and send mail that the Sabbath, except for the luck of a Special Delivery, is a grim day for him; and in his desire to hasten letters on their way, *any* visitor is temporarily impressed into the postal service; the President of the United States, if he were to come to lunch, would leave with two or three letters in his hand and Igor's request to "drop them in the corner mailbox." The humors of the day are determined by the contents of the morning post, which, with packages of books, music, letters, is generally large enough to fill a laundry basket. The bulk of the letters are from autograph hunters of the sort, "Dear Sir, I have signed photos from Christ, Socrates, Stockhausen, and Schweitzer, and would you please. . . ." These are destined for a special outsized dining-room wastebasket. (Igor allows himself to be victimized by the autograph racket only when it seems the easiest way to rid himself of a nuisance. I may add that he has managed to keep the public-institution attitude at bay better than any other eminent octogenarian, and in this age of the false-hero industry—Schweitzer, Casals, or this or that *chef d'orchestre*—he has luckily continued to be the arch anti-hero. He does not like the role of patriarch, either, and will not allow the neighborhood children to call him "Gramps," though he has willingly satisfied their curiosity about him when they brave our doorstep at Halloween.) Igor feels compelled to answer and file away every letter immediately, and he demands as much alacrity in his correspondents. He will even calculate the minimum time that an answer could take, and if it has not come by then he will send a copy of his original letter. His rooms probably contain as many filing cabinets as the state department of Liechtenstein, and no wonder. In addition to the huge dead-letter bureau, he has kept every program and article concerning his music since 1906. The articles are heavily underscored, incidentally, and the margins are filled with rubrics vehemently unflattering to the intelligence of critics.

The morning mail trauma leaves him only one or two hours' time for composition before lunch, but another three hours are set aside in the late afternoon, and sometimes three more at night. I can tell you nothing about the bio-chemistry of the composing process, of course, and little enough even about the habits which govern those hours. I do know that Igor's body temperature increases when he works—like Beethoven he has to open the windows afterward—and I believe him when he claims to prefer the activity of composing to the end product; he never savors a completed work in the same way as he does work-in-progress. He is now writing a cantata for baritone and orchestra, on a biblical text to be sung in Hebrew. He says that the musico-syllabic possibilities of Hebrew have charged his musical enzymes, and they must be highly charged, judging by the ardor with which he has composed in these past weeks. He begins by playing over the work of the previous day, and though he complains of his pace, each new opus seems to be written with the same facility that has marked his production all his life; the jinni never seem to fail him, and his genius shows no sign of weariness. From what I have said of his impatience to post letters, you will not be surprised to hear that as soon as twenty measures have been completed he will write them in score and send them to the publisher. He never rewrites in any depth, though he will recopy an entire page of orchestra score rather than leave a smear or an erasure, and never, in any enterprise, does he take a backward look.

Igor's studio is the most distant room from the kitchen. He cannot bear any odor while he is composing and he claims that pungent ones actually interfere with his hearing (a phenomenon which has been explained to us, though I don't understand the explanation, as an "interference of the functions of the amygdaloid nucleus with the computer functions of the cerebral hemispheres"). He composes at a tacky-sounding and usually out-of-tune upright piano that has been muted and dampened with felt. Nevertheless, and though the studio is soundproofed and the door tightly closed, little noises as though from mice on the keyboard penetrate the next room. A plywood drawing board is fixed to the music rack and to it are clipped quarto-size strips of thick white paper. These are used for the pencil-sketch manuscript. A few smaller sheets of paper are pinned to the board around this central manuscript, like sputniks. They are the navigation charts of serial orders, the transportation tables, the calculations of permutations—"here the twelfth note becomes the second note . . ."—and so forth. A kind of surgeon's operating table stands to the side of the piano, the cutlery in this case being colored pencils, gums, stopwatches, electric pencil-sharpeners (they sound unpleasantly like lawn mowers), electric metronomes, and the styluses with which Igor draws the staves and of which he is the patented inventor.

There are regular, established interruptions in Igor's day, such as the almost daily trips to doctors, the late-afternoon

visits of André Marion, Igor's son-in-law and secretary, and
the visits of his attorneys the Montaperts, with whom he is
closeted for hours at a time plotting new ways of reducing the
"fisc" (Igor's word for income tax); the current ways are a
fruit farm in Arizona and a "mineralogical development"
project (as the government describes the fossicking in "Veri-
gor," our California gold mines). Another regular visitor is
Robert Craft. Igor used to call him "Bobsky," I think because
of his Quiz-Kid eyeglasses; and, dropping a "ch" from Gogol,
"Bobinsky," a version first put into circulation by our friend,
the culture generalissimo, Nicolas Nabokov. Bobinsky comes
to help Igor with musical business, but he also contributes a
large amount of some not exactly coruscating conversation
on other matters. In the last few years, however, he has become as indispensable to Igor as his memory (which, in fact,
he is). He often stops to eat with us, incidentally (though
perhaps not entirely incidentally, as he is something of a chow
hound). Our meals are prepared sometimes by myself but
ordinarily by Evgenia Petrovna whose last name, Mrs. Gate,
is used according to whether we are being Russians or Americans. The cooking is regularly French but periodically Russian: *caviar blini, stroganov, kasha, kulebiaka, kissel, borscht,*
and *piroshki.*

To a casual observer some of Igor's habits at table would
seem odd, but what would probably be called the eccentricities are, as I see them, at least, partly "Russian." He relishes
dinnertime discussions of liver, bladder, and bowel troubles,
for instance, but so did Tolstoy (see the Countess Sophia
Tolstoy's *Journal*), and as the same unseemly inclination is
manifest in so many Russians of my acquaintance, I feel it
might almost be called a cultural trait. (One also finds it in
the French, though, as in the account by the Goncourts of a
dinner with Flaubert, Zola, Turgenev, Daudet: "We began
with a long discussion on the special aptitudes of writers suffering from constipation and diarrhoea.") On the personal

side, Dr. Glover (see his "The Significance of the Mouth in Psychoanalysis") would doubtless classify Igor as a "sucker" rather than a "biter," which would explain his preference for deep spoons, as well as his apparent dislike of the occidental system of impaling and lifting; at home, without guests, he sometimes feeds himself directly from the plate, aligning his head with it and bulldozing the contents to his mouth. He will eat directly from serving dishes, too, on occasion, and return leftovers *ibidem*, even though somewhat the worse for wear. He sets upon every variety of viand in such a highly distinctive manner, however, that with the exception of ragouts, which are dunked with bread and mopped in classic French style, the approaches are too individual and too extensive for cataloguing. A general characteristic is his abhorrence of any oleaginous substance. He will trim every rind of skin and fat, peeling a frankfurter and paring a piece of *prosciutto* so finely that the result will quality as a carving. This meticulousness is not especially "Russian," to be sure, but perhaps the large capacity for liquids is; and the sonorous sloshing of alcoholic beverages about the mouth (to flush the remoter taste buds); and the sound effects accompanying the intake of *potages* (rich fricatives that would greatly increase an *avant-garde* writer's store of siphonic onomatopoeia), though the ultimate stage, with the hoisting of the bowl like a wassailing Viking draining his meads, is culturally more Scandinavan than Slavic. Russian also, albeit obscurely, may be the habit of beret-wearing during meals, as though from a doctrinal duress like that of a pious Jew. Now, to a stranger all this must seem like the description of an outer barbarian, whereas to an acquaintance who sees him twice a month or so and on a different mettle, it will more likely appear as the "colorful idiosyncrasies of genius," a case of *génie oblige*. The truly singular aspect of it, however, is none of this but the spectacle of the Neanderthal appetite and energy.

Igor escapes from his work by playing solitaire; by looking

at television (he seems to be especially fond of the commercials, which are more "intellectual," he claims, than the features; he means the shaving-cream jingles that refer to Occam's razor, and so on); by listening to recordings; by catching by the scruff of the neck and caressing Celeste, our puss*partout* cat; by strolling in the patio (he is afraid to walk in Beverly Hills because of the danger of being run over by the Rolls-Royces of movie composers), though to walk at all has become difficult for him since his three "cerebrovascular accidents" (as the American euphemists describe a thrombosis; janitors here are called "maintenance engineers" and gangs of juvenile delinquents are "unsponsored youth groups"); and by talking with our gardeners Vassili Varzhinsky and Dmitri Stepanitch, old-fashioned gentlemen-refugees who look like character actors "on location" in a piece by Ostrovsky or Chekhov. In fact, some years ago a film talent scout approached Dmitri Stepanitch, who has a fine Kaiser beard, to play that monarch in a war picture. This person and a cigar-chomping agent had been casing our house for weeks, it appeared, but they could not know without closer evidence that, like all of our Russian retainers except our first physician here, Prince Galitzin, Dmitri Stepanitch could speak no English. But Dmitri Stepanitch is a great ham and his performance as the Kaiser would have been much too heavily scented. I should add that Dmitri Stepanitch has occasionally caused small flurries in the kitchen by his attentions to the American girls who help Mrs. Gate. They complain of his gallant hand-kissing, not because of the embarrassment, though, as I would, but because of the tickle.

Afternoon tea, served between siesta time and composing time, is another relaxation. Igor also drinks *infusions* or *tisanes* (*tilleul-menthe* or *camomile*), but he is inclined to lace these mild brews with a tumbler of some more potent potation. His managerial cortex is very powerful, and alcohol does not interfere with his work, unless, of course, he gets "squiffed." In the Swiss years he used to drink white wine (Neuchatel) while composing, and in his French years red wine. In America it is Scotch or sometimes a bumper of beer.

We engage in very little social activity here, but this was not always the case. In his *Dr. Faustus "Tagebuch,"* Thomas Mann suggested that Hollywood during the war was a more intellectually stimulating and cosmopolitan city than Paris or Munich had ever been, and improbable as that sounds to Europeans visiting our subtopia today—Hollywood now seems more like a cemetery with lights, as the Americans say, but, then, we come here only to recharge our batteries and to memorize the new telephone numbers and zip codes—I think it may almost have been true. The ferment of composers, writers, scientists, artists, actors, philosophers, and genuine phoneys did exist, and we often attended the lectures, exhibitions, concerts and other performances of these people. To compare *that* Hollywood with the Hollywood of today, consider the fact that the premiere of one version of Brecht's *Galileo*, with the collaboration of Eisler and Charles Laughton, took place here, and think of the inconceivably remote prospects of such an event now. Igor was so deeply impressed by the *Galileo*, incidentally, that the play was directly responsible for one of his rare public political acts. He protested Eisler's deportation because, as he said, he could see no possibility of harm from the man, and he thought the exile of the artist, or of any artist, a loss. But, then, at the time of the political fears of the immediate postwar years, culture decamped like Cambyses' army—culture as we knew it, that is, for Hollywood continues to boom unmindful of the phase I have tried to distinguish.

But I am rambling, not ranging, and I must stop. Remember me to Caterina and, if you chance to see her, to Anna Akhmatova. We both send our love.

Vera

2

Hollywood, February 25, 1965

Vladimir Ivanovitch Petrov
8 Pokrovsky Boulevard
Moscow

Dear Valodya,

We have changed houses! The climb from the street had become an insuperable obstacle for Igor and the lack of space was an increasing inconvenience for me. The move is not great, the new address being on the same street and only a two-minute walk away, but Igor was unhappy about leaving his old studio, and though the new one is better equipped (whether or not with muses I cannot say), he seemed for a time to regret the transfer, judging by his reluctance even to re-enter the old house—which we still own and which is still reigned over by Mrs. Gate. Igor was always deeply, even fetishistically, attached to objects, as you know, but not until this move did I realize how much security he has derived from them. Just as strongly as he possessed them, however, so now they have turned to possess him. Until he learned the relocation of them in the new house, a fuzziness was noticeable in the corners and edges of his ego, and during that transitional period the night light in his room had to be increased from a little blue *veilleuse* to two surgery-strength lamps.

The new property is more than twice as large as the old and it extends through the block to the next street, on which side we have a guest-house. We have many more trees than before, too, palms, pines, magnolias in front, and avocados and oranges in the rear—as well as contributions from a neighbor's scabious and ever-shedding eucalyptuses. We also have a swimming pool. Igor was never much at aquatics, and in fact he seems to have the fear of water said to be common to Russians, staying below deck when at sea, like Goncharov

on the *Frigat Palat*. But *I* like to swim, if such it is possible
to call my turtle stroke, and when the hot desert wind of our
California mistral dries our sinuses and the air for a hundred
electric miles around, the pool is a nirvana in a deliciously
palpable form.

We have two storeys now, or three, counting the basement,
which is a music room containing a piano, record-playing
equipment, music, and music books. At the well of the basement staircase is a wine cellar, and at the landing, conveniently
situated for emergencies from either floor, is a W.C., one of
five in the house. Salons, dining rooms, libraries are on the
ground floor, and so, of course, is the kitchen, which, with
gravity heat, push-button dishwashing, and garbage disposal
(a scary contraption), is a triumph of automation. The living
room contains no furnishings from our old house. Its chief
ornament is a black marble fireplace, on the mantelpiece of
which Igor keeps silver bowls of white asters and wax
gloxinias. In one corner of the room is a triple-fold *paravant*,
covered with an enlarged photograph of Igor looking over
the railing of a bridge at the Villa Manin.

The most effective improvements on our old house are
upstairs. There Igor has four connecting rooms as well as a
labyrinth of closets and alcoves, the Fort Knox of his filing
systems. He is now able to go from a central-bathroom-base-
of-all-operations to his bedroom, office, or studio without dis-
turbance by other inhabitants and without leaving his lair.
In the arrangement of furniture and bibelots, incidentally,
Igor's new studio is a near replica of the old, except that it and
all of his rooms are more spacious.

At this point I fancy you must be thinking of my description as the typical dream of the *petite bourgeoisie*. We ourselves do not feel thus tainted by our amenities, just as we
are not disturbed at being regarded by the neighbors as
"communists," as we were after our Russian visit, and by our
Russian friends as "imperialists," because of the mere fact of

residence in the farthest-"right" neighborhood of the left
part of America.

We were acquainted with the house during the tenancy of
the former owner, a remarkable lady who was a friend of
Igor's in ballet days and who, in fact, had paid for Diaghilev's
funeral and interment when no one closer came forward. A
colorful woman herself, one aspect of whose fame was established through the keyholes of a well-known *roman à clef*,
she had a genealogy from the time of the First Crusade, and
an Avignon Pope's dispensation of the ancestral right to meat
on Fridays. She had been immensely wealthy, too, but her
more tangible fortunes had dwindled through a long lifetime
shared with costly and impermanent paramours. Eventually
she was obliged to sell her homes in London, Paris, Venice,
Stra, until this was her only and, as it happened, also her last
property, though it dwindled, too, by parceling, and otherwise fell into desuetude. Toward the end, the living rooms
had become a kind of flea market in which most of the contents were for sale and even the ash trays had price tags.
Needless to say, the house had to be entirely refurbished.

※ ※ ※

You ask after Igor's health. He is stooped now, and walks
slowly and with a cane, which exaggerates the impression of
frailty. For any distance greater than a few hundred feet he
is constrained to use a wheel chair, which is the case in air
terminals. This must have been a hard climacteric to him at
first, as he was always an impatiently fast walker and only a
few years ago trailed me behind him like a Chinese wife, but
he seems to have become accustomed to it now and even to
enjoy the perambulation. Another impediment to locomotion
is a hernia, result of an accident eight years ago owing to a
partial paralysis on his right side which rendered him insensi-
ble to the strain of lifting a suitcase; he sometimes says that

he feels as though the right half of his body has been separated from the left, and that his right hand feels as though encased in a glove. Other parts of the dwelling are out of kilter, too, and there are other malfunctions, but the impaired walking upsets him more than anything else, and the threat of immobility, of the wheel chair as the only method of progress, is the most terrible of his forebodings.

Walking apart, Igor does not look his years. There is no admixture of gray in his reddish hair (at least on the top of the head, though it must be admitted that few hairs of *any* hue can be found in that location), and his eyes and ears are as attentive and powerful as ever. The face has gained in flesh and lost in angularity, but it is not striated with wrinkles as with others of his age. And the head is the most striking I have ever seen. For one thing, it is so small (a size-5 hat) and so unlike the genius types of the Beethovens and other behemoth highbrows (in the best sense) dear to nineteenth-century phrenology. The frontal lobes are "delinquently" low and concave, the glabella and jaw are "unheroically" recessive, and the nether lip is somewhat thick—a cranial picture resembling Shakespeare far less than those simian prototypes which Igor occasionally refers to and mispronounces as "aps."

The change in temperament in the last two years is very marked, however. The carapace over his feelings appears to be harder than ever, but the reason, I suspect, is that the contents have mellowed; and corresponding to this change is a loosening of the characteristic economy, in time, talk, money, and almost everything, in fact, but music. He is forgetful, too, and quicker to reverse himself, as well as unduly suspicious of any remarks he fails to understand, but these are ordinary signs of age. What is individual and unexpected is a new gentleness. Indeed, the word *"gentil"* appears so frequently in his vocabulary now, but was so rare in the past, that I accustom myself to it with difficulty.

There are no rages and no temper tantrums any more, but

only very small eruptions that quickly turn to embers. Contrast this with the bad old days when an explosion a week was the uninfracted rule; though what marvelous detonations some of them were, especially when furniture was overturned and crockery smashed *à la* Baba the Turk—though they could also be noiseless, as occasion suited, for Igor could fill a room with his black mood by the simple act of passing through it, like a cuttlefish spreading its ink. *That* Stravinsky wrote the *Rite of Spring,* we would think, as we retreated in awe until the dusky fluids had subsided. In truth, too, and as you can see, I am a bit nostalgic and would welcome a small, symptomatic cyclone from time to time. The gods are too easily mollified now, and the breezes are all too bland—in fact, the Trades are the prevailing winds nowadays.

Nevertheless, Igor's most striking quality at eighty-three is his energy. The other day I marked this passage in Jules Renard's *Journal:*

> What remains is to pick up the pen, to rule the paper, patiently to fill it up. The strong do not hesitate. They settle down, they sweat, they go on to the end. They exhaust the ink, they use up the paper. There are only oxen. The biggest ones are geniuses— the ones who toil eighteen hours a day without tiring.

Renard might have been thinking of Igor. The sound of his piano sometimes issues from his *sanctum sanctorum* while a party is still in progress downstairs, a party, moreover, at which he has imbibed at least as much as anyone else, though he alone is clearheaded an hour after and able to work. Last night, while I was riveted to the television, he typed two dozen letters. He has never known a holiday, in the sense of inactivity, and even when ill in bed he will study a score or read or write. I cannot tell you the exact yield of work that he wrests from his time, but I doubt many composers of his years have surpassed him.

I have often thought that the unkindest way to behave with Igor is to treat him, the person, as a being apart. Few people are "themselves" with Igor, which is commendable, of course, and probably desirable in most cases; but it is a different matter when the visitor performs three bows and three stumbles before entering the presence, and then gold-frames each word for a future conversation piece almost before it is said. Though the only possible compliment to offer such a man is the knowledge of his work, many people proceed instead to humiliate him with flattery; no wonder he enjoys himself so much in the company of people who have never heard of him. One would assume that isolation would have resulted from this kind of treatment, and an insusceptibility to what philosophers call "other minds," but in fact the contrary is the case. Igor is unusually aware of "other minds" and quick to see their contents. Some people even complain of his remarkable acquisitive powers, in fact, and of his habit of repeating their ideas back to them as though they were his, but I say that it shows he has an improving mind.

I have also thought, of late, of how oppressive to Igor must be the weight of posterity. It has hung around his neck for so long that for three-quarters of his life he must have felt as burdened with it as a belled cat. Imagine what it is like to know that your letters are destined to be collected and sold, or that your most unmeaning remarks are bound to reappear, distorted, in somebody's woolly memoirs. Igor tries to avenge himself on this fate by, so to speak, entering into correspondence with it. He will frame in red ink the idiocies in books and articles about himself, as if by this means he were able to rub posterity's nose in the dirt, but to tell the truth, Igor is fond of bad reviews and they are important to his security. Consider, after all, that he has hardly ever had a good one, and then look at those who have them all the time.

I have wondered recently if Igor's mind has ever been

darkened with a doubt as to his present relationship to "the times"—that "*in hoc tempore*" he talks about—but I feel that it has not. He is aware of a defection from his leadership by the so-called main currents, of course, but he is still too full of his own creations to give much thought to the shift, and perhaps it is a welcome anodyne after all those ovine imitators of the forties and fifties. But what if he does tell himself a necessary lie? Which of us has not done that, and not only in old age but all the time?

Now, at eighty-three, Igor receives about $10,000 for a concert—or, rather, half of a concert and part of a rehearsal (most of the work falling to Robert Craft, without whom no appearance of Igor's would have been possible in the last decade). I have noticed that few people listen with attention to the music in these concerts and that, in fact, few seem even to have come for that purpose. What they want is to be in the numinous presence. And though $10,000 may be a lot of money, so is Igor a lot of numen.

> With love,
> Vera

Concerning a Music Journalist in Los Angeles

I

Hollywood 69, California
January 5, 1962

Music Editor
Los Angeles Times

Sir: I have this instant received your reviewer's notice of the belated first Los Angeles performance of my *Rake's Progress* (*The Times*, Dec. 4, 1961). As I was unable to see this production, I have no opinion of it, though in fairness I confess that the fact that your reviewer found it of high quality is for me the worst possible recommendation.

I must protest his misrepresentation of facts about my opera. The final ensemble, he says, "borrows a page from *Don Giovanni*." It does no such thing. He states that Tom Rakewell loses at a game of cards with Nick Shadow. This is also untrue. Tom wins the game, and he wins it in plain English, the language your reviewer so fervently advocates for opera, even though he understands it no better than he writes it. Anyone who failed to follow that simple but crucial event in the plot could have understood little else about my opera.

Your reviewer calls my score "eye music." He writes, "On the printed page it reveals all manner of intellectual devices." This description proves that either his eye never fell upon the printed page or that he cannot read music—or, more likely, both together. "Intellectual" means nothing in your reviewer's sentence, though it does mark his inability to hear harmony and melody; that it is a pejorative word to him is for an all too obvious reason. "Eye music" *is* a useful term, however, which he doubtless picked up from a musical acquaintance and misapplied. *The Rake's Progress* contains no example of eye music by any definition, and the opera's one short canon could hardly be more obvious to the ear if it had been doubled with trumpets. I would challenge your reviewer to cite his examples, but I want no further contamination of him, even from the crossing of quills.

I repudiate your reviewer's errors of opinion no less than his errors of fact. "The singers are required to negotiate all kinds of unvocal passages," he says. This would have to be denied by the many singers who have scored notable successes in all the roles of the opera. To professional musicians, "unvocal," "unpianistic," "unviolinistic," and the like, are so many refuge-words behind which the reviewer vainly seeks to hide his ignorance of the uses of vocal and instrumental art.

Still, your reviewer remarks that Mr. So-and-So, as the Rake, "disported his fine tenor ably," which he could not have done if the music were "unvocal." If "disport" is what he did, though, he should have been censured rather than commended for it.

"The rhythms are tricky." Well, yes, if your yardstick is the overture to *Rienzi*. As for the charge that "never was an opera less theatrical or more undramatic," I can say that a few months ago in Stockholm it was one of the most dramatic theatrical experiences in my life, and as the performance I saw was the thirty-fifth sold-out one in four off-season months (in a city with, incidentally, one-eighth the population of Los Angeles), I do not think my reaction was entirely egocentric.

For many years now I have had to observe your reviewer stumbling through the musical world in quest of the absolute middle in mediocrity; serving as a mouthpiece for the opinions of the *pons asinorum;* consuming space about X or Y's interpretation without having the slightest notion of what was being interpreted; dismissing old and new masterpieces simply because they are invisible in his mole's-eye view of music history; denying the composers of yesterday and then using them as clubs to cudgel the composers of today.

The time has come to protest. In the case of this ignorant, errant, and smug review of *The Rake's Progress* I had thought for a moment that some of my colleagues might do so, especially those who profess to admire my work (and who have helped themselves to pieces of it). But I had forgotten how careers are made. So, then, *I* protest, and not only what your reviewer wrote about my opera, but his incompetence to write meaningfully about music of any kind.

Igor Stravinsky

2

Hollywood
March 18, 1962

Music Editor
Los Angeles Times

Sir: Not surprisingly, the qualities which distinguish the *Times'* appreciation of my new book are ignorance, prejudice, and error.

I will deal first with error. I have recently remarked your reviewer's inability to read, a conclusion I reached after he demonstrated that even with score in hand he was unable to follow the most important event in the last act of my *Rake's Progress*. Now, to bear out my conclusion, he exhibits his inability to read correctly a passage in my book. He has mistakenly attributed my comment about the late Deaf ("he tends to use the first person") for a remark about the late Langweilich. A small difference, he will say, but it is as significant as the late Deaf's failure to distinguish between a twelve-tone scale and a twelve-tone method—which is not, as your reviewer's fiction column claimed it is, a slight misuse of terms but a basic misconception of twentieth-century music.

And prejudice. Specifically your reviewer's prejudice against the vocabularies of educated people. I myself am quite naturally interested in words, if only because of necessity; I have had to become fluent in three languages other than my own and to learn to make my way in three more. But my interest in words is not merely philological. I recognize that words are the very instruments of thought and that a large vocabulary permits the making of distinctions. Your reviewer, as an aspirant writer, ought to understand this, and he should welcome being sent to the dictionary to learn. And not only to the dictionary: how could he, as a would-be music critic, have failed to learn "esurient" from the title of the eighth phrase of Bach's or any other composer's *Magnificat*? How could he have read any popular history of painting without knowing "wain," and how could he have done basket-weaving in kindergarten without learning "osier"? And how could he have turned his back on my later music without knowing that he was "tergiversating"? These words which he objects to in my book are at least spelled and used correctly, however, and this much cannot be said of his own excursions into what he calls a "sportive" vocabulary. He describes the late Deaf as a "Stravinsky apostate," which is an impossible verbal construction, and his double-errored "ola-prodida" certainly cannot be a printer's error of "olla podrida."

And ignorance. Your reviewer confesses that he has never heard of several composers whom I nominate as likely reviewers for a composers' magazine. Still, every one of them has been discussed in *Musical America*, an exoteric journal of which the local correspondent is none other than your reviewer. With that source of information so close at hand, it should not take much effort for him to keep abreast of musical activities. Such an effort would be worthier than the one on which he has spent so much energy recently—demonstrating that he is a dunce.

Igor Stravinsky

P.S.: I append some lines by Goethe. They were no doubt written with a simpleton like your reviewer in mind, and they should help him to a better understanding of his problems. "All great excellence in life or art, at first recognition, brings with it a certain pain arising from the strongly felt inferiority of the critic; only at a later period, when we take it into our culture, and appropriate as much of it as our capacities allow, do we learn to love and esteem it. Mediocrity, on the other hand, may often give unqualified pleasure; it does not disturb our self-satisfaction, but rather encourages us with the thought that we are as good as another."

Concerning Edgard Varèse

Hollywood, California 90069
November 18, 1965

The New York Times
Times Square
New York, New York

To the Music Editor:

Mr. Harold Schonberg's tribute to Edgard Varèse (*Times*, Sunday, November 14) employs some remarks of mine in a context they do not aptly serve.

I am quoted as saying that "the best things in [Varèse's] music—the first seven measures from No. 16 in *Arcana*, the whole of *Deserts*—are among the better things in contemporary music." Mr. Schonberg's comment on this is: "Yes, it became very fashionable to give blanket endorsement to Varèse." *That* is "blanket endorsement"? to choose seven measures out of four hundred and fifty, one complete work out of twenty, and qualify the selections as among the "better" things?

Mr. Schonberg further states that "around 1950 [Varèse] found himself in the enjoyable position of having all of his works called masterpieces. Stravinsky's reaction is typical." The typical reaction is quoted: "Varèse's music will endure." Around 1950? But I had heard nothing by Varèse until almost a decade later, and in 1950 no one could have called all of his works masterpieces, as no more than a handful of them were known. Where, in which publications, is this chorus of flattering opinion to be found? I knew nothing of it, at any rate, and though I was aware of a new respect for Varèse on the part of younger composers, my own regard for him was not directed by any fashion. After all, the two recordings which offered the first fairly comprehensive introduction to Varèse's music originated not in Donaueschingen or even Downtown New York, but in plain Los Angeles. My opinion of the music was formed during those recording sessions, and it was formed first hand. And I expressed that opinion in my *Memories and Commentaries* of 1960 not at all in a hedging manner as Mr. Schonberg says.

Mr. Schonberg additionally declares that "blanket endorsements" such as mine "did not help get [Varèse] performances." Perhaps not, but then again perhaps they did: I know positively of an instance in which a work by Varèse was played together with a work of my own precisely because of what I wrote; but the assertion is simply not probative. And the inference that the blanket endorsers might better have spent their energies promoting performances is also misdirected in my case. In fact, I gave a part of the recording time allotted to my *Renard* so that a recording of his *Offrandes* could be made. There was no sacrifice or virtue in this, to be sure, and probably I will be blamed for doing as I did; certainly it is deplorable that Varèse did not have a recording period to himself. Nevertheless the music *was* performed by this means, and by it has become known.

For the rest, I found Mr. Schonberg's piece most eloquent, especially the quotations from Varèse. It is regrettable that the *Times* did not devote a leading article of the sort to Varèse while he was alive, but by way of reparation Mr. Schonberg might still encourage some visiting foreign orchestra to interrupt the forty-year neglect of Varèse's *Amériques*; this way American orchestras can continue with *Finlandia* and *España* undisturbed. Or would that be too fashionable?

❊ ❊ ❊

I became acquainted with Varèse myself only at the end
of his life, and then only slightly, but that was enough to
know his genuineness and his unauctionable integrity. A big,
gruffly restless man, he had extraordinary power to vivify,
and I will not forget him as he moved about his basement
studio striking his beloved gongs, then rushed around the
block to buy a pizza. I remember him most clearly, however
—it was the last time I saw him—listening to the electronic
interludes of *Deserts,* which he had just revised (the machine
guns were made to enter at new places, I think) and pleading
with the sound engineer to increase the already fuse- and
brain-blowing volume: he could hardly contain his eagerness
to wiggle the dials himself. I am deeply saddened by his death.

Yours, etc.,
Igor Stravinsky

Some Observations on V.D.

Hotel Pierre
New York City
August 14, 1964

The Editor
Listen
1265 Broadway
New York 1, N.Y.

Sir: Owing to concerts abroad I have just seen your May-
June issue with the blasphemy captioned "The Deification of
Stravinsky." I cannot reply to such a spew—a hose or refuse-
removal department is the proper tool for that—and I agree
with the Koran that in religious arguments one should "have
patience under what the unbelievers say, and withdraw from
them gracefully." Alas, however, I not only lack Muslim

restraint but, to be frank, I rather relish the opportunity to
put on some war paint and knock this particular infidel flat;
and I would be bound to comment, in any case, if only to
warn readers with unsuspicious critical faculties that the article in question is unadulterated claptrap.

The spectacle of a bad composer going sour is not new,
of course, and there is nothing new in the sourness of the
very bad composer V.D.—to adopt his own system of ini-
tialing. What is different in the case of V.D. is an absurd
pretension to two modes of music making, "serious" and
"pop." Consider his masquerade as a "serious" composer. The
conspicuous failure of Diaghilev's 1925 season was a ballet
Zéphyre et Flore by V.D. The failure was none of my responsibility, though the fact that Diaghilev performed the
piece at all was to some extent my fault. Mistaking youth and
facility for talent, I had recommended the work to Diaghilev,
and for that kindness I am now visited with this curmud-
geonly, forty-year-belated thank-you note. I was probably
not the only one to blame in the matter, however, for Diaghilev was guided by other opinion as well as mine. The young
composer must have had admirers; and perhaps their hopes
were later justified by the success of "April in Paris." Diaghilev forgave my error, I should add, as we forgave one another repeatedly, during two decades of our association, for
unbrotherly acts; he did produce my *Apollo* a few seasons
later, and my early ballets remained in his repertory. I do
not think he ever forgave the composer of *Zéphyre*; at least,
he never asked him for another score.

That the composer of *Zéphyre et Flore* became the composer of "April in Paris" is, I think, the very definition of
the composer who fails and who, bitter and rebarbative, de-
votes his decline to Philistine diatribe. Any successful coun-
terpart to himself is suitable game for such a composer, of
course, but the ideal target would naturally be someone with

a similar history as, for example, another Russian who had also had successive French and American careers. It is significant that V.D. holds very strong feelings of animosity against myself, who succeeded in the field where he failed, but not at all against the composers in whose company a flummery such as "April in Paris" entitles him to a place. What I really suspect is that he could forgive me anything except my successes, even though those successes have been liberally punctuated, according to his documentation, with failures. But the composer of "April in Paris" was never a competitor of any "serious" composer, and certainly none of us was ever competing against him. In fact, his path crossed ours so very briefly and ineffectually that I am surprised to find him now elbowing his way into the company of the qualified chroniclers of those very exciting events in which he played so insignificant a part.

I am content, however, to let him suffer the delusions he has about my art. What agitates my bile is his vulgar impertinence in concerning himself with my personal income, and his suggestion that it is "wrong" of me to aspire to financial well-being. Let me say, once and for all, that I have never regarded poverty as attractive; that I do not wish to be buried in the rain, unattended, as Mozart was; that the very image of Bartók's poverty-stricken demise, to mention only one of my less fortunate colleagues, was enough to fire my ambition to earn every penny that my art would enable me to extract from the *society* that failed in its duty toward Bartók as it had earlier failed with Mozart. But the commercial failure of Bartók's music can hardly be blamed on the wildly overestimated commercial success of my own, the most popular of which, as V.D. well knows, earned me no royalties whatever during most of their existence because of the lack of a U.S.-Soviet copyright agreement.

Let me say also that now, in my old age, I enjoy being as

successful "moneywise" as were, for example, Puccini and Richard Strauss, though this success amounts to a small fraction of a film composer's earnings, or a virtuoso pianist's, or a popular song writer's—for in denigrating my musical ear because of its alleged sensitivity to the clink of money, V.D. has imprudently thrown the first ruble. I would wager that *his* income from "April in Paris," "March in Malibu," "June in Jutland," and whatever else of the sort he may have perpetrated, has exceeded my income from *Petrushka, Le Sacre du printemps, Les Noces* and *The Symphony of Psalms*—to list, by his count, my four acceptable efforts. The wager would be based on my certain knowledge of what a single semipopular song has brought a friend who is a Hollywood composer; that, and the fact that composing has accounted for only a small part of my livelihood. Even now, I am able to earn more for a soon-forgotten half hour of conducting than for a year's work at compositions which, at worst, will survive me and, depending on progress in medical science and morals, V.D.

Until recently. Now, however, I am able to refute on its own terms V.D.'s crudely materialist argument against all those works of mine which, he says, "cannot be called a lasting success." (V.D.'s informants among future generations are not named, but perhaps by "lasting" he means no more than a decade.) In fact, the popularity of *all* of my music, or call it the commercial interest (which I would be the last to claim as a measure of musical value, but which terminology expresses V.D.'s standards), has rocketed a hundredfold in the past few years, bringing me at long last exactly the kind of success—or is it failure?—that seems to be V.D.'s principal grievance and envy.

I am also irritated by V.D.'s suggestion that a composer is corrupted when he embraces a so-called serial or twelve-tone esthetic. This is not the first time in history that esthetics have been subjected to false moral judgments. It was wicked of Monteverdi to switch to the "second practice." It was immoral of Gluck to subject the note to the word. It was diabolical of Wagner to construct his music according to a system of "leading motives." So, today, music in the Soviet Union, afflicted with the weight of socio-political morality, has become perniciously anemic; and here in the Western world—or, rather, in the back-eddies still infected by various forms of V.D.—serialism is damned as a heresy, even though some of the musical miracles of the century are the work of serial composers. But one should not have to fight on that old ground so many years after *Lulu* and the *Lyric Suite*, *Moses und Aron*, and the Webern Symphony.

Even more useless and tired are the old Lambertian, Clarendonian, and Gray Cecilian charges against me now served up by the composer of "Autumn in New York." My hide has been toughened by half a century of lashing by inferior critics and envious colleagues, however, and it is absolutely insensitive to the blows now inflicted on me in the name of Prokofiev. I survived these attacks when they were fresh and I have no intention of succumbing to them now that they have grown stale. What surprises me, though, is that the composer of "London in Leapyear" has no new arguments of his own to use against me. He is a mere bottler of old vitriol; and, in view of the large number of witnesses he calls up against me, who gave their evidence during the four decades from 1915 to 1955, can he still pretend to be surprised that, on the occasion of my seventy-fifth birthday, I at last got around to speak my mind about some of the people who had been slandering me for half a century? Until then I had written books that were, in the opinion of the composer of "February in Fujiyama," merely dull. Now I decided to talk back and, though I am not truculent by nature, I certainly intend that my criticisms of Prokofiev, Rachmaninov, Glazunov, *et. alii,* should be not less lethal than theirs of me. All of us have our memories, and it is quite evident that the public is interested in them; even those of a minor actor but full-time busybody like V.D. must attract a certain audience. How boring it would be if all of us held the same opinion of everyone we met. My research staff, looking back into the files of music criticism during the past few decades, reports some rather damaging reviews of the "serious" works of the composer of "Christmas in Caracas," and I dare say that his own dossier is hardly more flattering to him than the one he has assembled on me.

Finally, I must defend my vocabulary. When I was quite young I realized that one's mental development was measurable to a certain extent in terms of vocabulary, and I have labored to increase my vocabulary all my life. It is also true that my written language is more elegant than my spoken, but I have noticed that I share this fault with Mr. Auden and Mr. Eliot as well as with most "public personalities" I have met. It is also true that my colleague and collaborator, who is co-author of my books of conversations, polishes my language when it is ungrammatical or ungraceful but, then, assistance of this kind is also common and has been celebrated in such examples as Pound's help to Eliot, or Perkins's to Thomas Wolfe, or Ted Sorenson's to the late President Kennedy. (Judging from the verbiage and the megaphone style in his article, V.D. would do well to seek similar assistance himself.) And, having mentioned the late President, I might say that certain presidential news conferences (though *not* President Kennedy's) that I have chanced to hear in the past decade have not made me ashamed of my impromptu remarks for the TV presentation of *The Flood,* apropos of which, incidentally, I must correct two of V.D.'s calumniating errors: I wrote only the music for the presentation, not the commercials, and the piece was commissioned by CBS, not by the cosmetics firm that eventually sponsored the broadcast.

In conclusion I should like to say that I was flattered at being placed among the "lares and penates" of the American Composer (though wrongly placed, I think), and that I was both flattered and rejuvenated by the realization that my "dehumanized" and "emotionless" music can still trigger so much very strong emotion. Finally, even a yapping at the heels, when it is so dedicated and tireless, is a tribute. For the remainder I am all sympathy and understanding. I am sorry for V.D. in his plight of musical impotence and, disliking father figures myself and being very tired of false representations of my own, I recognize the wish to attack them. Perhaps I can even understand and forgive V.D.'s ambition, now satisfied, to be noticed in my books. Yours etc.

Igor Stravinsky

P.S.: Kindly send me whichever future issue of your sheet happens to contain notice of the *completed* vital statistics of V.D., so that I may send an appropriate wreath.

INTERVIEWS

I chose Wystan Auden as librettist for my opera *The Rake's Progress* because of his special gift for versification; I have never been able to compose music to prose, even poetic prose. That he was a great poet others had assured me—I felt as much, but was too new to English to judge for myself—yet my first requisite was more modest and more specific; after all, successful collaborations between musicians and poets in dramatic works have been rare, and in fact Dryden and Purcell, Hofmannsthal and Strauss, Boito and Verdi (Boito was, rather, a great adapter, but that is almost as valuable), are the only names that come to mind. What I required was a versifier with whom I could collaborate in writing songs, an unusual starting point for an opera, I hardly need to add, as most composers begin with a search for qualities of dramatic construction and dramatic sensation. I had no knowledge of Wystan's dramatic gifts or even whether he was sensible to operatic stagecraft. I simply gave all priority to verse, hoping that we could evolve the theatrical form together and that it would inspire Wystan to dramatic poetry.

I think he *was* inspired, and in any case he inspired me. At the business level of the collaboration he wrote "words for music," and I wonder whether any poet since the Elizabethans has made a composer such a beautiful gift of them as the "Lanterloo" dance in our opera. Wystan had a genius for operatic wording. His lines were always the right length for singing and his words the right ones to sustain musical emphasis. A musical speed was generally suggested by the character and succession of the words, but it was only a useful indication, never a limitation. Best of all for a composer, the rhythmic values of the verse could be altered in singing without destroying the verse. At least, Wystan has never complained. At a different level, as soon as we began to work together I discovered that we shared the same views not only about opera, but also on the nature of the Beautiful and the Good. Thus, our opera is indeed, and in the highest sense, a collaboration.

Wystan has lived in Austria too long now, and I wish you could convince him to come back. After all, we cannot afford to give our best poet to the Germans.

In the Name of Jean-Jacques!
New York, January 1964

SHOW MAGAZINE: What did you think of *The Last Savage*, Mr. Stravinsky?

STRAVINSKY: I did very little thinking, I assure you.

SHOW: But did you enjoy it? Or, at any rate, did you enjoy it more than Mr. Menotti's last opera?

I.S.: A "no" to the first question, and to the second . . . well, it could not easily be otherwise. One sees everything miles away but has to wait eons while a mostly anonymous and never good enough composer at his not infrequent worst slowly brings it nearer: no expectation is ever confounded. The evening also began with whatever is the opposite of a flying start—a diving start, I suppose, so that the first scene took place, so to speak, under water.

SHOW: Well, how would you describe the work in general terms?

I.S.: It is slapstick without humor, and I should add that it is "farther out" than anything I have seen in a decade; in the wrong direction, of course.

SHOW: But is it so completely humorless? By all accounts the Metropolitan audience. . . .

I.S.: Exactly. The planted buffolas and dead-end rhyme jokes could have been written only with a Met audience in mind. One imagines the groans with which such descents of wit would be greeted a few blocks north, albeit re-confected with a genuine Broadway book and score. I would not deny that the subscribers enjoyed themselves, but that was because of the novelty and incongruity of hearing the American language (comic-strip variety) in America's principal arena of European Opera.

Still, the evening was not without fun—of an unintentional sort.

SHOW: Metropolitan audiences *are* rather special, you know.

I.S.: Agreed. Many of them would have come to the late Mr. Blitzstein's *Sacco and Vanzetti* expecting something in the line of *Romeo and Juliet*.

But is an audience entirely responsible for its ignorance? I grant that most of them "like what they know," but I doubt that they "know what they like." They know only when they have made a choice, and the Met audience in its forty-year isolation from new opera has never been given that opportunity. If instead of *"Cav"* and *"Pag,"* *Adriana Lecouvreur, Manon, Samson, Andrea Chénier* and so on through the last few seasons, it had been exposed to good productions of a few contemporary masterpieces, would it allow itself to be served with such an ear of corn as *The Last Savage?* The Met audience, or, at least, the subscribers, the underprivileged in ermine, is perfectly palateless. Naturally, it does not know how to evaluate anything new.

SHOW: But what *are* the masterpieces of contemporary opera?

I.S.: Busoni's *Arlecchino* and *Doktor Faust*—with Fischer-Dieskau a few years ago in Berlin, one of the major theatrical experiences of my life—and *Mahagonny, Lulu, Wozzeck, Erwartung* and *Moses und Aron;* perhaps even *Mathis der Maler* or *Cardillac* (I do not know them) or the *Angel of Fire,* which I heard in New York recently, or a Janáček (though the only one I have heard was the thinnest, longest, and least succulent noodle I have ever tried to swallow). Admittedly there is a paucity. But a contemporary masterpiece needs the support of a whole community of contemporary operas, masterpieces or not, and the Met and every other opera house should be mounting at least three or four worthy new works every season. It should already have secured and announced the American premieres of Krenek's *Golden Fleece,* Dallapiccola's *Ulysses,* Henze's *Bassarids,* Britten's *Lear,* the new Nono. *The Last Savage* deserves performance, of course, as part of the scene. That it is brought forth alone identifies it with standards, tastes, policies; in other words, puts the Met in a strong contender's position for the title of World's Most Provincial Opera House. Unless, of course—a Machiavellian possibility—the Met were promoting *The Savage* as a comment on the low state of opera, or as an alibi to prove that contemporary operas are not worth doing, and in this case they could hardly have made a better choice. Now, heaven help us, I read that an itinerant company is to carry Met tradition to the great unwashed.

SHOW: But did you find no merit in *The Savage* at all?

I.S.: I enjoyed one episode, the "dodecaphonic" string quartet. This is not good but it is better than any of the other music, and in his next opus the composer should plan to do an entire dodecaphonic movement. I appreciate that it was planned as a parody, of course, and I often sympathize with the composer's evident desire that the twelve-tone system should "drop dead." When an author means to behave like a pigeon on a monument, however, he should be certain that his wings will lift him high enough to make the gesture effective. A parody in a work of such length can be effective only as an excursion from a home style. But *The Savage* is only parody; and when the author tries to launch one of the ensembles with a rhythm from Verdi (that of "*Zitti, Zitti*" in *Rigoletto*), he invites and receives devastating comparison. I should add that "modern life" cannot be mocked successfully with a compost heap of Mascagni (it is considerably later, as the expression goes, than Mr. Menotti thinks); and that, in any case, an assault on the kingdoms of this world is not exactly suited to a composer who has made it all on this side.

SHOW: Then you do not agree that the subject had possibilities?

I.S.: No, at least not for a composer with Menotti's equipment, and for the reason just given: he is able to project the "natural savage" horn of his opera's dilemma, but not the "modern sophistication" horn. The only aspect of "modern life" suggested by *The Last Savage* is that certain subcortical activities should be turned over to the computer; or, in other words, that the latter two-thirds of this score should have been composed by feeding the first third to a machine. The "predatory female" idea might have possibilities, though—I am thinking of Mr. Robbins's ballet about her to the music of my String Concerto—especially to talented bachelor composers such as Britten, Henze, Tchaikovsky, and Menotti. In any case, a frank treatment of that subject could hardly fail to generate more tension. (I imagine a spooky atmosphere piece with an unexplained dread, as in *The Turn of the Screw*.)

SHOW: But surely you will concede that Menotti has personality. Isn't such a device as the repeated "Oh Mother, Oh Mother" in *Amahl*, and the "Oh Father, Oh Father" in *The Savage*—isn't it a mark of a real *persona*?

I.S.: Hm. Well, it is Menotti's bread and butter, at any rate.

SHOW: But you must have liked the sets. Everybody liked the sets.

I.S.: Impossible to say without sunglasses.

SHOW: In short?

I.S.: In short.

SHOW: An eye-closer?

I.S.: An eye-closer.

A Talk with Stravinsky
New York, January 1965

NEW YORK REVIEW: We hope you are enjoying your stay in New York, Mr. Stravinsky. Have you been to any interesting concerts or other performances?

I.S.: No concerts, but I heard a good *Falstaff* at the Metropolitan. And, oh yes, there was a television program, the wisdom of Pablo Casals, I believe. *That* was an interesting performance. In one scene the cellist and a sort of Hungarian composer, Zoltán Kodály, are shown together with their great-granddaughters—or so the viewer supposes until learning a blush later that they are the wives. And what are the two racy octogenarians talking about? Well, they are talking about the trouble with me, which is that I must always be doing the latest thing—*they* say, who have been doing exactly the same old thing for the last hundred and eighty years. Señor Casals offers extracts of his philosophy, too. It is a matter of some simplicities; of his being in favor of peace and against Franco, for example, and of playing Bach in the style of Brahms. But I have strayed. You wished to talk about music reviewers.

N.Y.R.: We wanted to ask why you bother to complain about them; what they say seems to be of such slight importance.

I.S.: I agree that what a reviewer says may be inconsequential, even in the short run. What I protest is his right to say it— Voltaire in reverse. Some people have earned the right, by knowledge and skill, but they are not the present—and yesterday's present, and, in fact, the perennial—crop of reviewers. To protest is to plead for higher standards, and it is my duty to do that. Incidentally, it has been said to me in argument that certain reviewers are wrong but honest. I find this illogical as a defense and alarming as an indication of the state of ethics. I am not concerned with the honesty of an opinion but with its worth. And what a condition we have come to that honesty is so exceptional as to deserve citation.

N.Y.R.: What are your principal strictures of the present system, Mr. Stravinsky?

I.S.: When the time limit imposed on the reviewer is very short, he should confine himself to reporting rather than snap-judging. I would also suggest that his investiture be made to depend on the possession of certain qualifications (a good audiogram report, to begin with). There is but one at the moment, the knack of delivering five hundred more or less readable words in the allotted hour or half hour. Under the present system, this ability to deliver the pulp, both the daily dose and the Sunday causerie, can win for its owner a throne of authority in each of several specialized fields, as we well know in New York, where the promiscuous hospitality of the leading newspaper has encouraged a sports writer to become both a music critic and a drama critic.

N.Y.R.: But does it matter? After all, there are critical organs of a different caliber from the dailies and weeklies.

I.S.: Cricitism, as distinguished from reviewing, is deliberated and therefore delayed reaction; as such it has less effect on the immediate and popular-minded commercial processes by which musicians live. A bad, meaning unfavorable, review may have disastrous consequences for a gifted young composer whose work probably cannot be evaluated on a single hearing in any case.

N.Y.R.: What sort of consequences? And does the composer's position in such matters differ substantially today from any other time?

I.S.: To the first question the answer is that performance and publications are very definitely affected by reviews; this is evidenced by their quotation (usually distorted) by impresarios and publishers. To the second, I would say that the position of the composer has changed radically in recent years, though whether it is more parlous practically and commercially I cannot say.

Performance outlets available to him are few, however, and the circuits heavily overloaded, which is why he has lately formed concert societies with which he can swap performances with other composer-entrepreneurs. The young composer's musical position, on the other hand, could be de-

scribed as a variety of dilemmas. "Long live chance," he hears
from one side, and "long live combinatoriality," from another,
yet his conservatory failed to inform him even of the existence
of the words, and his subsequent teachers, instead of helping
him, only bewilder him the more by their own ever more
cynical departures on the seasonal bandwagons. Never before
have composers been so unprepared by their schooling. The
compositional techniques still generally taught are as useful as
spare parts for machinery last manufactured about seventy-
five years ago. With this equipment the young musician must
steer between the Scylla of neo-classic serialism and the
Charybdis of Cage—though hopefully the metaphor may
lose its aptness for the reason that younger musicians are
showing a desire to avoid these particular straits in favor of
the open sea. At no other period has notation itself fallen into
such chaos that composers were able to confuse notational
gimmicks and musical invention. Contemporary music, the
life of it as well as the art, is a complex affair, and it should
not be ruled over at any level by amateur critics.

N.Y.R.: But composers *are* published and performed, some
good ones included, presumably, if only by accident or laws
of averages.

I.S.: Certainly, but you cannot absolve the industry by its
happier accidents. And in any case, the typical quantity arguments are specious at best, and at worst grossly misrepresenta-
tive. Some recent hoopla on the nation's culture reported by
Time magazine included the claim that our symphony orchestras have grown in number "from 800 to 1300" since 1950,
and that "eighteen million classical records" were sold in the
United States last year. Now, whatever the slant of truth in
these figures, it is as misleading as an outright falsehood. The
statements are, in fact, outrageously incomplete, and as such
are not harmless nonsense but culpable distortion. *Which*

classical records? 17.9 million Tchaikovsky retreads? (And why, incidentally, should they be called high fidelity records? Isn't fidelity enough?) The count of symphony orchestras, I can assure you, is close to a hundred percent inflated. Of those deserving the name, we have more likely grown from eight to thirteen, though I doubt that as many as thirteen offer full-time livelihood to their entire personnel, and I am certain there are not thirteen capable of preparing first-rate performances of the new works of our outstanding younger composers. In fact, I know of no combination of a major orchestra with its resident conductor (the failure of the New York Philharmonic to play the complete Wolpe Symphony last year is a crowning case in point) to which such a composer as Elliott Carter might entrust his new piano concerto, as he could so have entrusted it to Hans Rosbaud and the orchestra of the Sudwestfunk; but the lack of alignment between our composers and performers is another question, the question as to whether we prefer Centers for Performing Arts to Centers for Creative Arts. For the moment it is enough of a point to expose the disservice in most cultural publicity, and to warn the gulled readers of statistical fictions.

N.Y.R.: Would you care to comment on any other aspect of that culture cover story?

I.S.: Well, it confirmed the dowager as the dominating figure in American cultural life, and the fact that our muse looks suspiciously like Mother. Apart from that, the value of such a view of culture is in the need it shows of redefining the object—even the object of a Music Center, which, it appears, is not by any means music *tout simple*. Los Angeles, for example, chose to baptize its new Center with the beer of Strauss's *Fanfare* and Respighi's *Feste Romane*—both products, incidentally, of what not long ago was called the Axis. Now chauvinism has never counted even among the critics'

lists of my sins, but I will risk the suggestion that music by
Los Angeles composers might have been a more mature
choice, even possibly a piece by a refugee *from* the Axis—for
instance, Schoenberg, the fact of whose residence in the
movie village would be generally acknowledged in other less
remote parts of the world as the choicest flower the village
could have worn in its musical buttonhole on such an occasion.
To play Respighi instead of Schoenberg at the debut of a
Los Angeles Music Center would be comparable to the un-
veiling of a bust of Lysenko rather than Einstein at the opening of a museum of science at Princeton; or the dedication of
a museum of art in Cannes with an exposition of Buffet rather
than Picasso. In the dark of these antics the celebration of our
cultural "coming of age" seems a little ludicrous. Our culture
politics are in fact no more competent than our world politics,
and we are still playing at the game of American civilization
vs. European culture. America was already eminently "of
age" with Thoreau, C. S. Peirce, Ives, Wallace Stevens, and
others, I would think, and in fact it sometimes looks—the
view from the eastern side of the bridge, anyway—to be
growing the other way. But I am discursive—an old man's
fault. You must stop me.

N.Y.R.: May we return to our question about reviewers, Mr.
Stravinsky? Are they alone responsible, or are they also victims of the system?

I.S.: They are both, sometimes, but I have tried to impute to
them no more than their share, and I certainly do not hold
them guilty every time. In fact, only yesterday I found myself defending them. This remarkable occurrence came about
as a result of listening to a tape of the new *Wozzeck* at
Covent Garden, and at the same time reading a file of reviews.
To compare the performance with the reports of it was to
be struck by the universal failure of the latter to mention the

fact that the singing was at least half of the time very wide of the mark in respect to pitch. But can one blame the reviewers? The vocal parts in the denser passages are difficult to follow even now, and, anyway, is the reviewer not justified in assuming that at some point in the preparation the conductor would have discovered and arrested a wholesale tendency to sing wrong notes? The picture must be restored to *status quo*, however, and I will therefore conclude with another instance, fresh from my own experience, in which I think the reviewer is at fault. At the recent New York performance of my *Abraham and Isaac*, a hireling of the newspaper which knows what is "fit to print" described the piece as "monotonous" and "minor." Now, both words may very well be "true" (I have no doubt that they represent the "honest opinion" of the person who scribbled them), and surely the point of view of them can be sustained and justified (I could do it myself; I might also add that I have grown quite a garden with the flowers that reviewers have thrown at the supposed graves of works of mine over the past fifty years). But they have to be explained. The reader deserves the dignity of argument, and if the reviewer cannot supply one, he should give the facts of the concert and other bits of reportage about it, and no more. The two words, just by themselves and thrown like mud, are nothing.

N.Y.R.: Do you, Mr. Stravinsky, have any further observations to offer concerning the approach to criticism?

I.S.: Well, conception comes first, of course; you must be able to listen to what you are hearing. And you must find a point of balance between past and present. This is difficult even in considering the work of a single individual, where the new cannot be isolated from the old, yet must not be judged entirely in terms of it either. Perhaps the central problem, then, is to measure the individuating newness. I have been thinking about this in connection with my new Variations, and wondering how to describe whatever in it is new, but all I can say is that this newness came to me naturally, and that it cannot seem natural to a critic, even to one who knows me in the form of my entire past, for the simple reason that he is not me. The standard approach to any aspect of the new consists in identifying so-called influences, a device that in my case has resulted of late in some jejune comparisons with isorhythmic motets. With the Variations it will no doubt be discovered that I have been sideswiped by Stockhausen, or received major transfusions from Boulez.

N.Y.R.: Surely the practices you deplore will be corrected, Mr. Stravinsky, on the accession of a new generation.

I.S.: For what reason, by what training and what example now in operation? No. In fact, I am tempted to fly to the other extreme of *"Plus ça change . . ."* though that is an equally unlikeable complacency. Just suppose for a moment that it was not complacency, however, but a matter of biology? Suppose that someone were to discover a kind of Bertillon measurement for reviewers? After all, there has been no change in cockroaches these 150,000,000 years.

A Perfect Total

"I would rejoice in it more if I knew more clearly what we wanted the knowledge for. . . ."
—W. H. AUDEN, *After Reading A Child's Guide To Modern Physics*

SEVENTEEN: Mr. Stravinsky, what are the general problems in the path of young people who wish to pursue careers as composers or artists—not the timeless problems of art but those peculiar to our age of science?

I.S.: Generality itself may be the greatest problem, but before I attempt to explain let me say that I consider it a mistake to think of *making* in art, as distinguished from *selling* in art— newspaper reviewing, lecturing to women's clubs, conducting orchestras—in terms of a career; the making itself is its own end, and there can be no other. As for the problem of generality, it is simply that whereas the arts in past cultures interpreted, symbolized, or adorned general ideas—call them religious beliefs, or merely "ends"—the general as well as the particular ideas of science are incomprehensible to most artists and are likely to remain so in the near future. How, then, is an artist who aspires to associations of science to make his arrangements with (how interpret, symbolize, and adorn?) general scientific beliefs that he is able to apprehend only through paraphrases in an intermediate and inexact language of words? In fact, how is he even to make his representations against them in the event that, like myself, he objects to being taken on a ride to an unannounced destination as a straphanger to concepts he does not understand? Speaking for myself, I can say that *my* generalities—cosmological, philosophical, theological—are those of a remote and comparatively primitive past; or, alternatively, that my art is my generality. But this is no help to young people whose work is yet to be fashioned. Thank heaven (or some other generality) that you only ask me to name the problems, not to try to solve them!

Another large one, one in which I have had some experience, is the increasing domination by technical processes— call them "means." Closely related to this, in fact a chief consequence of it, is the problem of the increasingly rapid turnover of artistic conventions. And I should stop at these two, on which I have some views, and try to disentangle myself from the wool of my own generalities, except that there is one more "problem" on my list, and it is the only one on which I am really qualified to speak. This is the problem of old age, of continuing to grow from your seventeen to my eighty-three. The new science of gerontology is of no avail here, and old age is more than ever a nightmare, even to the few near-nonagenarian newsworthies like myself who have escaped that neglect which is the fate of the elderly. As I see it, much of the responsibility for this state of affairs lies with the news-drugged public's obsession with novelty, for our society tends to glamorize, rather than merely encourage, the newest and youngest, the first novels and the opus "1"s, and always at the expense of mature work. This, too, is a side effect of the disintegration of those general ideas.

SEVENTEEN: Would you explain what you mean by encroaching technical processes and the consequences thereof?

I.S.: The present development of recording technique is the nearest example to hand, though the technical aspect of recording is only one of the problems created by an industry that will soon be bringing the most "in" composers' latest gimmicks to Djakarta, Stanleyville, and Des Moines directly from the launching pads in the European fashion centers. The distribution of printed music has little effect today in comparison with the distribution of recordings, not only because recordings can be broadcast, but also because most new music cannot be heard in the imagination simply by reading the score, as was once the case. Still, the prospect of world standardization dismays me less than the prospect of the complete technical domination of the musical performance itself. Recording processes, which are determined by wasteful competition, have already arrived at the stage at which the manufactured performance has supplanted the true one and at which, on choice, most of us would reject the true. We are so well accustomed to the refinements of technical processing even now, if fact, that we find the natural to be less and less allowable. Natural balance, natural dynamics, natural echo, natural color, natural (and endearing) human error—such as the cracked horn-notes that disappeared from recorded per-formances a decade ago, but still occur in concerts—these have been replaced by added echo and reverberation, by a neu-tralizing dynamic range, by filtered sound, by an engineered balance. The resulting product is a super-glossy chem-fab music substitute that was never heard on sea or land, includ-ing Philadelphia. Now, obviously, gross and distracting errors must be edited out, and some other improvements should be allowed if the vital cohesion of the performance is not thereby intercepted, but sound engineers and tape splicers have ex-ceeded this kind of minor surgery by so much that they are, in effect, reconducting the performances. And it is already too late to complain, for fake phonography has overtaken fake photography, and a recording nowadays has been so thor-oughly "corrected" technically that it is as unlike a live per-formance as a painted corpse in a Hollywood mortuary is unlike a living human being.

SEVENTEEN: What, Mr. Stravinsky, do you mean by conven-tion?

I.S.: Something quite comprehensive, and as my idea of it probably impinges on other concepts, I doubt that I can offer a definition. I could begin by saying that I am a conventional composer myself, for instance, but that would shed no light as I am unable to imagine any other kind. Or I could turn to some of the labels habitually cast in opposition to "conven-tional," like "revolutionary" and "spontaneous," but the artists who would profess to attitudes thereunder invoked would soon prove to have their conventions too, however different the emphasis they would put on the word. Let me try defini-tion *per differentiam*, then, and discard some meanings which are *not* mine. First, the conventional is often equated with the old-fashioned, wrongly to my mind, not because of the "old," but because a fashion is a lesser phenomenon. Thus, automobile tail fins, jazzy glasses, snoods, were fashions of the fifties, but the principle governing the incidence of their occurrence is a convention both of our economic life and of a certain area of our artistic life. The word is also applied to a kind of art which carries over from its immediate legacy with little change—a description, by the way, of most commercially successful art (Rachmaninoff is an example). And it is used with still another sense by cartographers, as I have lately learned from *The Vinland Map,* a "conventional" outline being a mere copy, the contrary of one that is "realistic" or empirically determined. As I said, however, these are not my meanings. To me, conventions are codes of agreement. As such they are carriers of tradition (and of genre, though that is another question). Conventions differ from traditions in that they are modified rather than developed, and in that they are tied to this or that time, whereas traditions, as major lines of descent, are timeless. Traditions may be thought of as the universal and the hard facts of art, conventions as the local and the soft facts.

Perhaps you recall the discussion of this subject in the *Cratylus,* Socrates refereeing at first, then refuting Hermogenes' argument that names are not attached to things by nature but are conventions of the users. I confess that so far as my art is concerned I agree with Hermogenes, even though modern philology opposes him, holding that word conventions are anything but arbitrary and that all names possess "echoic value"; and modern physics as well, if I understand anything of what Dr. Oppenheimer means by "prejudices of nature." In art, the agreements of the users, the mutual understanding of the parties to the artistic transaction, are enough, it seems to me, or at any rate they are all the artist need bother about. Profound derivations in nature are not his affair, and Nature itself is only another convention to him.

SEVENTEEN: Why does the rapid acceleration with which conventions are modified disturb you, Mr. Stravinsky?

I.S.: Because, like all old men, I am portentous (though prescient is the way old men prefer to think of themselves). Nevertheless, from where I stand (and my geography may be at fault), the community of criteria which has always existed somewhere in the background appears to be crumbling. Now, you may say that this does not matter, that posterity will sort the sheep from the goats, but to me such an answer is complacent. I have no confidence in the justice of posterity and have never understood the logic of the argument that though what *is* may be wrong, the consecration of it through time will make it right. To me all histories are deterministic. They offer not "what was," but a choice governed by the determinations, conscious and unconscious, of the choosers. I myself have lived long enough to have known a few of these histories of my own music, and to have seen the complexion put upon the very same pieces turn from Revolutionary red to Establishment gray, though, of course, the music was guilty only of re-ordering the conditions of its environment, of creating reaction and being reacted upon in turn according to laws of social biology which the historians did not take into account.

SEVENTEEN: Would you say that changes in convention are brought about in a similar manner?

I.S.: I suppose that a kind of biological process must take place, the succession of modifications at some point producing a new species, and that the metaphor might be extended to describe electronically fabricated sound as a mutation. But this is picture language, no more, and therefore a contribution to the semantic mess.

SEVENTEEN: Where do you find the greater semantic obstructions, Mr. Stravinsky, between yourself and your audience, or between yourself and your colleagues?

I.S.: They are about equal, I imagine. At any rate, I seem to be about equally estranged from my youngest and oldest competitors.

SEVENTEEN: And how do you envisage your audience today?

I.S.: It has no visage for me, which is why I no longer have any audience in mind when I compose. Though audiences exist for my past works, they have yet to be developed for my present ones. I deplore this breach, but unlike some of my more "socially conscious" colleagues I do not believe that it can be closed by a *rapprochement* in a musically backward direction. To me, any attempt to return to past safeties is as futile as the proposal a few years ago to return to "conventional" (still another meaning!)—pre-H or A—bombs. We can neither put back the clock nor slow down our forward speed, and as we are already flying pilotless, on instrument controls, it is even too late to ask where we are going.

SEVENTEEN: A final question, Mr. Stravinsky, concerning the last of the "problems" you mentioned, old age: how do you see yourself in relation to the youth of today?

I.S.: The youngest generation is not very respectful of age, as you know, and younger composers tend to regard me with about as much interest as speeding motorists give to a discarded automobile in one of those above-ground roadside graveyards. I do not mind the relegation, though, and I have not become cynical (well, not very) observing each year's crop of these youths as they arrive and unpack their suitcases full of, or so it seems for a while, bright new ideas. We— these young people and myself—are a necessary equation, and so are the two of us, your seventeen and my eighty-three. Together we make a perfect total.

A Decade Later

*When sounds are smooth and clear, and have a single pure
tone, then they are not relatively but absolutely beautiful.*

—PHILEBUS, 51

*Music unites the contrary attributes of being both intel-
ligible and untranslatable.*

—LÉVI-STRAUSS: *Le Cru et le Cuit*

UNIVERSITY OF WASHINGTON INTERVIEWER: You were
complaining about Anton-olatry, Mr. Stravinsky, and assert-
ing that it is time to replace cultism with criticism.

I.S.: Yes, but we should not altogether despise cults. As prime
movers they are far more useful than critics, after all, and in
Webern's case the cult, rather than the critics, is responsible
for much of our knowledge of the music. But cults tend to
become dome shaped, and domes exclude the light. Worse
still, the Webern cult made the mistake of switching from
the music to the musician, a barren devotion in any case, but
especially so in this one because of the unexploitable nature
of the mahatma-to-be. The pendulum has started back,
though, and there are signs of tastes and discriminations coming into operation. Soon we will have to listen from a new
angle. But poor Webern!

U.W.I.: What do you mean by that?

I.S.: I was merely musing on the destiny of composers and
the depredations of amateur appraisers, with their cycles of
inflation and deflation. The fact that Webern is suffering from
the latter at present is simply the result of an oversupply of
simulacra produced by cheap, or rather—Foundation wages
being generous—superficial labor. No doubt even the thought
of such a commerce would have horrified the composer, but
the heliocentric position accorded him (above Schoenberg!)

by, for example, the Domaine Musical with its anti-Brahms deaf spot (and hence, the Brahmsian heredity in Schoenberg), would have given him a mortal shock. Nothing was more absurd in those appraisers of a decade ago than the Schoenberg-Webern syzygy. Over to you, U.W.I.

u.w.i.: Do you think the state of the market is the only reason for the deflation, Mr. Stravinsky, or were we guilty of some inflating of Webern himself?

i.s.: Whether or not our estimations of Webern were somewhere askew is not of great moment. There is nothing surprising in errors of musical judgment in confrontation with the radically new. What does amaze is the wholesale commission of that most obvious of mistakes, the attempt to multiply originality. The more original and individual, so the more unrepeatable and inimitable, yet multiplication quickly became the *carte du jour*, not only of "abstract structural devices," as music reviewers are fond of scribbling (and what musical device is not abstract and structural?), but even of the tone of voice. I know something about pseudo-Webern, for at the time it was being manufactured I came under the spell of him myself, though I think I was faithful to Webern, to my discoveries in him, longer than anyone else.

u.w.i.: Are you suggesting that others who found their direction in him have betrayed him?

i.s.: Not that, not that. I would say, however, that the group which sprang from him and into prominence in the fifties now tends to regard him too lightly, as something they like to call a "precursor," a tugboat which, now that it has brought to shore such mighty liners as themselves, may be sent to rest in shallow waters (where for company it will find a few old skiffs like myself). At times I have had the impression they still program his "precursory" music along with the grander confections of their own establishments simply to show how they have "turned it to account" or given it more "scope." At any rate, there is no doubt that their improvements are meant to supersede, the authors of them already having acknowledged the futility of those cranky old "serial" formulas Webern was so obsessed with, and consigned them to completed history (Vienna between the wars, according to the dates on the tombstone). Disregarding the fact that in the absence of other differentia it is an unarguable proposition whether "serial" music represents a decline from the previous stage, today's progressives have formed a coalition with yesterday's nonstarters, and we may expect to be hearing again from the latter about the substitution of an "arbitrary order" (those Draconian twelve-tone laws) for a "natural gravitational system," as if both the arbitrary and the natural were not equally artificial and composed. Like all *ars nova / ars antiqua* debates, however, this one is of little use to practicing composers, and as always the music to come will be determined by other factors than the rules of the rule-makers.

u.w.i.: To go back to the question of scope, Mr. Stravinsky, do you consider Webern's to be too narrow?

i.s.: Not for Webern—which is no answer, of course, but I cannot understand the word in musical terms. Webern's time-scale is tiny, his quantity is minute, the variety of his forms is small, but whether these are measurements of scope I am unable to say. If, for example, scope is also a question of depth and not merely of width and expanse, then Webern's can be very great, and it is in any case perfectly circumscribed, which I say to remind you that we can only judge what the composer has done, not what he did not set out to do. To begin with, can we be certain that the scope we are looking for is really Webern's and not your own Beethovenesque idea of what it should be? Admittedly, Webern often seems to have put a low premium on his listener's sense of involvement. His music is wholly unrhetorical, and in that sense unpersuasive. There is no movement from simple to complex, no development of subsidiary parts or integration of counter-themes, second subjects, fugal episodes, and the like. The listener is definitely not invited to participate in the argument of the creation as he is in the symphonies of Beethoven. On the contrary, each opus offers itself only as a whole, a unity to be contemplated. Now obviously such an art work is essentially static, and obviously, too, the cost in subjectivity is high. Naturally I concede that it is possible to feel constricted when listening to a succession of, especially, the very short pieces, and to attribute this feeling to lack of scope, but I consider the very attempt to follow a chain of, as I say, unities, to be a quantitative mistake; I mean, just because they are clock-time short. For a test you must try the single opus and in the neighborhood of other music. Thus, in Venice a few years ago I heard the Parennin Quartet struggle through some forty minutes of Boulez's *Livre pour quatuor*, then play the four minutes of Webern's *Bagatelles*. I assure you that since then scope has never seemed to be a matter of size.

U.W.I.: What are your present criticisms of the music, Mr. Stravinsky?

I.S.: They are mere differences of palate, mostly, and doubt-less more revealing of myself than of Webern. Those *molto ritenuto, molto espressivo,* and "dying away" phrase-endings weary me now, and there is a touch of cuteness in the vocal music which I dislike: the too-frisky piano figure at the beginning of *"Wie bin ich froh!"* for instance, and the *"Glück"* at the conclusion of the Chinese choruses, though the *chinoiserie* is also less subtle than in the early Li-Tai-Po song, and in fact the whole opus reminds me of a musical snuffbox; but the worst example is surely that wretched *"Bienchen"* in *Gleich und Gleich* (did Webern know Hugo Wolf's setting of this poem?), which should have been a large wasp with a good sting. These are minor dyslogistics, however, simple conflicts of temperament which you will understand better when I add that I also prefer unhappiness to happiness and misery to gay spirits in a great deal of German music besides Webern, since, and emphatically including, *Die Meistersinger*.

u.w.i.: But do you have other, more basic, criticisms, or larger criticisms of specific pieces, that you had not felt a decade ago?

i.s.: The String Quartet left me with a slight feeling of aridity when I heard it recently, but if the performance had been better, my report of the music might have been very different. Then the saxophone Quartet, when I heard it last in Paris a few seasons ago, sounded somewhat soiled by the years in the first movement, and somewhat scatty in the second. This performance also was poor, but only part of the blame can be laid to it, I think, for the hammering succession of down-beats that labor the second movement is also the fault of the notation: the note-values are too large and the measures too small. As you know, the silent or suspended beat with the notes on the anacrusis is one of the devices of this movement which Webern was to employ again in later works, though with a degree of success that is still hotly contended. Its for-mation near the end of the Concerto disturbs no one, but many think the use of it in the final twelve measures of the piano Variations mere *Papiermusik*, owing to attenuating changes of tempo. The metrical accent obtains here only if the listener is looking at a score or watching a conductor, they argue, and therefore toward the end of the passage the ear perceives the notes not in relation to silent beats but as beats themselves.

Another criticism I might mention is that sometimes We-bern's choral harmony strikes me oddly, for example the *"Im Dunkel"* near the end of the First Cantata, and the parallel-interval passages in the fifth movement of the Sec-ond Cantata. I think I see the interval logic and the "purity" of these constructions, and I am at least willing to believe

that they derive from a "teleological" conception (in practice, a mania for total identification) of the form. But it *is*
harmony, after all, even when described as a "refracted expression of the horizontal interval structure" (a commen-
tator's concettism), and in the case of the "*Im Dunkel*" it is
very banal harmony indeed.

u.w.i.: You have acknowledged that the quality of a performance is vital. How in your opinion, have performance
standards changed in the last decade?

i.s.: But there have *been* far too few performances, apart from
the Five Pieces for String Quartet and the Six Pieces for
Orchestra, to allow anyone to speak of "standards." It is
worth repeating, though, that performance can make the
hundred percent difference of comprehension in this music,
as it can no longer do in the case of a popular classic, and
even with such a simple and accessible piece as my own Symphonies of Wind Instruments, I would not have blamed anyone who had taken it for an ugly duckling on the strength of
its London debut (though I see that I have launched an un-
suitable metaphor, for the work is no swan even when perfectly played). The other day, leafing through programs of
the concerts of Jean Wiener and others in Paris in the early
twenties I was surprised to discover that songs and chamber
music by Webern had been performed together with some
of my own music. I have no recollection of it, however, not
even of a circumstantial nature such as whether the few
squeaks and twitches the music was then generally reputed
to be excited any derision;[1] and I can account for this blank

---

[1] This nonawareness of Webern is especially painful to me now when I
read him in a letter to Berg dated June 9, 1919. "*Strawinsky war herrlich.
Wunderbar sind diese Lieder. Mir geht dieser Musik ganz unglaublich nahe.
Ich liebe die ganz besonders. Etwas so unsäglich Ruhrendes wie diese Wie-
genlieder. Wie diese drei Klarinetten klingen! Und 'Pribaoutki.' Ah, mein
lieber, etwas ganz herrlich! Diese Wörtlichkeit (realismus) führt ins Meta-
physiche. Strawinsky-Lieder waren ausserordentlich gelungen.*"

only by doubting the performances. As an idea of what they could have been like, I refer you to a recording of the *Bagatelles* made a quarter of a century later (Dial Records, 1950) by the Kolisch Quartet. Here the performers were the highest authorities, the ideal interpreters from the very *sanctum sanctorum* of the composer, yet their performance fails even on the level of accuracy. Now I beg you not to misunderstand me. I do not intend this as criticism of the players, who were in fact far ahead of any others at that time in their mastery and understanding of the music. It is, rather, a contribution to the history of performance, and the example can be made again with the Boulez recording of the Webern Symphony —at a much less remote date—and with Columbia's "complete" Webern, now twelve years since the making. These efforts are mere curiosities now, studies of the performance limitations (and possibilities) of the time rather than revelations of the music, though on occasion they were that, too, even if only, in some cases, as maps to still undiscovered treasure.

u.w.i.: To me the "curious" aspect of the Columbia recordings is that some of the pieces actually received their first auditions this way, among them the Goethe choruses which, judging by the difficulties of the music even now, must have been a baptism of fire. But the prediction, published in that album, that the Six Pieces For Orchestra would become a conductors' Bucephalus, while most of the other music languished, has come all too true.

i.s.: The Columbia project, to which I was witness at every stage, is an incredible chapter of music history, one that makes a decade seem a very long time. To begin with, as most of the musical materials, scores, and parts did not exist, the conductor had to extract them himself from poor photostats of the original manuscripts; the publishers were eventually

obliged to print the music because of the demand created
by the recordings. A second difficulty was in the fact that
while chamber music could be rehearsed in conjunction with
concerts (rehearsals for recordings directly must be paid for
at full recording rates), the orchestral music could not be
rehearsed at all because the conductor had no orchestral concerts. The only recourse was to rehearse each player individually until everyone had learned his own part like a cipher;
and this is in fact what the conductor did, for the three
cantatas, the orchestra Variations, the Six Pieces, the Passacaglia, the Ricercar, and the Symphony had to be and were
recorded in only two three-hour periods. A third handicap
was the absence of any assistance from a musical or engineering supervisor. Not only the musical performance, therefore,
but every aspect of the production as well was the responsibility of the conductor. Still, recording companies can hardly
be expected to believe in such ventures, and they are no more
to blame, certainly, than the conductors who had orchestras
and who could have found the money to purchase the time,
but who lacked imagination. In this context of my little history, it now seems unfair to complain that in some of the
performances notes were not always played as nodes, yet I
wonder when we will again hear such better-than-violin distinctions of pitch as those of Miss Marni Nixon. (Not from
Miss Nixon herself, to be sure: she has graduated from
Webern to Liza Doolittle!)

u.w.i.: As you have noted some of your criticism, Mr. Stravinsky, would you also evaluate the high points?

i.s.: After the Five Movements and the Six Pieces, the next
peaks come a decade later, with the Trakl songs, the Canons,
the Volkstexte, the clarinet and guitar songs. But for me, the
Trio, the Symphony, and the orchestra Variations are Webern's greatest achievements.

u.w.i.: Has your estimation of Webern's position changed appreciably in the last decade, Mr. Stravinsky?

i.s.: Not mine, but certainly that of many others. "With it" composers have now turned away, or developed away, from his influence, though their music often continues to be a *catalogue raisonné* of derivations from his. But all of us owe something to him, if not in rhythmic vocabulary, then in our sensibility to musical time, for I think Webern has raised everyone's sense of refinement in this regard (well, *nearly* everyone's). Whether there are "great," or only new and very individual, feelings in his music is a question I can answer only for myself, but for me Webern *has* a power to move, and no moment in contemporary music has haunted me more than the Coda of the Symphony. In spite of what I said at the beginning of our talk, then, if you are "seeking strange gods" you might do worse than to continue to revere St. Anton.

Hollywood, November 5, 1965

OBITUARY

Some Table Talk of T. S. Eliot

I met T. S. Eliot for the first time on a December afternoon in 1956. I was in London for a concert of my music in St. Martin's-in-the-Fields, and I invited him to tea. He arrived ahead of me and was waiting with Stephen Spender in the Savoy Grill Room when I appeared. A long time later he said that from photographs and views of rostrums he had expected a taller man. Conversely, I had anticipated less imposing proportions; his big, rather stolid and cumbrous frame seemed an unnecessarily large refuge even for such overendowed shyness and modesty as his. Conversation was not ready or easy, and at times I could almost hear the waiters silently polishing the silverware as though for a wake. The Savoyard sandwiches were a help, however, and so was the "tea" (whisky, in practice). Eliot turned his head from speaker to speaker with a slight jerk, emitting a nervous-tic "yes" or "hm" every few seconds. You felt he was registering unfavorable impressions. "Hm, well, perhaps, yes, though not precisely in that way," he seemed to say, and when once he actually *did* say "Then you really think so?" you were certain of it. The inflection made you doubt you would ever

again be so rash as to think or assert anything at all. Even the
pause after you had spoken seemed deliberate, as though to
give you a chance to savor the full fatuity of your remarks.
Now, my "you" is only myself, of course, and the account
of the remembered experience is colored by the perspective
and the need to enhance a point (to write about a man is to
make him pose), which is that I revered Eliot not only as a
great sorcerer of words but as the very key-keeper of the
language.

We managed to talk that afternoon, nevertheless, and
though I hardly recall the topics, I remember that Wagner
was one; Eliot's Wagner nostalgia was apparent and I think
that *Tristan* must have been one of the most passionate experiences in his life. We also talked about *Cymbeline*, which
I was on my way to see that evening; about Rudolph Kassner,
whose "On Vanity" Eliot had published in an early *Criterion;* and about ballet. Eliot was an able critic of several
kinds of dance technique, and, in fact, a critic with more
varied interests and versatility than one would think.

Eliot has drawn his own portraits, however—Old Possum,
Tiresias, the churchwarden, Sweeney—and the only com-
posite picture will remain the one painted by himself. And
why should we look for another, or ask what was he "like"?
The creations are the man, and the proof is a parody of
Prufrock I have just produced in attempting to describe
him ("impenetrably punctilious, deferential but a bit severe,
and yes, somewhat restless, somewhat weary, somewhat
grave"). He may also have been a great actor, of course, with
a secret life behind his words, but I do not know. His prepared faces, as he called them, are enough for me.

❊ ❊ ❊

My recollections of our last two meetings are more distinct.
The earlier occasion is connected with a fiftieth-anniversary

commemorative performance of *Le Sacre du printemps* in—
of all changes of venue—Albert Hall. The Eliots, who lived
nearby, had invited me for a drink after these depressing
revels. As I crossed the threshold of their apartment, Eliot
applauded me. He had heard the concert "on the wireless"
(he was fond of horsedrawn phrases) and he went on to compare the "ovation" with "the shaky reception of 1921, when
the audience refrained from demonstrations but was in a
violent mood."

In the vestibule I saw a hat-stand with a Homburg and,
more optimistically, a straw Stetson for the Bahama beach.
The walls here were graced with drawings of cats by Eliot's
father, and an autograph letter by Coleridge framed together
with a *précis* of his life and work which Eliot had written
for a BBC program during the war, and which Mrs. Eliot,
then her future husband's secretary, had retrieved from his
wastebasket. The display of art in the other rooms included
a water color by Ruskin, in the manner of Turner, for which
Eliot used the *mot juste* "gradely"; a water color by Henry
Moore; an Edward Lear landscape; some Wyndham Lewis
drawings; Jacob Epstein's head of Eliot; and several towers
of books standing on the end tables like modern sculptures.

Conversation started with the Derby, which I had watched
on television in the afternoon and on which I had lost a bet.
Eliot said he "used to wager in the Calcutta Sweepstakes, but
never drew a horse. During a short visit to Stockholm in 1948
I put some money on a long shot called Queen Mary—out
of loyalty, of course; it was not a hunch—but we came in
last." He was keen to hear whether I had remarked many
changes in Russian pronunciation during my trip to the Soviet
Union some months previous, and he asked me for examples.
He had himself received the poet Evtushenko a short time
before, he said, but "the young man's eyes were frightened,
and he was too careful of what he was saying and of what

I would think—though, in any case, I myself am quite unable to speak through a translator unless I know him." One of my Russian "r's" reminded him of the variety of "r" sounds in Sanskrit, "which Indians do not recognize as differentiations, even though they pronounce them." Talking about his own work, Eliot observed that while rereading his doctorate thesis on F. H. Bradley he was able to identify Bradley as a primary influence on his own prose style. He said, too, that the best parts of his new essay on George Herbert were the quotations, and he regretted that he had not had a "sense of his audience" while writing it; though, as he certainly knew, his audiences were the "lit" departments of several hundred thousand American universities. "Herbert is a great poet," he went on, "and one of a very few I can read and read again. Mallarmé is another, incidentally, and so is Edward Lear." And with this he boasted of not having read any serious prose fiction since 1927. "I think the last novel was *Middlemarch* . . . no, I am forgetting *The Heart of Midlothian,* which I enjoyed in the hospital a few years ago. But I confess that I never finished *War and Peace.* Shouldn't say so, however; remarks like that cut the critics' cake in half."

I tried to provoke him to talk about Joyce, with, as a stratagem, the fact that I had a concert in Dublin the next week; but all he could be made to say was that the account of their meeting in Wyndham Lewis's *Blasting and Bombardiering* is accurate. "When I lectured in Dublin," he added, "almost every Irishman to whom I was introduced told me that almost every other Irishman was not to be trusted." And the thought of lecturing recalled the tour in early postwar Germany during which he read his lecture on Goethe. My memory is ajar, however, and I recall only that he complained about "official receptions at which totally humorless people tried to shout ultimate philosophy back and forth with me"; and that he asked if, on the other hand, I had noticed how "English people laugh when confronted by something serious that they do not understand, because above all they want to be polite."

I described an excursion to Hampton Court that I had taken the day before, telling him that the portrait there of Isabella d'Este by Giulio Romano is remarkable for the effect of the snarl produced by the everted lower lip (whereas Titian's portrait, for comparison, reveals the woman's extraordinary intelligence). We then talked of Ferrara, of the emanations of the Romagnol hemp which are supposed to addle the natives, and of the Estense Court at the time of Pirro Ligorio and Gesualdo. Eliot said that he was once bitten by Ferrarese fleas, and though details were not forthcoming I assumed the event must have occurred in a "one-night cheap hotel." I remember he used the word "transpadane" in this discussion and though it may have had to be dredged up and artificially resuscitated, like all of Eliot's words it became beautiful.

That night I was greatly moved by Mrs. Eliot's devotion to her husband, and by her gentleness with him as he would rest his head on her shoulder for a moment, or squeeze her hand. His marriage was the happiest event of his life.

❋　❋　❋

What was destined to be our last meeting came about in New York seven months later (December 12). When we called for the Eliots at the River Club on East Fifty-second Street, T.S.E. was swathed in mufflers, pullover, heavy blue cashmere overcoat, while Mrs. T.S.E., who entered the limousine complaining of overheated American hotels, wore neither coat nor wrap, but a silk summer frock which exposed pleasing patches of milky, faintly freckled skin. As we drove away from the Club, Eliot confessed a fondness for East Fifty-second Street—"the fact that it is a dead end makes it so convenient"—and as we caught a view of the United Nations

Building he said he had lately come to suspect "an anti-European conspiracy" was afoot there.

But all was not well. His walk faltered to such an extent that the revolving restaurant door had to be held back for him to pass through. And there were other tokens of his progressing illness in the more frequent and now somewhat convulsive throat clearings, and in his cinereous complexion. The poor man bent over his plate, drinking a little but eating hardly at all. He raised himself bolt upright only at wide intervals—during which moments, however, the force of intelligence in his clear hazel eyes was undiminished. His voice had dwindled to a scrannel murmur, and his most powerful sound was a wheezy "ee, ee" laugh which had a rather sinister effect, like a "bronc's cheer." Because of his low resonance, other speakers tended to jam him with their louder equipment, myself included, for I have a defensive habit of talking too much when I find my neighbor difficult to understand. The first part of the conversation was concerned with Joseph Conrad. I do not remember how it began, though it might have begun with me. Conrad is especially interesting to me because of his Polish-Ruthenian background, which was partly the same as my own[1] (he had lived for some years as a child in my father's birthplace, Chernigov), and because he was—dare I say "also"?—a man who in his mature years moved from a Slav culture with French inlay to an English one. Eliot described Conrad as "a Grand Seigneur, the grandest I have ever met, though it was a shock after reading him to hear him talk. He had a very guttural accent." I asked if it were like mine and Eliot replied that mine was easier to understand—which did not quite answer me. He was rereading *Nostromo* at present, he said, and he declared "Youth" and

[1] A letter containing my political views on the Ukraine (I opposed autonomy for it) was published in the *Gazette de Lausanne* at the end of 1916 or the beginning of 1917. Some of my statements excited a great deal of controversy.

"The End of the Tether" to be "the finest stories of that kind I know."

Eliot also professed an admiration for the late Louis Mac-Neice, saying that he "had a very warm feeling for him, though he was a disappointing person to meet." And he said that what he most liked about St. John Perse was "his handwriting and his intelligence," which both raised and forbade one to ask the question whether he meant he did *not* like the poems. A mention of Apollinaire drew him to remark that he thought *Alcools* greatly overrated. As always, a part of our conversation alighted on languages themselves. He told me (no, Eliot never "told," he imparted) that at the time of his employment in Lloyds' Bank his Italian was fluent, "but it was Dantean Italian, not the most suitable source for modern business phraseology. I had a smattering of Romanian and modern Greek, too, which for some reason had convinced the manager of the bank that therefore I must also know Polish. He was incredulous when I said I did not, as if it were illogical not to know Polish when one knew Romanian and Greek."

We drank gin martinis (but Eliot took a daiquiri), a Pouilly Fumé, a Cheval Blanc, an Armagnac (but Eliot took a Drambuie). In the Armagnac stage he suddenly sat straight up and, using my first name for the first time, proposed a toast to "another ten years for both of us." Perdurability on that scale seemed so improbable, however, that the phrase sounded rather sad and in fact rang more like a farewell. But he seemed to feel closer to us than ever before, and he was certainly more affectionate. Warmed by the wines, he decided halfway through the meal to shed his pullover. Flamboyant flannel braces were exposed in the process, and a ringside of Le Pavillon patrons (*luxe*, *calme*, and lots of fat bank accounts) gazed on aghast.

The assassination of the President was referred to, whereupon Eliot said that during the winter in Nassau he had received two telephone calls from the White House inviting him respectively to a dinner for Nobel Prize winners and to another, general gathering. "And now, of all the horrible coincidences," he continued, "can you believe that I was once made an honorary deputy sheriff of Dallas?" And, no, I could not see Eliot with boots and spurs, badge and a ten-gallon hat.

At every meeting with the poet the conversation was sooner or later drawn to the subject of the Mississippi, perhaps as much because of me as of him; the lure of the river was instilled in me by a Russian translation of Mark Twain, which I read as a boy, and when I came to America the high points of all my transcontinental train trips were the crossings of the "strong, brown god"—though the god of the poem, as Eliot once corrected me, was actually "the muddy 'Mo.'" I remember his recalling how in his boyhood home in Missouri the housekeeper used to come to his room on cold mornings, lighting a fire to heat a kettle of water and pulling a tub from under the bed. And he went on to say that when he gave the Yeats lecture at Trinity College, Dublin, during the war, "an old charwoman came in the morning, lighting a fire in my room and pulling the same kind of tub from under my bed, which made me feel as though I were a boy again, and back in Missouri."

Eliot was a touching figure that night, and so was Mrs. Eliot, with her perpetually cheerful voice, her heirloom jewelry (was it the gift of a favorite aunt?), and her new "Mrs. Eliot" versus her former, secretarial, manner. As we called for our coats, the *maître d'hotel* told the *vestiaire* that "there you see the greatest living poet." I do not know whether Eliot overheard, but my wife saved him from embarrassment. She said, with just the right tone and tact, "Well, he does his best."

BOOK REVIEWS

Schoenberg's Letters[1]

THE OBSERVER, *October 18, 1964*

"By regarding the artistic innovator as abnormal, we accorded ourselves the luxury of believing that he did not concern us, and that he did not put in question, by the mere fact of his existence, an accepted social, moral, or intellectual order."
—CLAUDE LÉVI-STRAUSS, *Totemism*

M ost contemporary composers' letters must be crude and grubby, or so I imagine from my own epistolary labors and from my observation that the letters composers of today are most likely to trouble over are directed to publishers, concert managers, conductors, and other industrialists. The letter as communication to friends is an unnatural medium to him, or

[1] *Arnold Schoenberg: Letters.* Edited by Erwin Stein. Translated by Eithne Wilkins and Ernst Kaiser. (Faber, 63s.) The translators should be congratulated, thanked, and quickly re-employed to translate the *Harmonielehre*. My only criticism of the book would be to express the wish for a more complete collection (including the letters to myself in 1919) and with fewer asterisks for fewer deletions.

at any rate, one he lacks the leisure to develop. A contemporary composer must rarely undertake to say in a personal letter what he has in mind to say to the people to whom he would like to say it. (If he takes time to address himself to a disobliging journalist, that is only because it is so much easier to do as well as disproportionately, if only momentarily, gratifying.)

There are exceptions, of course, in our day, most notably Richard Strauss, who from time to time stands up to Hofmannsthal—an incomparably greater effort for him than the other way around—and gets the better of it, I think, by sheer straightforwardness. (There, I have done my bit for the 1964 Strauss millennium celebrations!)

But Strauss by then had already withdrawn from the center, from then on only living through a time or, at worst, traveling through in luxury class a time that Schoenberg lived and formed and that now to some extent—for centripetal as he was, other developments were and are possible—lives in and finds its form in him. And Schoenberg, in letter after letter, does undertake to speak his mind, for which reason his letters are also an autobiography and, because not meant as such and not dependent on recollection, the most consistently reliable in existence by a great composer.

In fact this is one of the few great books by composers, and no one concerned with music—not merely contemporary music—can afford to be without it. But others should read it, too. An artist's record of his struggles may fail to engross or edify a reader who does not feel the necessity of art, but not in this case, I think, for the reason that the lenses of Schoenberg's conscience were the most powerful of the musicians of the era, and not only in music. Indeed, he seems to have seen a length ahead in nearly every question to which he gave his attention, so that one rubs one's eyes at, for example, the dates of the letters to Kandinsky, with their references

to Hitler—that they were written in 1923, not 1933. And the
Kandinsky letters, together with those to Gustav Mahler
(which include a Schubertian rent-begging one) are worth
the price of possession.

But non-specialist readers should not shy away from the
musical discussions merely because what they may have tried
to read about Schoenberg up to now seemed to have been
written in Fortran or intramuralese. The composer himself is
clear and plain and his letters are stocked with insights rather
than with the principles of analysis.

Unfortunately, the first chapters, the longest in most auto-
biographies, are missing, and the first postmark is 1910, by
which time Schoenberg's name (at least) was already known
and about two-fifths of his music had already been written.
From one of the earlier letters a random remark to the effect
that an orchestra is richer in treble than in bass instruments
shows him thinking polyphonically at a time when no one
else did; for observations such as that I regret the absence of
more material from this period. And the decade and a half
after 1910 is also too meagerly represented, the arguments of
those years being the best parts of the book. Here is a reply
to a conductor who wished to blue-pencil a passage in an
early work of his:

I am against removing tonsils although I know how one can
somehow manage to go on living even without arms, legs, nose,
eyes, tongue, ears, etc. . . . . A work doesn't have to be performed
at all costs either, if it means losing parts of it that may even be
ugly or faulty but which it was born with. . . . Cutting isn't the
way to improve a work. Brevity and succinctness are a matter
of *exposition*. In this case the details are not conceived com-
pactly; it is all long-winded. If I cut some such details, the other
long-winded ones remain, and it remains a work of long-winded
exposition. It will not take so long to play, but it will not really
be shorter. A work that has been shortened by cutting may very
well give the impression of being an excessively long work (be-

cause of the exposition) that is too short in various places (where it has been cut).

In the letters of this period, injustices merely rankle him, are not yet the torture they were to become after another decade of that indignation which accompanies every page of the book like a *basso continuo*. Now, in the early twenties, he even appears to be resigned—"I realize that I cannot be understood and am content to make do with respect"— though, of course, he was not nor ever could be.

And the wit is not yet all bitter. When a newspaper asks him for a list of five people he would save if he were a present-day Noah on the eve of another Flood, Schoenberg replies by enclosing a self-addressed postcard, "to let me know of anyone who decides to rescue me so that I can remain in his vicinity." On another occasion he writes that "I usually answer the question why I no longer compose as I did at the period of *Verklärte Nacht* by saying 'I do, but I can't help it if people don't yet recognize the fact.'" And in one of the most valuable statements in the volume he tells a publisher that "music never drags a meaning around with it, at least not in the form in which it [music] manifests itself, even though meaning is inherent in its nature."

The tone changes *ca.* 1925. The facile music lately come to fashion paid him little homage, of course, and the now Old Master had lost patience with the slow corroding of the second-rate. The attacks on the first "12-tone" pieces seem to have exceeded even the harshest receptions of the early years, at which time, in any case, such things are easier to take. He now begins to distinguish "true-born" musicians from those who have merely "become what they are," and he would not have subscribed to Sartre's "genius is a way out that one invents," but most certainly would have thought it a description of an altogether different activity—the cult of *kairos* and The Room at the Top.

He looks to left and right in anger, though never in that temper "back," for he had an exceptionally forgiving nature. And he sometimes sounds like the Leader of Righteousness. "Laws of loyalty" are invoked and disciples warned not to acknowledge other gods or to keep compromising company (myself above all; the shoe of his satire on C-major endings fits five of my works at that time and perhaps twenty since, but it is clear that Schoenberg thought of me as a mere Russian exotic, at first, and later, as a *modiste,* or *maître* of *assemblages*).

Some of the letters during this phase are about as cordial as traffic citations, and one, to the late Hanns Eisler, during the time when Schoenberg was trying to keep the serial idea under wraps, seems a shrill castigation to have been based on no more than a rumor. Contrast this with the letters, a few years earlier, to J. M. Hauer, who had arrived at a "12-tone theory" of his own. Here Schoenberg generously proposed an exchange of ideas and possible joint publication, like Darwin and Wallace.

But even in this time of public and personal difficulties the letters continue to exhibit the chief quality of the music, which is the passionate development of the argument. What they lack of the music, of the Serenade, the Quintet, the Septet, is the songfulness and the humor, hardly surprising omissions when one considers that the aim of so many of them is to burn dry rot and expose dead standards—the standards, it follows, of the very people who could have given him preferment. But this still leaves for admiration a book containing hardly a received idea and none that Schoenberg allows to pass without an overhauling. And if all this merit does not seem to contain much promise of entertainment, the injury of that impression should be outweighed by the statement that the letters are the most refreshingly unliterary I have read.

It is in the American years that they become painful and

occasionally pettish. More conscious of his "Jewishness" with each new act of Nazi aggression, he complains of neglect by Jews. They "have never shown any interest in my music," he writes in 1938, "and now, into the bargain, in Palestine they are out to develop, artificially, an authentically Jewish kind of music, which rejects what I have achieved," though near the end he expresses the wish to emigrate to Israel.

Nor did the great American ostrich pay him any more attention than the small Viennese ostrich had done. "It is my most intense desire to depart from Vienna as unnoticed as I have always been while I was here," he tells a friend in 1925, and Viennese love-hate continues to the end which, however, came too soon for Schoenberg to say "I told you so" and is still a little soon for the reader to do the same. But the improvidence of a young man in unpunished Vienna and of an old and, moreover, famous one in the opulence of postwar America are very different humiliations.

The lack of money is the lack of time. After having shared so much of his life with pupils, he now complains that teaching wearies him, leaving him no time for composition. Some of the letters are chits to a college president begging $200 or even $150 with which to buy books for his students. But the nadir comes in a letter the seventy-year-old master addressed to the Guggenheim Foundation asking for assistance so that he can finish *Moses und Aron*. Though even a few more measures of this opera would have been worth a whole catalogue of music the Guggenheim Foundation did sponsor, Schoenberg's request was denied.

By 1939 the Schoenberg movement, to all appearances, had ceased to exist. Berg was dead, Webern was silenced—though he had never been loud—and Schoenberg himself was writing either tonal music or nothing at all. "I have not composed for the past two years," he informs a friend, and gives as the reason, "unbearable depression."

The last letters hint at the recrudescence, but no more. It

began during the war in Schoenberg's own renewed crea-
tivity, but gathered momentum only in the year of his death,
by which time he had stopped priding himself on his unplayed
music, clinging instead to the achievement of not having given
up the struggle. But there is something triumphant in the
old man.

Wagner's Prose

The first question raised by a reprint of Wagner's writings
is whether or not they are useful to the understanding of his
art, and to me, any affirmative answer would have the familiar thin sound of academic barrel-scraping. The second
question is in the failure of the first. Of what use are they
then? For it can hardly matter that Wagner had little talent
for theoretical argument, and few people are likely to be
disturbed any more by the disparity between his egregious
and clumsy apologetics and *Tristan and Isolde*. The only answer I can find is that the writings are effective evidence of
the split between a man's genius and the accessory parts of
his mental *mise-en-scène*.

The book is not all or uniformly bad, of course. Wagner is
always better with cases than on theoretical rambles, and he
is an acute, if injudicious, critic of the theater of his time and
of other composers, as the discussions of Mozart and Rossini
in the first part of the present volume[2] will show. Wagner's
criticism is remarkable, too, because it is governed by a consistent historical point of view. He is the first great composer

[2] *Wagner on Music and Drama.* A compendium of Richard Wagner's
prose works. Selected and arranged, and with an introduction by Albert
Goldman and Evert Sprinchorn (E. P. Dutton and Co., Inc., New York,
1964).

to have begun with an analysis of music history from the outside, and from that perspective to have determined his own place in its future progress. He seems to have possessed this view as early as the awakening of his musical talent, moreover, and it was to remain the "drive" (Bayreuth or bust) behind all of his writings. With spectacular simplicity, his reading of history pointed straight home to the Fatherland and unfalteringly to the Wagner front door. No matter, however, that it is historically absurd. It directed him away from "absolute" music (though in the galimatias of his discussion of the term one is unable to discover what he really meant by it) toward a "unification of the arts" in a new form of "dramatic expression." This, however, may only be a long way of saying that he had the knowledge of his own gifts. Finally, it can hardly matter whether or not the historical diagnosis is exact when the prognosis is *Tristan* or *The Ring*.

The trouble is with the manner in which the great conception plods along. Wagner exhorts and coaxes, rather than argues, and he has no other quality for relief. Though he labors mightily to be explicit, the only result is laboriousness. "Let me out with it in one phrase," he cries at one point, strangling from his own periphrastic disease, and for once the reader is in full sympathy. But it will not come out except in a prodigious verbosity, here rendered in an incredible dialect of Quakerisms, archaicisms, and syntactical Germanisms invented for him by his first translator, William Ashton Ellis. Though the literary merit in this tumble of unpruned talk must be nearly nil in the original, Ellis set out to and, alas, probably did succeed in finding an "equivalent style." Wagner's sentences can break all endurance records without so much as tempting Ellis's fidelity. The reader backtracks at first, but after a few tapeworms of a hundred or so collectively unintelligible words, decides that skipping is the better method. Item:

". . . the will is longing to become pure knowledge, but this is possible only in so far as it stays stock-still in its deepest inner chamber: 'tis as if it were awaiting tidings of redemption from there outside; content they it not, it sets itself in that state of clairvoyance; and here beyond the bounds of time and space, it knows itself the world's one and all."

It? They? Here? Where? Who? And there are still further impediments to legibility, including an addiction to metaphors—as many "stormy seas" are "sailed o'er" in these essays as ever in Hakluyt—and to impossible compound words: Mozart, for example, is the "early-sped" and the "song-glad" (slap-happy?). The grotesque style and the special pleading are obstacles few readers are likely to leap.

The selection and ordering of the texts seem admirable to me, though I judge without having read all of Wagner. More excerpts might have been drawn from the letters, particularly from those to Frau ("my child") Wesendonck and Judith ("the overflowing cup of my intoxication") Gauthier, if only for the reason that the composer's amorous style would at least be a contrast. As the occasions provoking the writings are important, too, some circumstantial information might have been added at the head of each piece. This deficiency is partly offset by an introduction relating the writings to Wagner's biography and practice, an excellent summary on the whole, and incandescence itself compared to what follows. I do not agree, though, that Wagner is a "brilliant exponent of Beethoven." To my mind his program notes on the symphonies are rubbish, the worse because these misrepresentations of music are by a very great composer. Wagner tries to establish in words the "real" subjects of the symphonies because a "real subject"—rather than a merely musical one—is necessary to a "real understanding"; and, of course, these attempts result in descriptions of a surpassing fatuity. Item: the composer of the "Pastoral" Symphony "turned his steps toward life-glad men encamped on breezy meads . . . kissing, dancing, frolicking beside the tender gossip of the brook. . . ." And the Ninth Symphony, says Wagner, is "the redemption of Music from out her own peculiar element into the realm of *universal art*"—but, then, Wagner is always yearning to go beyond music and regularly serving notice that the "Art Work of the Future" will not indulge music for its own sake.

Nor can I concur with the editors' claim that the "basic argument" of the pamphlet *Jews in Music* (wisely placed near the beginning of the book so that it colors the idealism to come) "contains as much truth on the subject as anyone could have seen during the nineteenth century." Nietschze, for one, saw more "truth on the subject," but never mind; the question is whether Wagner saw any at all, and I will labor it myself because I suspect that though everyone has heard of the pamphlet, few people have actually read it. In fact, Wagner's attack is personal as well as theoretical and far more virulent than one would suppose. It is also so surprisingly contemporary that a good deal of it could have been written by Rosenberg or Goebbels. "Judaism" is "the evil conscience of our modern civilization," he says, and the "Jew" is "the most heartless of all human beings," and the great radical from the barricades of 1848 even goes on to discriminate a "commoner class of Jew." But where is his "truth on the subject"? In the logic which attributes a composer's failure in the "formal productive faculty" to his Jewishness? Then what of the same failure in all the others? And where is the "truth" in the contention that "imitation" and "mimicry" are peculiarly Jewish characteristics in music? In fact, critics of my own music in the nineteen-twenties might have taken their cue from Wagner's tirade on this subject: "The Jew musician hurls together the diverse forms and styles of every age and every master." The substance of the argument is less shock-

ing, however, than the intolerably mean manner of it, above all
in the reproach to Mendelssohn for modeling himself on "our"
Bach.[3] The unpleasant truth, which even Thomas Mann could
not whitewash, is that Wagner might have been created to
the Third Reich's specifications. His writings appeal again
and again to those tiresome virtues of the uncorrupted "folk";
to the "direct expression of emotion" vs. "intellectualized"
(Jewish) "speech"; to the "inwardness" of the German soul
in its "war of conscience" against French, Italian, or other
outwardnesses; to the necessity of purging the world of politics that it may again deserve a Wagner (a "true poet").

The other papers in the first section set out to analyze
some aspects of "The Cultural Decadence of the Nineteenth
Century," but the most effective of them are concerned with
opera itself ("the personnel of a first class orchestra consists,
for no little part, of the only truly musically cultured members of an opera company"). The difficulty here is that Wagner's satire is flat; his arsenal contains only heavy artillery
and his shells are too big to load—as one sees when one compares him to the Berlioz of *Evenings in the Orchestra*, which
covers some of the same ground; not only is the French master's narrative skill far superior, but also his human landscape
has a richer variety. The section on "The Origins of Modern
Opera" contains matter of more value, and on Mozart, Weber,
and Rossini it is very good indeed. Item:

Criticism, which at bottom always waits upon the public voice,
has never dealt with *Euryanthe* in the measure that its uncom-
monly instructive content deserves. Yet, never has there been composed a work in which the inner contradictions of the whole
genre have been more consistently worked out. These contradictions are: absolute, self-sufficing melody, and unflinchingly true

[3] It is an interesting point of Eric Werner's recent book on the *Elijah*
that Mendelssohn's cadences were influenced by the music of the Hebrew
Sacred Services.

dramatic expression. Here one or the other must necessarily be sacrificed—either melody or drama. Rossini sacrificed the drama; the noble Weber wished to reinstate it by force of his more judicious melody. He had to learn that this was an impossibility.

The Rossini chapter is insufferably condescending, but it reveals Wagner's ambivalent feelings toward Italian music, elsewhere exposed in the Italianate melodic strain, with its curious apparatus of appoggiaturas, that curls through the whole of his music from *Das Liebesverbot* to *Parsifal* (and on to *Verklärte Nacht*) without ever being digested. Discussing the new quality of Weber's melody in *Euryanthe*, Wagner remarks astutely that "one might almost say the melody was ready before a line of its poem"—which, incidentally, was the case with *Pelléas*, as we now know from a sketch score in the Meyer collection. In another passage we see Wagner condemning action and the "lust of the eye" that requires "constant changes of scene," as though he were already preparing his audience for the statuary of *The Ring*.

The section of excerpts from the *Art Work of the Future* is a muddle of Schopenhauer and phenomenology, in the main, but there is an inquiry into the relationships of spoken vowel sounds and sung tones, a kind of musical "*alchémie-du-verbe*" which Wagner abandons at the exact point at which our interest is caught. For a lighthearted page or two at the beginning of the section called "Wagner's Development" the master seems about to do what Nietschze correctly said he could not do: laugh at himself. These autobiographical writings are otherwise notable in exposing the fact that Wagner's musical training was the skimpiest of any of the great composers, and that he had the widest interests in everything else; but, after all, music is "the art which is easiest to learn," as he had said of certain "Jews" who had learned more of it more easily than himself. The remaining sections are concerned with "The Art of Performance," which contains some still-pertinent comment (he stressed the importance of tempo above all else); "Bayreuth," which is Wagner on top, sounding off like a world minister of arts and sciences; and "Politics." His later politics are at best whiggish, thanks to the fact of his royal patron, and at worst a parade of philo-German sentiments. He had already expressed the former point of view in *Das Rheingold*, in that unintentional comedy scene where Wotan refuses to pay the giants for building Valhalla (the monster had promised them his sister-in-law). Fasolt, the spokesman of the giants and a prototype labor leader warns Wotan that *"Was der bist, bist du nur durch Verträge"* ("What you are, you are only by agreement"), which is a most unmythological intrusion of the idea that Godheads and monarchies are constitutional, as well as a threat, in the context, that Valhallas may be combustible.

The thrall of Wagner has abated for reasons as different as the shortage of Flagstads and the decline of the narcotic effects of the music itself owing to the circulation of stronger drugs. (And it *was* an opiate at one time capable of giving Baudelaire, for one, a considerable bhang.) This book will not rehabilitate the man, but the Wagnerite will deny that he needs to be. For them, it is enough, as Nietschze said, that "some things have been added to the realm of art by Wagner alone."

ON CONDUCTORS
AND CONDUCTING[1]

"*The Imperial Kapellmeister gave the beat.*"
—QUANTZ, *describing a performance of an opera by J. J. Fux in 1723.*

Conducting, like politics, rarely attracts original minds,[2] and the field is more for the making of careers and the exploitation of personalities—another resemblance to politics—than a profession for the application of exact and standardized

[1] Thoughts and recollections tape-recorded for the London *Observer*, June 1962, in answer to a question about "eminent conductors I have known," but the tone and real provocation of my remarks are to be traced to a recording of the Brahms First Symphony given to me at that time and which I had tried to follow but could not because the second beats of the 6/8 movement were so delayed that the time signature might have been 6½/8. I imagined how the conductor would call the distortion emphasis, though it is only weakening exaggeration; and expressive freedom, though the natural rhythmic vitality is corrupted. I began the conversation in the mood of a composer rebelling against the fact that one cannot hear Johannes Brahms without the editing and the uninteresting comments of Conductor "X" *about* Johannes Brahms.

It is probably unnecessary at this date to warn the reader that no part of my soul is a diplomatist or politician.

[2] Mahler, Strauss, Boulez are exceptions.

disciplines. A conductor may actually be less well equipped for his work than his players, but no one except the players need know it, and his career is not dependent on them in any case,[3] but on the society women (including critics) to whom his musical qualities are of secondary importance. The successful conductor *can* be an incomplete musician, but he *must* be a compleat angler. His first skill *has* to be power politics.[4]

In such people the incidence of ego disease is naturally high to begin with, and I hardly need add that the disease grows like a tropical weed under the sun of a pandering public. The results are that the conductor is encouraged to impose a purely egotistical, false, and arbitrary authority, and that he is accorded a position out of all proportion to his real value in the musical, as opposed to the music-business, community. He soon becomes a "great" conductor, in fact, or as the press agent of one of them recently wrote me, a "titan of the podium," and as such is very nearly the worst obstacle to genuine music-making. "Great" conductors, like "great" actors, are unable to play anything but themselves; being unable to adapt themselves to the work, they adapt the work to themselves, to their "style," their mannerisms. The cult of the "great" conductor also tends to substitute looking for listening, so that to conductor and audience alike (and to reviewers who habitually fall into the trap of describing a conductor's appearance rather than the way he makes music sound, and of mistaking the conductor's gestures for the music's meanings), the important part of the performance becomes the gesture.[5]

---

[3] Orchestral players are not the most reliable judges of conductors.

[4] See the excellent analysis of the orchestral conductor in Canetti's *Crowds and Power*.

[5] To quote a recent *New York Times* review: "Here was the young man vigorously beating time when his hands were not occupied at the keyboard. His beautiful fingers cued everybody in, his beat was strong and sturdy, his eyes darted hither and thither.

If you are incapable of listening, the conductor will show you what to feel. Thus, the film-actor type of conductor will act out a life of Napoleon in "his" *Eroica*, wear an expression of noble suffering on the retreat from Moscow (TV having circumvented the comparatively merciful limitation to the dorsal view) and one of ultimate triumph in the last movement, during which he even dances the Victory Ball. If you are unable to listen to the music, you watch the corybantics, and if you *are* able, you had better not go to the concert.

I have other complaints against the conductor cult, but I will mention only two of them. First, it stultifies the repertory. Each conductor must make his mark in the standard pieces, the Strauss tone poems, *La Mer*, and so on, and though you may have had Herr Professor von Schnell's versions only a few months ago, you must now endure the aberrations of Herr Doktor von Langsamer; no wonder that the type of conductor whose work is mostly repetition easily develops an occupational indifference to music. Second, the typical conductor is a delinquent, quickly rusticated and lost to the new musical ideas of his age; or perhaps *arriviste* is a better word, in the sense of no progress, for to progress would mean to sell a stock that is paying handsome dividends. Think of Bruno Walter, who was Schoenberg's contemporary and who should logically have been his champion.

* * *

I have admired the work of many conductors during my long career as a listener, but I am not sure I would admire that work now. Felix Weingartner, for instance, was a near idol

---

"But when he was playing the piano, the orchestra did just as well without the cues of those beautiful hands, those expressive eyes, those rhythmic shoulders. The entrances in the last movement were just as precise, the ensemble just as coordinated, the shadings just as accomplished. People may get the idea a conductor is not really needed."

of mine in my youth. I heard him direct a Beethoven cycle in Berlin in 1900, and was thrilled by it, and in later years I attended his concerts on several occasions. But I think that of all the conductors I have heard I would nominate Alexander von Zemlinsky as the one who achieved the most consistently high standards. I remember a *Marriage of Figaro* conducted by him in Prague as the most satisfying operatic experience of my life.

As for the better conductors of today, I was never good at passing out testimonials, as you know, and I have certainly not become an encomiast in my old age. However, I will name a few of the, in my opinion, better craftsmen and more conscientious musicians: Szell, for instance, who can give prophylactic performances of the standard classic repertory; Reiner (*"l'amico* Fritz"), who made the Chicago Symphony into the most precise and flexible orchestra in the world and who, incidentally, was an effective antidote to the windmill and grandstand schools; Rosbaud, who was the most scrupulous of musicians and one of the few non-delinquent conductors; Ormandy, who gave the Philadelphia Orchestra a chinchilla echo, and who is an ideal conductor of Johann Strauss, as well as a specialist in posthumous music such as Tchaikovsky's Seventh (and even in such prehumous music as Webern's *Im Sommerwind*); Lorin Maazel, to name the most gifted of the middle-aged conductors, who has ability in a wide range and who has survived the publicity attending a debut at the age of one and a half, but who conducted a *Don Giovanni* I heard recently at the Met exactly as though he were a drum major; and Scherchen, who in spite of eccentricities or protective discolorations (the supersonic "finale" and the adagio "andante") can give clean bandmasterly performances of Haydn and convincing ones of Bach, even though he is without a clue to a Bach style. (It is unfair to single him out for censure on this point, though, as all "great" conductors' performances of Bach are grotesquely anachronistic, the reason being that there is no room in Bach for great conducting.)[6] I have not yet heard any *Wunderkind* of the younger generation, none of the Beatles (non-coleopterous) of the Classics, though we may be certain that the public will be only too willing to sacrifice the values and experience of a mature craftsman like Rosbaud to whatever new notion of glamor there may be for sale. I think, however, that the better conductors will continue to be bred in the field of the elastic beat—opera—and that we can look for them in the same old Mittel-Europa mill in which a student may acquire the routines of a dozen masterworks while still in his apprenticeship. Opera repertory is so much more extensive than symphonic—compare Verdi with Brahms as material—and the revival of opera is a mark of the present age.

When I played my piano concerto under Furtwängler's direction in Leipzig and in Berlin, he was at the height of his reputation ("the last of the great tradition," people were saying, though I thought myself it would be better to call him the first of the small). Nevertheless, he conducted it badly, even worse than Koussevitzky at the premiere. I was surprised by this because other musicians of his generation, and of older generations still, had guided the orchestra without difficulty. A few years after the Berlin performance, while on vacation in the Villa d'Este at Como, I received a telegram from Furtwängler requesting first-performance rights to my *Capriccio*. I replied that the piece had already been played twenty times (this was in 1931), but that he was welcome

[6] As nobody wants to hear more than once most (if any) of the music now being composed, it is in *"continuo* period" music that an intelligent musician might best make his mark as a conductor today, though not by resurrecting deservedly forgotten baroque operas in concert performances, or by forming chamber orchestras dedicated to the performance of yet more minor *ottocento* Italians. Bach himself is the most fallow field, but there are other good fields, too, such as Biber and Zelenka.

to play it for the twenty-first. I blame his telegram, and my
less than perfect sobriety, for the misdemeanor that has troubled my conscience, though slightly, in the years since. That
night, walking between a pair of "Greek" statues on one of
the Villa's garden paths, I saw that the marble figures were
covered with tourists' signatures, and took a pen myself and
scrawled WILHELM VON DER FURTWÄNGLER on the *gluteus
maximus* of the most obviously *ersatz* Apollo.

My memories of Mengelberg are also not among the most
deeply cherished. At our first rehearsal of the *Capriccio*, he
began to conduct in an impossible tempo. I said I was unable
to play at that speed, but I should have specified, for he could
not tell whether I had meant that he had been too fast or too
slow. He was flustered, though, and instead of starting over,
he embarked on a self-justifying oration: "Gentlemen, in
my fifty years of conducting I think I have learned to recognize the proper tempo of a piece of music, but Monsieur Stravinsky would like us to play like this—tick, tick, tick, tick";
and he cocked his forefinger to mimic Herr Mälzel's very
useful invention.

But Mengelberg was always a speech-maker, an after-dinner
Demosthenes of impressive volubility. I remember a banquet
in Amsterdam honoring Respighi. Mengelberg delivered the
toast, but glancing at me somewhere toward the end of it
and probably finding me staring at my watch, he pronounced
my name at the climactic moment instead of Respighi's. Mengelberg was not wicked, of course, or ungenerous, or even
totally devoid of musicianship. He was only morbidly dependent on flattery.

I met Otto Klemperer in the early 1920's in, I think, Leipzig or Dresden. He was regarded as the most skillful of the
younger German conductors, and as the most sympathetically
devoted to contemporary composers, a reputation he managed to uphold throughout the 1920's as well as in his first

American years. Klemperer was sometimes guilty of erratic *tempi*—they raced in the twenties, as now they are inclined to mope—but his musical impulses were often amazingly right. He is the only conductor who knew how to build the measure-and-a-note upbeat to the 6/8 *allegro* of the "Clock" Symphony, avoiding not only a strong but also a weak downbeat on the first measure, and saving the thesis for the second full measure. Klemperer, that great gaunt Polyphemus of a man, was also, and surprisingly, a profoundly droll character, though one could never be certain that drollery, in fact, was what he intended.

The performance of my piano concerto with Bruno Walter, in Paris in the late 1920's, was an unanticipated pleasure. I had not expected this *"Romantiker"* from an older generation to be able to count my scrambled meters or, knowing how he would slow down for the second subject of a symphony, to be able to keep my metronomic *tempi*, but he followed me as nimbly as anyone with whom I played the piece.

We saw each other next in New York in 1935, at a League of Composers concert, and after that in Hollywood, where we were neighbors for twenty years. Though our tastes and tempers—his melting, Viennese manner and my characteristic explosiveness—could hardly have been more unlike, we were drawn together in some way, if only because octogenarians naturally come to respect each other as counterchecks in the elimination game.

Bruno Walter called on me a few weeks before his death, inviting me in the name of the Vienna Philharmonic to conduct in Salzburg. I knew he was ailing and I offered to come to him instead, but he would not have it that way. He was animated, warm, and, as always, laboriously gentle. We talked about Tchaikovsky's operas and he told me his impressions of Leningrad during a trip there in the 1920's to conduct *Pique Dame*. He also talked about Rudolph Steiner—not critically as I do about that sort of thing, but, then, Steiner belonged to Walter's background. In parting I expressed regret that we had already had to wait too long for his *Fidelio* recording, and he said that he hoped I would hear it one day. But that day will not come. Shortly afterward he lay in his coffin, the "he" still incarnate, as Steiner would have it. On the wall above was a framed invitation to Beethoven's funeral.

I cannot add to what I have said elsewhere about Pierre Monteux except to remark that of all the conductors I have known he was the least interested in calisthenic exhibitions for the entertainment of the audience, and the most concerned to give clear signals to the orchestra.

My first experience with Koussevitzky as a performer of my own music was his London execution—in the firing-squad sense—of my Symphonies of Wind Instruments. He came to see me in Biarritz after that, to mend relations and to invite me to conduct my *Octuor* in one of his Paris concerts. Twenty years later he commissioned a piece from me as a memorial to his wife, Natalie,[7] but the performance of this Ode, as I called it, was another disaster. The trumpet player misread the key of his instrument in the third part and played the whole movement a major-second flat. Moreover, two systems of score from the final page had been copied erroneously as one. They were played that way, too, and my simple triadic piece concluded in a cacophony that would now win me prestige at Darmstadt. Not only did this sudden change in harmonic style not excite Koussevitzky's suspicion, however, but some years later he actually confided to me his preference for "the original version." But Koussevitzky filled an extraor-

---

[7] A worthy woman who naturally and unfortunately looked irate, like a hen, even when in good humor. Koussevitzky's career was purchased with her money. The subsequent Mrs. Koussevitzky was a different sort entirely, a woman of supererogatory goodness and zeal.

dinary role in America. He tried to, and did, establish an American version of the Rimsky academy, a nationalist movement that insured his popularity but probably retarded the course of new music. But with it all he was an extremely generous man who did more than any conductor to help composers financially.

Ernest Ansermet introduced himself to me in a street in Clarens one day in 1911 and invited me to his home for dinner. Although I had heard of him as a schoolmaster and amateur musician, his appearance—the beard—gave me an unpleasant turn; for a moment I took him for someone masquerading as the Charlatan in *Petrushka*.

Shortly after that Ansermet became the conductor of the Kursaal orchestra in Montreux, and our next encounter was at the home of the *chanson* composer Henri Duparc, a morose gentleman living in retirement near Vevey (in fact, near a hotel in which I had stayed as a child in the 1890's and in which I had once seen the Empress Elisabeth of Austria). At about this time, and I think with Ansermet, I also met the Geneva composer Ernest Bloch, an egregious type of man whom I saw rather frequently in my first years in Switzerland, and again many years later in Portland, Oregon.

When Pierné and Monteux had left the Russian Ballet in 1914, I recommended Ansermet to succeed them. He was skillful in regulating orchestral balances and he understood the Franco-Russian new music of that day. I was on close terms with Ansermet in the 1920's and 1930's and, in fact, until 1937 when he made an unauthorized cut in *Jeu de Cartes* and began, some years after that, to criticize my revisions of earlier pieces—though he had been the first to perform the 1919 revisions of the *Firebird* and the *Nightingale*. Since then he has been decrying my new music with *a priori* and "The Emperor's New Clothes" types of arguments, and he has even had the temerity to express himself in a heavy but not very weighty tome on the subject, one which uses phrases such as "*conscience logarithmique,*" but which only proves, and sadly, that he cannot hear or follow this music. In spite of all that, however, I am still fond of him, and I cannot forget many merry hours shared together. I remember one evening when, after we had drunk a bottle of *Framboise* together, he pretended to be a dog and began barking like one, under my studio piano in the Salle Pleyel. It was a very convincing performance.

Leopold Stokowski came to see me in Biarritz in 1922. I remember him as sympathetic and charming. He looked like a sleek Russian wolfhound then, and only later, in his film-star years, when he must have spent an hour a day trying to find the perfect bisexual hairdo, and disheveling it in exactly the right way, did he ever appear to be ungroomed. He made a handsome cash offer for the first American performance rights to my future works, and he actually paid an installment on the proposed sum, though he must have had afterthoughts about the agreement, as I did not hear from him again until the time of *Persephone*, which he also wished to introduce in America. I attended a Stokowski concert in Carnegie Hall in 1935 or 1937 and greeted the "maestro" backstage at intermission. I saw him next in 1942 in Hollywood, when he came to study my Symphony in C with me before attempting to conduct it with the NBC Orchestra. Few conductors can have done as much as Stokowski to gain a hearing for new music, and now, in his eighties, he has crowned his achievements by his patient preparation and performance of that astounding work, the Fourth Symphony of Ives. No conductor has been as good an orchestra-builder, either, and from basic sticks and stones to chromium plate. For better or worse, the tricks he taught still survive (along with the popular image of conducting as a kind of legerde-main) as, for example, the way cello sections stagger their bowing in the *Tristan* Prelude to produce a smooth and consistent *crescendo*.

I had little knowledge of Sir Thomas Beecham's musicianship, and I never heard him perform any of my music, but I did know his generosity. At the beginning of the 1914 war, he sent me 2,500 Swiss francs in the event that I should be cut off from my sources of income in Russia. The money came like manna, as I had to pay my mother's passage back to Russia on the Brindisi-to-Odessa boat, the only route still open. Beecham was my first friend among English musicians, and he was, first and last, the most spirited. We continued to see each other in later years and, whether in spite or because of the fact that we never shared a concert together, were always friends. I often saw him during the 1940's and I remember very clearly two particularly lively evenings in his company, one with Percy Grainger in New York, the other in Mexico.

But I would like to mention two other English conductors, Edward Clark and Eugene Goossens and, if I may do so, to honor their memories. Clark was the first English musician to have had direct knowledge of the Schoenberg school, and one day when his efforts on its behalf are made known, his name will be engraved in English musical history. Clark was a jolly man and a wonderful friend.

Goossens was a natural musician from a family of born musicians, and he was a master of orchestral technique. I recall with pleasure his brilliant performance of *Le Sacre* in London in 1921, and Diaghilev's jealousy at a triumph that, even by reflection, was not his.

Mitropoulos had performed *Petrushka* and *Histoire du soldat*, but as a missionary of Mahler and as a specialist in the *Alpine Symphony* (in which he was as sure-footed as a chamois) he could not have been generally interested in my music. I was therefore surprised when he came to call on me in Hollywood one summer evening in 1945. His speech, French mixed with a few words of Slavonic, as well as his wobbly movements, quickly endeared him to me. We talked about the Orthodox Church, and he examined my icons. The next day, in Hollywood Bowl, I heard him conduct and play Prokofiev's Third Piano Concerto, an amazing display of virtuosity. Mitropoulos was gentle, humble, and very kind. I was deeply moved by his death. (But I see that these remarks are turning into a necrology and that I am too inclined to praise the dead and damn the not-quite. But then, most readers will in any case come away with the impression that my remarks are intended to flatten out the country around so that I will stand up myself like a mesa.)

Leonard Bernstein came to see me in New York one day in 1945. His visit was to have lasted a few minutes, but it filled the entire day: the young Bernstein was articulate and readily likeable (he still is), and he obviously adored music (he still does). He was also very personally attractive, not yet leonine or English-sheep-dog, but wearing a most becoming pompadour. Since then Mr. Bernstein has made himself well known—in fact, one suspects guided missile experts of studying his career for basic technique. I would not be surprised in the near future to hear of his conducting several concerts at the same time, giving an opening downbeat in Carnegie Hall, then flying off to lead the first measures of another concert in Lincoln Center, and so on, while subordinates—for he has become a department store—rush in and bring the various pieces through to the end. But how dull New York would be without Leonard Bernstein. A few days after our first meeting I went to his performance of the Symphony of Psalms. WOW!

PART II

From the Diaries
of Robert Craft,
1949–1966

An inquisitiveness into the minutest circumstances and casual sayings of eminent contemporaries is indeed quite natural; but so are all our follies.—COLERIDGE

NOTE: In the present book, as in DIALOGUES AND A DIARY, *part one is the wheat, part two the tattered tares. I regret that all of the books did not appear in this form, or in their original form as diaries with no separation of materials. But I failed to see the value of circumstances and only lately realized that had I retained my own account of, for example, the lively encounters of Stravinsky and Pierre Boulez in 1957, the context, maladroitly composed though it was, would have given a different and I think more attractive complexion to Stravinsky's remarks concerning Boulez in the first book of* CONVERSATIONS.

In choosing this second series of diary excerpts, I sought to avoid a certain facetious type of entry by which, I fear, the earlier anthology was characterized. At the same time I risked the inclusion of a few close-ups of character and habit; aberrant habit, as it may seem to some, though if such be the case the only reason is that it was easier to observe. To avoid duplication, minor cuts and conflations have been effected.

But whatever the contribution of these off-duty observations to the background of the subject, they contain too much of the landscape of the writer and too little of his principal figure. This, together with a more imperative reason, is why there will be no more of them. Diary-keeping, a mental metabolizing activity at one time, now appears to me like a bad habit. To the addict it could become an end in itself, and one for which he might not only exploit experience but force it as well. For myself, then, and touching wood, this will be nunc dimittis.

R.C.

1949

July 27

Los Angeles. Aldous and Maria Huxley to dinner, she petite and eager, with large, believing eyes in a small, pinched face, he even taller than anyone had warned. But one looks first at his silver-point features, especially the slightly hooked, slightly haughty nose, and rarely away from them thereafter. The right cornea is covered by a milky film, like clouded glass, and it is the unflawed but rapidly nictitating left eye which he turns to us, though its powers of sight are hardly greater. His skin has a desiccated appearance—from the desert sun during his anchorite period, one would suppose, except that it is also deathly white. Everything else about the man except the big weedy brows suggests not the out-of-doors, however, but the tightly sealed edifices of intellectual respectability. What strikes one next is that he seems so absurdly out of scale in the diminutive I.S. house. He crouches under the low ceilings, ducks through the doorways, flinches by a chandelier, stoops at table, until we feel as though it may *really* be unsafe for him here, that he *could* actually trap himself in one of I.S.'s tiny W.C.'s and never get out.

At table we are more precisely aware of his visual limitations: he *feels* for his knife, fork, and plate, with the palpations of the blind. His wife helps him to find the food, and she continues to direct him throughout the meal in almost unnoticed *sotto voce* asides. *"Un tout petit peu à gauche, chéri,"* she whispers when his knife fails to find a purchase on the meat, and in the same voice she advises him how long to uptilt the salt shaker, but I think he would not welcome, indeed would resent any sign of solicitude from another source.

Conversation is in French. This is partly because Mr. and Mrs. H. obviously prefer to talk in that language, but principally because I.S.'s ear, having been exclusively confined to my backwoods American, is not attuned to Huxley English. (The word "issue," for example, a clean, sibilant "iss-u" in Mr. H.'s mouth, a gooey "ish-shoe" in mine, must confound the I.S.'s as it distracts me.) In any case, I.S. seems to think of Mr. H. as an English-born Frenchman whose manners may be the quintessence of Englishness (this is good in I.S.'s book), but who is in other important respects more civilized (French). Language apart, the two men inhibit each other. If Mr. H. is the wrong size, he is also the wrong culture. That sovereignty of scientific rationalism, the very blueprint of his intellectual heredity, is a planet away from I.S.'s mystagogical view of human existence. I.S. has not followed any science or philosophy of science since his reading of Bergson a half century ago. It is for this reason, also, that he lives in terror all evening lest Mr. H. dwell on scientific deeds and books of which he has never heard. Yet I think that Mr. H. is as self-conscious of his own limitations in being unable to stem the flow of his thoughts long enough to approach the world of the other from the other's bias. The two men watch each other like champions of two mutually incomprehensible games; for basic toe-holds rather than gambits or feints.

Mr. H.'s voice, a lambent, culture-saturated purr, is as

memorable as his head. When he tells a story, it ripples musically through pursed lips. The longer anecdotes begin in low
dove-tones, rising toward what promises to be a loudly ex-
plosive finish but knotting into a *Knödel* instead, or fizzling
out at the climactic high notes. And what a storyteller he is!
As family history alone, his autobiography would contain the
richest material of any living writer, but judging from tonight's tales of Joyce, Pound, Eliot, Yeats, such a book promises to be one of the most amusing for the twenties and thirties
as well. Best of all, he betrays no mark of the repertory company, and good as these performances are, the most astonishing occurs in a more difficult line—in confrontation with
I.S.'s collection of sea shells. Holding each specimen under
a magnifying glass two inches from his left eye, Mr. H.
casually sheds a mass of recondite conchological learning
about it, and when dropping a Latin name, he begs our pardon with exquisite punctilio.

The hunching and cringing from the restrictions of Lilliput
begin all over again on the way to the living room, though
having charted the chief dangers in his memory, he now
moves with a more gliding and rubbery walk. We ensconce
him in the largest chair, from which, however, he seems to
squirm away—parts of him, anyway—like a cornered cepha-
lopod, now stretching its peripatetic tentacles to alarming
lengths, now cupping them in. As he listens to us, his fingers
plait and unplait, or tickle the fenders of his chair, but when
he talks, his arms move continuously and rapidly in large
illustrative gestures so that he seems, like Vishnu, to have
several pairs of them. And what does he talk about? The
finding of bacteria at ocean depths; the heightening of erotic
sensibilities through breathing exercises; the sexual customs
of the American utopias, especially the Oneida experiment
of training adolescent boys on women past the menopause;
Baudelaire's Latin poems, which "demonstrate wide reading

in the type of poem but show complete ignorance of stress and merely duplicate the number of syllables"; problems of multiple meanings in Pali "which, after all, is not a very subtle language but neverthelss has thirty different words for 'knowledge' "; Augustus Hare, whose taste for oddity is very like Mr. H.'s own; the possibility of flights to the moon within a decade if enough money were to be diverted to the project, though Mr. H.'s only interest in going to any other planet would be "to establish contact with an older civilization." This river of information is continually nourished by tributaries of quotations—a couplet by Trumbull Stickney, a clerihew, the whole of *"La vierge, le vivace, et le bel aujourd'hui,"* which he recites as though he were reading from an oculist's chart, except for one small stumble of memory from which he picks himself up with an air of surprise that none of us had caught him as he tripped. One feels confident that Mr. H. would have as much Bartlett no matter what the topic, and that every volume in the anthology will always automatically flick open to the right page.

Brilliant as it is, we are a little relieved when it comes to an end; *I* am, anyway, for I have resolved a dozen times an hour to keep my Boeotian ignorance to myself and never to expose it in public—at any rate not in *this* public. But he is the gentlest human being I have ever seen, and the most delightfully giggly.

August 19

To the Huxleys' for tea—parsley tea with crystal sugar, and a tray of molasses cookies, wheat germ, raw carrots, small wedges of non-fattening fruit cake. Architecturally the house would satisfy the taste for mansions of a retired Kenya colonial; and it is a contrast in most other ways as well to the I.S. house, which, like the composer himself, is small, snug, brightly lighted, not forbiddingly private, as packed as a provincial museum. The lights are off as we enter, drawn curtains notwithstanding, and the sole evidence of Edison is a lamp in Mr. H.'s study that would seem more suitable for third-degree interrogations. The walls are bare, except for a few of Mr. H.'s own water colors (landscapes of trees and rocks somewhat in the manner of Cézanne), and the furniture, what there is of it, is severe. I.S. does not scintillate in such surroundings. And when Mrs. H. withdraws, taking V. with her so that the boys may have a smoking-room chat, he is not only uncomfortable but positively frightened of facing Mr. H. without V.'s support. As I know I.S., he is whetting for a whisky, but the display of health foods and Mrs. H.'s gingerly proffering of a carafe of sherry (after a slightly snickering reference to booze) intimidate him and he does not ask for it. The sepulchral lighting and raftered baronial hall dampen the conversation, too; Mr. H. is serious here, and we are reverent and hushed—though for my part I could not have contributed more than five or six twigs to the blaze of Mr. H.'s talk anyway, and these are held back less by the bleakness of the *décors* than by self-consciousness for my pawky verbal congestions.

Mr. H. alone and uninterrupted is not easily bettered, in any case, and I regret no tape recorder preserved him today, especially his descriptions of the culinary mortifications of St. Philip Neri. He is more engaging to listen to than to read, the conversationalist being superior to the writer in at least two definite ways. First, the talk is wholly free of the late-Tolstoy type of sermonizing that has become such a heavy part of the books; second, the talker embroiders his main thematic paths with a luxury of odd links, an anastomosis of curious connections (the Huxley style is beginning to affect

me!) which the writer could not—no writer could—afford
to follow.

What is Mr. H. to I.S.? A kind of handy, neighborhood
university, whatever more besides. I.S., like a radio quiz master, is forever wanting immediate answers to random matters
of fact. He will leave the dinner table to trace some scrap of
information and return thirty minutes and two cold courses
later—empty-handed more often than not, for lack of a
methodology. But if Mr. H. is in town I.S. need only pick up
the telephone, as he did yesterday when he wanted a run-
down on the history of scissors. He is convinced that Mr. H.
suffers from his encyclopedic erudition, incidentally, and
that he is a prisoner of it. I believe that this is true, even to
the extent that the Tao of his seemingly unquenchable quest
is freedom through possession.

And I.S. to Mr. H.? A "genius" or, as scientists prefer,
"hopeful monster," is the simple but, I think, complete answer: one of a sacred few invested with the divine power of
creation. Not only does Mr. H. prostrate himself before the
mystery of this power, but he seems to regard it as a justifica-
tion for the existence of the mass of humanity. D. H. Lawrence was Mr. H.'s genius in the early years, and whatever
qualities the word represents for him now, Lawrentian or
otherwise, he thirsts for them still, as others do for religious
inspiration. At the same time, he would disclaim even a pinch
of these qualities as his own, I think, and allow the designa-
tion "creative writer" to be applied to himself only if he
were attempting to explain his low income to a tax collector.
He writhes when anyone so much as hints at a reference to
his work, and actually groans aloud when V. alludes to a
dramatization of *Brave New World;* a direct question about
a book-in-progress would doubtless dissolve him altogether.
Contrast this with I.S., who beams with satisfaction at the
mention of *his* tiniest opus. But, then, I.S. *is* a creator.

But Mr. H. also looks to I.S. as a source of knowledge *about* music, and not only for the so-called secrets of art but, curiously, for the plainest of lexical facts as well. His appetite for this knowledge appears to be insatiable, moreover, though he already possesses a huge store of music history and a tune-humming acquaintance with the repertory which is (on that level) at least as wide as I.S.'s. He does not seem to consider that such knowledge has little interest for, or bearing on, the mind of the composer, or that the composer's stock of prejudices can be narrow and cranky because of creative preoccupations of the moment. How long, I wonder, will it take Mr. H. to discover that I.S.'s genius is wrapped—for protection from musical data—in a vacuum?

1950

July 5

Hollywood. Not only angels fear to tread! After my visit
with Schoenberg today, I am aware of having walked from
the street to his house on the grass, instead of the gravel
driveway; of tiptoeing to the door; and of waiting there in
hopes of being seen in order not to have to ring the bell. In
fact, Schoenberg's pretty daughter does see me, and she leads
me to the living room, abandoning me there except for a few
peeps at me from the kitchen. There is only one picture in
the room, a photograph of Kokoschka, and the only furniture
is a gravy-colored leather armchair, a sofa, and a piano set
like a table with the tennis trophies of Schoenberg's elder son.
The composer enters, walking slowly and with the help of
his wife. He is stooped and wizened, but sun-tanned like an
athlete. He seems thinner than last time—that pained, too
sensitive face, difficult to look into and impossible not to look
into—and the bulging veins in his right temple are more
prominent. Perhaps from the same cause his ears appear to
have grown larger; they *are* larger (the concha and outward
antitragus) than I.S.'s, which I remark because the oversized

hearing apparatus of both composers is their outstanding sculptural feature. He seats himself in the gravy *fauteuil*, on the edge of the cushion and without repose; and seated he seems even smaller, and older, than his years. Then, as we begin to talk, he adjusts caster-thick eye-glasses heretofore dangling from his neck by a ribbon and rubber bands. The voice is soft, but as pained and sensitive as the face, and at moments it is almost embarrassingly intense.

He tries to convince me to use an English translation for my forthcoming New York performance of *Pierrot lunaire*, and he recommends the version by Ingolf Dahl. To my question about performing his *a cappella* male choruses, he suggests that I double each line with an instrument and wire the instruments to the singers from offstage through individual earphones. As I also intend to perform the Septet-Suite, Opus 29, he proposes that we listen to a recording of the work made in Paris at the time of the premiere. The fact that he conducted the performance does not stay him from censuring it briefly during nearly every page-turn in the score, and at length during each pause to change the record side. "This is the most difficult of all my piano writings," he remarks at one point, though I am thinking that the clarinet parts are far more of a problem. He listens to the music (what can be heard of it beneath distractingly crepitant surface noise) as though he had forgotten having written it, and the rediscovery leaves him radiant. And afterward, in spite of his criticisms, he gives me the records to copy, which is very like I.S., who will also play acetates of his radio broadcasts and lend them out to prospective performers.

A question of mine concerning the *Lieder*, Opus 22, seems to surprise him—agreeably, I think. He wants to know how I know them, and with absolute ingenuousness he confesses to his guilt "in using too many instruments, though orchestras of that size were not impracticable at the time the music was composed." With no tone of complaint he remarks that the songs "had to wait twenty years for a performance," and at that I want to tell him that I think they are the most beautiful orchestral songs ever written, but do not, partly because of the text of his canon for G. B. Shaw and partly because one does not gush to Schoenberg—though I regret later that I did not say it. He is much more surprised to discover that I know the score of *Von Heute auf Morgen*, and less able to conceal his pleasure in recalling that long-buried masterpiece, the largest completed work of his mature years. But the fact of these reactions is also shocking evidence of the neglect of his music. How, in this age of . . . ? Yes, but that's it, exactly.

He knows of my association with I.S., but does not allude to it, and I refrain from doing so myself because I have not come on I.S.'s account. I think he is curious, though, and would at least like to inquire after I.S.'s health—even though his own is so frail and though age has so suddenly crushed him. At one point his younger son tears through the room yelping like a bloodhound. Schoenberg calls after the boy, makes a show of shrinking from the noise, and begs him not to play in the house. It seems to me that anyone observing this incident who was not already aware of the relationship must naturally suppose the composer to be the grandfather instead of the parent. As I prepare to go he autographs my score of *Pierrot lunaire*, adding the phrase "expecting a good performance"; and he invites me to visit him again next week. My feeling of lightness outdoors is a measure of the almost unbearable intensity of the man, as well as of the strain created by the danger of crossing the circle of his pride, for though his humility is fathomless it is also plated all the way down with a hubris of stainless steel.

1951

April 17

An afternoon with Universal Knowledge. Aldous calls, asking me to read to him; he has overtaxed his "good" eye. I find him typing the witchcraft book, nevertheless—in the den at the end of the darkened corridor, and on a table stacked ominously with publications in Braille. He is wearing his "Chinese glasses," black cellulose goggles with perforations in place of lenses: they force the pupils to perform a kind of stroboscopic movement, and consequently prevent staring; Aldous has taped a bandage over the pinholes on the right side, which means that he no longer has any sight at all from his opaline right eye.

He seems pleased to be interrupted, but is clearly less hungry for a dose of reading than for a discussion of the substance of his work—except that he refuses to talk about it as *his;* he will give himself no credit, even for the discoveries of his own research. Without any steppingstone small talk he pulls me into the deeps of the *Malleus Malleficatum* and the "appalling materialism to which it testifies." Developing this thesis, he seems to shirk no opportunity for scatological descriptions and, of course, the torturing of "witches" provides an abundance of such occasions. But there is no Swiftian compulsiveness in this, I think; it is merely the yeast in his argument on the naturalness of human vileness. At one point, telling of the use of bellows and tongs to exorcize the Devil from a child's stomach, he is put in mind of a cartoon by Wilhelm Busch, and the thought of that fellow misanthrope leaves him gay and exhilarated. "Has anyone ever detested humanity more?" he asks, and his voice glitters mordantly and as heartlessly as the ice cubes at a cocktail party.

A thought strikes me today, as it has before, that two of Aldous's most prominent intellectual qualities are clarity and, at the same time, credulity, and that they make a very odd team. On the one side is an apparently unshakable *credo ut intelligam* (which includes logic and the analytic disciplines), and on the other, a radical susceptibility to the nostrums of quacksalvers and spiritual confidence men. The clarity side is descended by school from the Victorian philosophers for whom there could be no unruly ideas, and one cannot help remarking that this instrument is not quite the right one for the verbally elusive "perennial philosophy." But what of the teammate? What school is *he* from, Paracelsus High? Where was he keeping himself at the time of *Antic Hay*, one would like to know, and what has befallen the author of same that he can now look for salvation in a pill? For he who was always hurrying to expose the *Paradis Artificiels* of yesterday has become the readiest exponent, even the guinea pig, for those of today. Why, as it appears, is he grasping at straws?[1] As a so-called uncommitted liberal he is committed to try everything, of course, and give every idea its due, but a profounder explanation will have to delve back to Victorian roots. Aldous is a shocked Victorian, it seems to me, and even a shell-shocked one, as much as the poets of the trenches. And

[1] Part of the answer will be found, I think, in the sad events of his own life. See the entry for November 24, 1963.

he is capable of being shocked by what to most people are common happenings. His hardest-worked word is "extraordinary," and the runner-up word, "absolutely," operates as its geminate. Only the extraordinary and the exaggerated interest him, in fact, and at times one thinks that he has ceased to believe in ordinary human beings. There are only Mozarts and imbeciles in his world, only extreme aspects of humanity, and these aspects continually shock him. Now, it must be allowed that some of the shocks, such as the creations of Mozart, are ennobling, even though most of them (and with so much more satisfaction for anti-meliorists such as Aldous) are the contrary. Irony is the surfacing trick of the shocked Victorian, but irony stales with the speed of yesterday's events, and how much of Aldous's will outlive him?

The point about ordinary and whole people is the crux of Aldous's failure as a novelist—though "failure" is unfair for in this sense he never set out to succeed and, anyway, why should he not write about extraordinary ones? A readable journal is rarer than a readable novel, and its characters and records of events, being "true," are at least as likely to endure —the characters and events in a journal by Aldous Huxley, at any rate. And such a journal by him—the unfictionalized raw material, the ideas and speculations, the thumbnail portraits, the highlights of conversations, the commentaries about books (his annotations in Evans-Wentz's *Tibetan Book of the Dead* which I have just borrowed contain a whole library implicit in the cross-references)—this would be a treasure indeed. As far back as *Point Counterpoint*, Philip Quarles's musings indicated this type of journal as Aldous's own form *par excellence;* except that Aldous in first person is far superior to Aldous under any guise—being surpassed, in fact, only by Aldous *in* person.

[*Postscript, 1965.* I cannot excuse the impudence of these arguments which I had manufactured out of some no longer remembered necessity to myself, but I might try to improve my appearance by emphasizing the fact that the true subject here is not so much A.H. as my own growing-pains. A.H. had had a considerable influence on me long before I knew him, and in my prep school and early college years the appearance of each new book by him was an exciting event that would bring new notions and new bearings for old ones. I should add that in the year of my discovery of him, his reputation had begun to suffer because of his pacifism—more that, I think, than his espousal of a religious philosophy which was already on its way to a wartime vogue. He had recently published an *Encyclopedia of Pacifism*, together with a shorter tract which attempted to argue pacifism as a practical policy. The argument broke ground with the claim that "feeling, willing, thinking are the three modes of ordinary human activity." The statement derives from Fulgentius, I think, or from Ficino and the Florentine Neoplatonists, but it seemed deliberately to overlook another very ordinary mode, action —though as Kierkegaard says somewhere, "In Greece, philosophizing was a mode of action," and it was certainly that with Aldous himself. But the oversight was polemically unfortunate and so was the title of the pamphlet, *What are you going to do about it?*, which fairly begged for the rejoinder it soon received, C. Day Lewis's *We're not going to do nothing*. For more on A.H. see the entries for July 27 and August 19, 1949 (pages 159–65) and November 24, 1963 (pages 299–304).]

April 28

Tonight's Russian Easter Midnight Mass is presided over by a bishop, for which reason, probably, the crowd is greater than in other years. In any case, there is no room for us in

the little white church with the blue-onion dome, and we join
two or three hundred other latecomers now packing the
grounds and spilling into the street, to which the service is
relayed through a spluttery public-address system. The majority of this outdoor congregation are "D.P.'s" with close-
shaven or *en brosse* heads, ill-fitting donated clothes, and far-
away eyes. The others are the white Russian regulars, a loud
clan locally with whom the I.S.'s have little traffic and by
whom, in consequence, they are snubbed. Both factions appear to be deeply homesick tonight, the flamboyant professional exiles no less than the timid and indigent D.P.'s—or so
I judge from their soulful singing of a hymn; not only soulful, either, but drastically out-of-tune, like an "atonal" version of the beginning of "*1812*." Even the mire—we have had
a week of heavy rain—seems to contribute to their nostalgia,
responding to their footsteps with Russian-size squelches.

Shortly before midnight all of us in the open-air congregation light tapers. Then at twelve exactly the church doors
open and the clergy and congregation pour forth into our
already dense and now literally inflammable human chandelier. A deacon in a newly starched alb heads the procession,
swinging the censer with a vengeance and spreading incense
over us as if he were crop-dusting. Behind him, the bishop,
in a scarlet, white, and gold samite, pauses on the top step
and sings "*Christos Voskreseh*" ("Christ Is Risen"), to which
the whole crowd responds with "*Vīeestinoo Voskreseh*" ("He
is risen indeed")—though it comes out not like that, but
tumbling around the church letter by letter, like noodles in
alphabet soup. Next in the procession is a priest carrying a
tall cross, and a train of acolytes displaying icons, "*haroogvee*"
(holy banners or icons made of cloth), the globe and scepter
of Christ the King; all of these clerics have long soft beards,
like Spanish moss. Three times around the church they parade,
and thrice, in tow, follow the "D.P.'s," whose attention, however, is directed more and more to their wilting and dripping

candles. "*Christos Voskreseh*," cries the bishop as he launches each successive trip, and each time the "*Vīeestinoo Voskreseh*" wobbles around the church in response. The ritual concludes with an orgy of congregational kissing, in the sequence left cheek, right cheek, and again left, and with everyone you know or cannot escape, Easter kisses being unrefusable.

At the I.S.'s afterward, the Lenten fast is symbolically broken—not having been physically observed—by eating *kooleetch*, the Easter bread with a paper rose; and *paskha*, the million-calorie (sugar, milk, cheese, eggs, raisins, tutti-frutti) Easter cake. After draining in its obelisk mold for almost a week the *paskha* was taxied to church today to be blessed. The mold and a cheesecloth wrapper are now removed revealing the imprint "*X.B.*"—"Christ Is Risen"—on the front of the decanted cake, as well as Easter flower designs on the sides.

June 18

I.S.'s birthday begins, as it does each year, in a bad mood. This, however, seems to be owing to nothing more grave than the deprivation of breakfast until after Confession; it is characteristic of I.S. to complain of cramps at the first crinkle of hunger, and to demand food immediately, no matter where he is or in what company. On the way to church this morning, in any case, he growls from time to time like a hungry tiger; and I might add that this being the second most sacred day in the year (next to Christmas), the growl is the only sound permitted. The birthday Confession and Mass following it consume two hours, most of which time has to be knelt through on an uncushioned floor. As we enter the church, I.S. goes directly to the altar rail and prostrates himself. After a while an acolyte appears, rattling his thurible and fumigating us. A priest enters next, half-concealing himself behind a rood screen, like an intrigant in a Restoration comedy. He signals I.S. to approach the screen, where he asks him—furtively, as though he were demanding the password in a speakeasy—the name of his patron saint. And from this point I.S. is "Igor" (correctly pronounced "eager" only by V., who, at the same time, is the only person he will allow to pronounce it). "What, Igor, do you have on your conscience?" the confessor inquires, and whatever it is, I.S. tells him standing. For the Absolution, the priest holds a partlet over I.S.'s head, recites a prayer over it, extends his pectoral cross to the penitent's lips. The doors are opened, after this, and a few stray people enter to join in the Mass and form a chorus, of sorts, in the *"Gospodi Pamili."* A second acolyte now carries the monstrance for the priest and follows the Communion cup with a red cloth with which to wipe pendant drops of wine. After taking the sacraments, I.S. prays with his head to the floor.

The ride from the church is silent, like the ride going, but at least the odor of sanctimony is dispelled by the smell of whisky and cold Russian cutlets. At home I.S. goes directly to his studio and prays as though to a fertility idol before the icon that watches over him as he composes. From noon on, friends call, bringing gifts and offerings while more than a hundred telegrams from the far-away faithful pile up on the hall table. I.S.'s mood is unaffected, though, and he remains removed and untalkative to the end of the day.

July 7

Call on Schoenberg to return a tape of his Violin Concerto. There are two sculptured heads of him in the living room now, one full and robust from *ca.* 1936, the other, of recent date, shrunken to two-thirds, it seems, of the size. He is unwell today, and unable to come downstairs, but his voice is audible from the bedroom, and from there he inscribes my scores of *Erwartung* and *Die glückliche Hand*, besides sending me a gift of the facsimile of *Dreimal tausend Jahre*. He also sends a message inviting me to stay and listen to the Concerto (I have been doing little else all week), while Mrs. Schoenberg explains that "he likes to hear it, whatever he can hear of it upstairs; it is his favorite of his orchestral works, as the String Trio is of his chamber music." After we listen twice through, she shows me Schoenberg's studio, which is as small and crowded as I.S.'s, but without I.S.'s finicky aesthetic arrangement of working paraphernalia, and without the tinsel and *décors*. The desk is tinted with red, yellow, and blue light from a stained-glass window, which is eery, though not more so than the self-portraits, obsessive about eyes. Manuscripts and papers cover the desk, a table, and an old harmonium, and every bit of shelf space is stuffed with music (I notice orchestra scores of *Otello* and *Falstaff*) or bound sets of books (Strindberg, Ibsen, Byron). A mandolin, wistful reminder of the Serenade and *Pierrot*, hangs from a peg on the wall.

1952

February 23

At Aldous's request I witness and sign his Last Will and Testament, in token for which he presents me with a volume of risqué verse, an inducement to improve my French, he says, adding that the book had been given to him in his youth for the same purpose.

He has returned today from a trip in the desert, and as always after a spell in depopulated regions he is refreshed and in high spirits. He has brought back a garland of rare-blossoming—once-in-a-decade—lilies, but he himself is a far more spectacular and rarer burgeoning. "Cacti," he says, "grow no more than an inch in five years and are therefore, the large ones anyway, some of the world's most venerable plants." But he is more excited by the discovery that "desert 'poorwills' hibernate. They are genetically related to hummingbirds, you remember" (oddly enough I do not) "and hummingbirds were the only species heretofore positively known to hibernate, which is why the early Hindu philosophers called them 'sleeping birds.' " He then digresses for a fascinating quarter of an hour on the Trochilidea family, "what the onomatopoeic Mayans called the Dzunuum. . . ."

I drive him later to the summit of Doheny Hill, the start of one of his favorite rambles (but definitely not one of mine; though only three minutes from the center of Beverly Hills, it has a reputation for rattlesnakes). We follow rutted tracks into a wilderness, the daddy longlegs easily ahead. But the intellectual pace is faster, and here he keeps a good sprint in front, without trying, which makes my pursuit feel mentally pigeon-toed—and I am trying very hard. He dispenses dendrological information along the way, as if we were on a botanical tutorial, and I learn and forget all sorts of things about florae to right and left of the path, not only the tallest pendunculates but the tiniest sessile organisms as well—though one wonders how he, purblind as he is, can tell. Not until the return trek does he switch to a subject I am able to follow, "the 'lit'ry' cult of dirt, Auden's

'Who would love me be not too clean.' "

From this conversation it would appear that Ford Madox Ford was the least frequently washed of modern novelists. My unique contribution is to quote the dirt-specialist historian Lecky, though I realize afterward that I have mistakenly attributed the remark to J. B. Bury, whose name I mispronounce, as though it had to do with graveyards; Aldous is greatly taken aback by his ignorance of this author until dawn breaks on him and it is discovered that "Oh, you mean Professor Bewry." But his most interesting remarks of the afternoon are about "Tom" Eliot. "The marriage in *The Cocktail Party* was inspired—if that is the word—by Tom's own marriage. His wife, Vivienne, was an ether addict, you know; her face was mottled from it, like ecchymotic spots, and the house smelled like a hospital. All that dust and despair in Eliot's poetry is to be traced to this fact and, of course, *The*

Family Reunion is a play about murdering one's wife." And he compares Eliot's criticism to "a great operation that is never performed: powerful lights are brought into focus, anaesthetists and assistants are posted, the instruments are prepared. Finally the surgeon arrives and opens his bag—but closes it again and goes off."

After the walk we drive to an ice-cream parlor in Beverly Hills and—at Aldous's suggestion—eat banana splits. He says that "cerebrotonics should eat bananas every day."

May 2

Paris. *Wozzeck* at the Théâtre des Champs-Elysées, and afterward a dinner with Albert Camus. He is uncommunicative at first, annoyed, no doubt, because of our talk about the music. At one point he attempts to turn the conversation to Melville, saying that he plans to devote an essay to "this greatest American writer, an infinitely more important writer, incidentally, than the *pederaste voyeur* Henri James." No one takes the bait, however, and the Büchner-Berg talk continues. But if the opera made little impression on Camus—in comparison with the permanent dent in myself—he is attentive to whatever is said about the play. I.S. offers the thought that "the only one of Büchner's contemporaries with whom he might be compared is Gogol, but Büchner succeeded in throwing off the social blinkers of his time with more power of poetry than Gogol, though he lacked Gogol's sense of humor; I am thinking of Wozzeck's line, 'People like us, if we ever did get into heaven, they'd put us to work on the thunder.'" I.S. then says that in his opinion the last orchestral interlude is a mistake. "Until this point the composer has stood behind his constructions, but here he comes up front to tell us exactly how he feels about it all and how we should feel, as if there had ever been any doubt about how anyone felt. The opera should have ended with the Doctor's *'jetzt ganz still'* or the Hauptmann's *'Kommen Sie schnell,'* and avoided this apotheosis." Camus then remarks that the profoundest dimension in the play is Wozzeck's endowment with earth spirits. "Like Caliban he sees and hears with an animal being, a radar reaching into Nature itself, and the fact that he is under the spell of an (to him) enchanted Nature is established if not completely at the beginning of the opera, then already in the foraging scene, where he sees a strange fire while his companion sees only a man suffering visions. In the scene with the Doctor, too, the sense of this Nature that Wozzeck so desperately seeks to understand is hardly ever absent. 'If only one could read the lines and figures in the toadstools,' he says, but the medical materialist discourages him, telling him that *his* Nature is the merest superstition. At times Wozzeck sounds as though he were describing the effects of a hallucinatory drug. 'The world gets dark,' he tells the Doctor, 'and you have to feel around with your hands and everything keeps slipping, like a spider's web.' The Fool is also subject to visions, incidentally, and though he is only a stock character, they put him, briefly, on the same wave-length as Wozzeck." I.S. remarks at this point that the great feat of the Fool's scene is in the music. "Berg really does succeed in creating the impression that the apparatus of the concertina, the band, and the soldiers' chorus has been improvised then and there for a one and only performance. And this, I think, is the greatest achievement of the opera as a whole: that the listener always has a sense of a totally spontaneous expressive freedom from a score that makes the most profound use of so-called abstract formal devices, and which is the most in-depth-calculated, as they say, in the history of opera."

Camus considers *Wozzeck*, the play, to be one of the first

"existentialist" masterpieces. "Less than a minute after the curtain is opened, Wozzeck's existentialist isolation is defined. He talks to the Captain and the Captain talks to him but without any communication. And in the next three scenes it is the same between Wozzeck and his comrade, Wozzeck and his wife, Wozzeck and the man of science, that proto-Nazi doctor who is the most astonishing creation of all—though Büchner's doctor is not quite the same as the Nazi scientists who treated men as experimental objects because he still has to tell himself not to 'let a mere man upset you.' The technique of the Doctor scene, of the psychoanalytical catechism, is a no less amazing anticipation, incidentally, and the way the name of Marie comes to Wozzeck's lips is a stroke of genius. One should also note the fact that the Doctor, the scientific materialist, fails to perceive these now so-called Freudian slips. When the man of true human nature—'the dumb soul of humanity,' as Rilke described Wozzeck—is delivered to his tormentor, it is the tormentor who is destroyed, who disintegrates as a human being as he progresses in his indifference to suffering. Thus the Doctor in this scene, and thus the Captain at the end of the play when he says 'come away, it is not good to listen.' That statement stands as the antithesis to all those questions in which Wozzeck seeks to discover Nature's meaning."

1 9 5 5

March 15

Lisbon. The Aviz Hotel. I.S. is not yet awake this morning
when a reporter calls to say he has won the Sibelius Prize, a
sum of $18,000. To escape an interview he pretends to have
a cold (superstitiously fearing to catch a punitive one immediately thereafter) and adds that, in any case, if he receives
the money he intends to sell it to Calouste Gulbenkian, the
oil millionaire who is gravely ill in the rooms adjoining ours
and whose low, dry cough comes through the wall, like that
of the goat in *Gerontion*.

On the way to Evora for lunch, we stop to see the "Golden
Coaches of Belem," a museum of horse carriages with heavy
rococo furbelows. Lifting a seat cushion and discovering a
privy-shaped aperture underneath, I.S. is delighted to find
that the passenger could relieve nature in transit "just like
the horses."

As we enter the Evora restaurant, the proprietor is ab-
sorbed in a newspaper on the back page of which we see a
photograph of I.S. illustrating a story about the Sibelius
Prize. Soon the paper will be turned around, there will be

glances in our direction, and we will be caught—the consequences of which could be the gift of a new *specialité de la
maison* (the old one is a soup of rancid olive oil) which we
would somehow have to eat. But in the event, the proprietor
merely sends for a certain professor, the most learned of the
guides, indeed the only one worthy of us. Stupefied with the
local wine, a drop of which would have cured the insomnia
even of the thane of Cawdor, we struggle against sleep. The
professor arrives, however, and makes clear at once that there
will be no *Reader's Digest* version of *his* tour. We follow him
to a church with a famous charnel house in which we are
meant to shudder (and do); to São Braz, a cathedral with
wide buttresses and knobbed finials like the legs of a colossal
grasshopper; and to a convent school whose classroom walls
tell the story of Portugal's heroic age in bright blue *azulejos*.

Returning to Lisbon, we stop at Arrabida to walk on a high
road overlooking the sea. Then, back at the Aviz, I.S. receives
a batch of telegrams congratulating him on the Sibelius Prize,
some of them at the same time requesting contributions and
one asking outright for a loan.

March 18

To Seville via Badajoz, where the Spanish customs house is
filled with photographs of El Caudillo as well as a considerable contingent of his soldiers. The clerk ignores us and our
declarations until he has finished reading a magazine. Then,
after stamping the papers and allowing us to return to the
car, he suddenly detains I.S. with a request for an autograph.
(The Sibelius Prize? A suspicion that I.S. might turn out to
have been a famous violinist or film producer?) The narrow

Guadiana bridge is choked with purple pigs who turn in panic as they see our car and curdle the air with their squeals.

Reaching Seville at dusk, we go directly to the Cathedral. There, groping in the gloom, we are startled by a man's voice shouting, *"Estravinsky? Estravinsky?"* *"Q'y a t'il, mon Père,"* says I.S., when we see that the cries are coming from a priest. *"Vous êtes riche maintenant, n'est-ce pas?"* is the excited reply. *"Comment?"* says I.S. *"Le Prix d'Esibelius,"* the padre hopefully explains, but I.S. tries to dampen his enthusiasm with, *"Peut-être je suis riche, mon Père, mais je suis très avare."* This seems not to daunt our new companion very deeply, however, and he is soon proudly revealing himself as the organist, which could account for his descrying I.S. in the *noche oscura* of the Cathedral but does not unravel the mystery of how I.S.'s presence in Seville was discovered in the first place, since we have not yet registered in a hotel. Later the padre tells us that he had as quickly recognized Richard Strauss and Ravel when they visited the Cathedral— and no doubt surprised them as much as he did us. We follow him, enveloped in his cloud of garlic, to see the paintings and the treasuries. He is at least able to unlock doors and light lights.

March 26

Madrid. We spend the morning in the Prado, but the day is dark and the primitives are the only pictures within reach of lights. The most memorable of these are a *retablo* showing a Saint Vincent being fished from the sea by his nimbus; and an Ascent into Heaven in which the Holy Feet protrude below a dark cloud in one panel, but have been pulled out of sight in another, leaving a fiery wake. I.S. dubs it "the first 'before and after' advertisement."

At noon we drive to the Escurial with Prince Eugenio de Bourbon, a nephew of Alfonso XIII. The mountains and pine forests are still snow-covered, and in spite of our heavy coats we shiver both outdoors and in—though Prince Eugenio, in a light suit, appears not to notice the cold. We follow him across freezing pavements and down drafty corridors to the icy vaults and the royal tombs which begin with Charles V and end with an empty niche for the uncle of our host.

Back in Madrid, Ortega y Gasset calls on us, accompanied by the young Marquesa de Slauzol, who warns us that Ortega is hard of hearing and who helps him with words he fails to catch. Everything about the man is vivid, his clothes—natty blue jacket, bow tie, pearl cuff links—as well as his mind. He is extremely resonant, however, and so, obeying the Marquesa, are we. Moreover, our chorus of deaf men's voices grows louder as we ply each other with whisky, two bottles of which are emptied before Ortega departs, leaving us wonderfully elated, not to say "high."

The Zamora Club, where we watch flamenco dancing from midnight until two, is a small room full of Americans and smoke. The dancers and singers sit in a semicircle flanking two guitarists, an old man and a boy. The men help their songs with their hands, tracing aerial patterns as elaborate as the melismas and arabesques of the music. They also clap, stomp, and shout *olé*, to liven the long limbering period, but the performances drag on according to a worst-first protocol. The male dancers affect not to notice the audience, but every bump and grind of the females, especially of one Rosa, the beauty of the troupe in spite of her blemished skin, is directed exclusively there.

1 9 5 6

July 26

Istanbul. A motorboat excursion on the Bosphorus. Decaying palaces and villas line the shore the whole way, and the only buildings in trim condition are the embassies of Egypt and the U.S.S.R. The characteristic villas are made of wood, are unpainted, and have a large number of shuttered windows. The plainest of them remind V. of Sebastopol and the Crimea, but to me they are like the early frame structures now being torn down in downtown Los Angeles. Not many of them *are* plain, however, and the architectural motives are as varied as Gothic spires and Alpine roofs. About half of the buildings imitate Venice and put their feet in the water, but others approach it stepwise or through a kind of Ganges ghat. We stay close to the European shore as far as a cordon marking the channel to the Black Sea, then cross to Asia until we come as far as the pink villa of Pierre Loti. Back in the Golden Horn, we dock in time to see the President of Pakistan debarking from a Turkish battleship, and I.S. notes with glee that "the anti-American reception parade awaiting him is a solid line of Cadillacs." We drive to the hotel through a street called "Pig Alley" because of a shop which sells pork to Christians.

The Paracleseion of Kariye Camii (Zhamee), near the Adrianople Gate, was damaged by earthquakes, and about a third of the frescoes have washed away in the resulting leaks. Moslem pargeting has preserved the others, though, and, most perfectly, a portrait of a Resurrected Christ joining with Adam and Eve in a jubilant dance. Next to this is a Last Judgment in which the Hell is too small to receive the large company being driven there, and the Paradise is a cool white park full of rivers, birds, and beasts; but bandage-like scaffolding partly obstructs our view. A young American restorer says that this very morning a Simeon Stylites was discovered on a pillar in a fresco that had just been cleaned. But the building is richer in mosaics, especially in the right vestibule, with its twenty-four pendentive portraits of the ancestors of Christ and its pictures of a leper with black sores, of a donor in oriental hat and costume, and of a Baptism in which a white eel is being swallowed by a large fish (is this a marriage symbol?). The mosaic restorers work like dentists and in fact use dental tools.

The exterior of the Blue Mosque is the same gray as the sacred pigeons in its yard, but the interior is flooded with blue light from tiles in the direct aim of the side and dome windows. I.S. talks about the sense of unity in the single large room which is missing in a many-chapeled church, but he objects to the absence of iconographic representation and adduces it as a sign of "the intellectualism of the religion." The legs of the Mosque are four great columns, sequoia trees in girth. Grandfathers' clocks, gifts from Queen Victoria, stand by the two front shins, where they look odd indeed as furniture though the fact of them, of clock time in a place of prayer, impresses I.S. more profoundly than anything in Istanbul. Some worshipers enter, carrying their shoes in their hands, then kneel, touching their heads to the rug-covered floor. The men congregate on a large dais at what would be the place of an altar in a church, while heavily veiled and shawled women squat in a corner as far from the men, it seems, as possible. When an imam enters, shouting, everybody stands, including a small boy who amuses himself by running over the floor in his stocking feet. Near the right wall is a hassock for the Koran reader, and in front of it a circle for the ulema, the exegetes and disputants; according to I.S., we are to take this as further evidence of intellectualism and scholasticism. A pulpit-shaped paladin projects from the center wall next to a balcony in gold lattice for the sultan's wives, a kind of hen yard on stilts. A muezzin is chanting from one of the minarets as we leave, and along the stone troughs of the outer wall the faithful are washing their feet.

Hagia Sophia, in comparison, is an empty, dirty, stale-smelling turn-of-the-century railway station. Large round plaques, green like the Prophet's robe and inscribed in gold with mottoes from the Koran, hang like banners from the aisle columns. A guide in a tarboosh wishes us to recognize the features of the Empress Theodora in the grain of one the marble walls, and he is abusive, calling us giaours when we fail to do so. We climb a dark ramp to the balconies, but the upstairs floors seem to weave and sway and the columns to thrust out from the center.

July 30

Venice. An open-air *Tosca* in the Campo S. Angelo. The Scarpia is a seasoned wobbler with a blubbery *crescendo* on every note, and the Tosca has a tremolo that will soon be spreading to a major third. The better spectacle is not in front, but around, where every window with a view of the

Campo is a loge in a large family circle. I.S., speaking of theaters indoors and out, says that what impressed him most in Bayreuth was "the weblike blending of the orchestra from under the stage; *Parsifal* was still a headache, but it was a headache with aspirin." This leads to a remark about singers of the roles of Tristan and Isolde: "Most of them look like the results of crash programs in electronic mating. Naturally such monsters have to swallow philters before they can *do* anything."

August 9

A windy morning. Sea-size waves beat against the Fondamenta and the sky rumbles like an empty stomach until rain falls, turning the Grand Canal deep green and Palladio's white faces even whiter. We spend the day in museums and churches, beginning in the Correr with the illuminated manuscripts (one of them, *Marco Polo in Tartaria*, a picture book meant to inspire terror of the Turk, shows people being skewered through the extremes of their digestive systems). Antonella's *Christ Lamented by Angels* in an adjoining room is one of the most affecting pictures in the world, but the dead God is an Adonis and His beauty is too fleshly. The glowing *morbidezza* of the Christ in the center of the picture is surrounded by the shadows of the angels, one of whom, directly behind the Christ, seems to have given Him his wings.

Some of the tapestries in the San Marco Museum are woven *in toto* with different tones of gold. Gleaming gold angels have been threaded on faded gold backgrounds, as have gold lions-of-Saint-Mark on gold maps of Venice, which are then framed, in turn, with ropes of purled gold. But the most striking tapestry is one composed entirely of geometric patches, a collage of squares, arcs, circles, half moons, all differently dyed; and another, a Resurrection from Arras in which the white diaphanous light of the Christ dazzles the waking Roman soldiers and corrupts their motley. But the Venetian climate is unkind to color and we remember how luminous in comparison were the tapestries in the cold, dry Escurial.

The first church we visit, S. Francesco della Vigna, is in Palladio's best First National Bank style. V. considers the façade "pompous," but I.S. prefers to call it "imposing," and whether one or the other, it would look better in the large open place it once commanded (see the Canaletto of 1744); it is so encroached upon now, in any case, that from the end of the Campo only half of it is in view. San Lorenzo, nearby, also needs a wider dominion and is also rudely crowded by newer buildings, though its façade has long since been stripped of stone and its brick underclothes are now a hanging garden of weeds. San Pietro in Castello, another Palladian master-piece of the neighborhood, is dying of dilapidation, too, but its white, tipsy *torreloggio* is the most beautiful in Venice. Yet even these are in good condition compared with Santa Maria Maggiore, a church praised by Burney for its music: the exterior is testudinarious with skin disease, and the interior is a rat-infested ruin. The Rio di S. Maria Maggiore leads to a prison, whence the name of the street changes to "Rio Terra of the Thinkers," though whether or not with didactic intent I do not know. Lively radio music flows over the walls, but a dark-faced guard on the parapet scowls and motions us on.

August 10

An audience with the Patriarch, Cardinal Roncalli,[1] to seek his permission for the concert in the Basilica of San Marco. The Cardinal's gondola fetches us at noon, ferrying us to a

[1] Elevated to the tiara two years later as John XXIII.

tunnel on the Rio Palazzo, where we are led through passage-
ways and up flights of stairs. Ushered into the presence,
I copy I.S. in bowing and kissing the proffered ring
hand. After that the principal problem is in adjusting one's
eyes to scarlet: the scarlet skull cap on the Cardinal and the
scarlet *galero* on a table by the Cardinal's chair; the scarlet
cape of watered silk, the scarlet-lined soutane with scarlet buttons, the scarlet stockings, the scarlet-bordered and scarlet-
beaded slippers, the scarlet ribbons goffered on the left waist,
the scarlet-tasseled scarlet sash over the stomach—the stomach
of a woman about to be rushed to a maternity hospital. The
Cardinal converses in fluent French, but unlike most conversation with Frenchmen, this is easygoing. And His Eminence is quick and well-informed, which surprises me, as I
have imagined such a man living in a greater measure of
seclusion. He can spring stronger surprises, too, though he
does not do so for that reason, as when he remarks, apropos
of his years as nuncio in Sophia and Istanbul, that "orientals
are more profoundly religious than we Catholics." While telling us that he officiated at vernacular Masses in these cities,
he observes that "stupidity is stubborn, intelligence is resil-
ient," and it is clear that the remark is meant for the Church.
He is curious about I.S.'s Russian Orthodoxy and, I think,
would like to debate the Filioque Clause with him, but I.S.'s
relations to both the Roman and Russian churches are a
mystery at present even to himself. As to the matter of the
meeting, the Cardinal wishes to know why I.S. has chosen a
passage from the "Song of Solomon" for the *Canticum Sacrum*
and "for use in a Christian Church." I attempt to answer this
myself with a history of the *Sinfonia Sacra* form in the
Cardinal's own San Marco, but as I talk, His Eminence
twiddles the gold cross dangling on his stomach, and this
epigastric play almost distracts me from my subject. The
explanation appears to satisfy him, though, and, hoisting his
huge croup from the chair—it is another surprise that such

a figure and all of that tropical plumage moves—he gives his
blessing to the concert. We exit genuflecting, again bussing
the ring, sidling and scraping *al rovescio,* but before we leave
the palace he escorts us to the great throne room, site of the
Doges' ambassadorial dinners. From here we have a view of
San Marco's unexpectedly plain brick back.

A motorboat trip to Torcello, stopping to place a wreath
on Diaghilev's grave at San Michele (but without I.S., who
superstitiously refuses to go near the island); the church of
San Michele, so white from the lagoon, is the darkest sepul-
chre inside. The Laguna Morta, in spite of its name, is alive
with barges, and the rhythm of the boatmen as they lever
their poles in the mud and walk from bow to stern is hypnotic
to watch. We follow a channel marked by telephone poles
and buoys, but are obliged to stop every thousand yards or
so to free our propeller of seaweed. The sky is a mass of
Turner-like billowing movements, and at times the horizon
seems to be high in the air and our boat to be sailing upward.
In the lagoon near Torcello we see a gondola with a lone goat
for a passenger, an Edward Lear image.

September 1

I.S., after working all morning at the pink piano of the hotel
nightclub (apparently undeterred by ghosts of dance music
and odors of half-smoked cigars): "A series is a facet, and
serial composition is a faceting, or crystallizing, a way of
presenting together several sides of the same idea. But it is
too difficult to write my dry music in this Venetian hu-
midity."

Venetians have no soft "j"; they say "Zulian" and "Anzelo"
(pronounced "tse"), and *"ze ne peux pas"*—which reminds

I.S. of Manuel de Falla's "h" for "j" (and of his inability to begin a word with "st"): "*He ne peux pas, mon cher Estravinsky.*" Other Venetian pronunciations are similar to Spanish, too (not just Zuans and Juans, Zans and Sans), as for example, *stelle,* which comes out as an extremely palatal "stey-ye." English "ch" and "sh" sounds are difficult for Venetians, as well, thus they say *Petruska* and Marzeria (for Merceria); and the "n" is silent in certain positions, as in Fracesca da Rimini or Artur Rubistein, and dropped altogether as the double consonant, as in "*Madona.*" The sharp-edged "c" is avoided, too, as in "*portego*" (replacing *portico*), and "*mi digo*" (the accusative) which is used instead of "*Io dico.*" Even the word "*Doge*" is softened to "*Dose.*"

A regatta. Rival brass bands begin to play in the Piazza long before the races commence, while at the same time (!) a concert of opera arias blasts forth from a loudspeaker near the Bucintoro. By mid-afternoon nearly every boat in Venice is gathered in the Grand Canal, from gaggles of gondolas and flotillas of other small craft, each bearing the standard of its patron saint and *sestiere* or island, to all of the city's official boats except the fire department, and such leviathan relics from the Arsenale Museum as are still buoyant or bale-able— caravels and galleys with gold-leaf Tritons and baldachins on the poop decks which trail velvet canopies in the water. The crews of these museum pieces are dressed in tabards, doublet and hose, piebald caps and other antique garb, and they carry arquebuses and culverines, but they are as encumbered and ill-at-ease as an opera chorus at a first costume fitting. The actual races are an eternity in getting started, and except for a heat of some long pod-shaped barks, are extremely dull.

Venetian night sounds: the lap of waves on stone; the plash of oars in water; the grating of oars in tholepins; the clatter of the *saracinesca,* the iron-shutter shop fronts; the cries of gondoliers and gondoliers arguing; the hooting of ocean liners as they arrive or depart from the canal of the Giudecca; the soft singing of women from the darkened houses in the *calli* (strong and vibrant in the morning when they are at their laundry, but now quiet and gently palpitating); the bells in two speeds of S. Trovaso, at nones and complines, and the bells of San Marco at midnight. At midnight we go to the bridge corner of the Doge's palace to see the frieze of Noah's drunkenness. Noah, eyes closed in semi-slumber, swoons and holds the trunk of the vine for support. We count twelve birds singing in the vine.

1 9 5 7

September 2

Venice. Lunch with Giorgio di Chirico, who looks exactly like his innumerable *autoritratti:* the subtle brown eyes, the quiet, well-manicured fingers, the pale, womanish skin, the soft silver hair parted as it was in the pictures of forty years ago—which is when he made the acquaintance of I.S.[1] Later in the day we meet a colleague of Chirico who tells us that the "decadence" of the Italian master "must have begun a few minutes after birth . . . Chirico had a great vision as a young man, but it quickly lost its force. After that he began to devote himself to techniques, filling canvas after canvas with displays of them, but without a single idea. When I first knew him thirty years ago, his notebooks were covered with drawings copied from old masters, and he soon began to copy anything that attracted him in anyone else's work and to use it without acknowledgment as his own. The reason for this is only partly in the fact that his own imagination had dried up; it is equally because he was so vain: 'I can paint like Giotto

[1] Chirico was I.S.'s, but not Diaghilev's, choice of a painter for *Apollon Musagètes* (R.C.).

or Raphael, or even like early Chirico,' is what he seemed to say. In fact, I was with him one day in the thirties when 'Argyrol' Barnes came to his Paris studio to inquire if he had a painting for sale similar to one that Barnes admired from 1911. Chirico thought a moment, then answered that he did just happen to have another one like it, which could be recovered in a month or so from such and such an exhibition and sold to Barnes. He then set to work copying the 1911 picture from a photograph and signing it 1911. But what a subject for a 'Freudian' biography! Consider all those self-portraits as Don Giovanni or Apollo, and consider the tragedy of a man given a few years of lucidity during which he is a great painter and after which he denies he has ever been the former person, being unable to live with the knowledge. But Chirico is aware even of this. I remember an exhibition in Paris just before the War of his latest and most academic paintings. They were so bad no one could find anything to say, and we all left the gallery silently shaking his hand. Di Chirico described this to me afterward saying that 'It was as though I were dead and the visitors were mourners who came to pay their respects but knew I couldn't hear.' "

1958

August 8

As we near Genoa on the *Cristoforo Colombo* this morning, an elderly couple who have been eyeing I.S. ever since New York are finally emboldened to address him. (All first-class passengers are elderly, and throughout the voyage we have looked longingly from our superior deck to the progressively poorer and livelier decks of cabin and steerage class.) The man makes me think of a well-groomed Afghan, except for the rosewood walking stick and the gardenia in the lapel, but his wife is a different kind of canine altogether, and her manner is that of a huntress toward social big game. She does all of the talking, and at one point says something in French, adding the information, "that's French," as though I.S. might have taken it for Swahili. As they move off, we hear the Afghan angrily bark at his bitch for "trying to catch *him*."

Genoa is enveloped in dense fog in which small boats move in and out like phantoms. Excited gulls seem eager to guide us, as other birds guided Alexander to Siwa, but they disappear when twin tugboats siphon us between the breakwaters and then escort us to the dock, one on each side, like a mustache.

The display of temperament in the hotel dining room is a striking contrast to the imperturbable routine of the boat. Here the service is clamorous, sweaty, melodramatic. Our waiter mutters "*Mamma mia*" or invokes the Virgin on each trip from the kitchen, and his state of nerves is such that when we merely point out the shortage of a spoon he smites his breast and cries "*mea culpa.*"

The Campo Santo, "*il più bello cimiterio del mondo*" as the souvenir hawkers claim, is now a major tourist stop, equipped with guides who interpret and extol as if they were in the Bargello. Most of the monuments are sculptured family groups "taken" at the bedsides of the dying, the husbands and sons with their hats in their hands, the wives and daughters with tears in their eyes. In one *tableau mourant*, a young wife is shown drawing the bedclothes over her expired husband's face. In another, a widow holds her infant son for a farewell *bacio* on its deceased papa's cheek. Resurrection scenes are common, of course, and in the standard one the dead are shown setting out for Heaven with angel traffic policemen pointing the way. The *fin de siècle* marks a trend to Resignation (what horrible poses of Resignation there are!), to Philosophy, and to the Nude (Eves and Niobes with fig leaves held as coyly as strip-teasers' fans). Of the philosophers, Socrates (in an Inverness cape) is a surprisingly popular saint for a Christian cemetery, but then Christ Himself is often made to look like Hegel, a Hegel surrounded by brooding, pinions-folded, philosophy-student angels. I.S. recalls a monument in a similar cemetery at Padua, a sculptured reconstruction of the actual automobile accident in which the entombed family was killed. "A careening 'life-size' automobile was carved on the grave, with a goggled chauffeur and a woman in the back seat screaming through her veil. It was as real as Madame Tussaud's. Surely *taste* is a moral category." But not in all these thousands of sarcophagi is there a single figure with any beauty of expression comparable to those serenely smiling Etrurians on their tombs.

October 18

Schloss Fürstenberg, Donaueschingen. We stay in the "Kaiser's Suite," which is on the third floor, a five-minute walk from a shuddering lift, through galleries of royal portraits and an armory large enough to sustain an old-fashioned Central American revolution. My room contains a cheval glass, a flocculent bed, a console table on which charts are displayed for the seating of luncheon and dinner guests—Prinzen, Grafen, Barone, composers—and a copy of the intra-castle telephone directory (104 numbers). A concierge leads us from here to the dining room which is a half mile hike back to the cruelty-to-old-machines elevator, and then through corridors gory with battle paintings and bristling with antlers of slaughtered stags. I am seated at table next to Olivier Messiaen, a humorless man with a loose physique but profoundly preoccupied eyes. Discussing him afterward with I.S., who will never forgive his criticism of *The Rake*, I try to argue that a part of his mind and emotion would be more at home in the century of Francis of Assisi, and that he might be called a mystic or a Holy Roller rather than a *naïf*, which is I.S.'s classification. But I.S. really does dislike Messiaen's music, what he knows of it, and he describes it as "improvisation which is the slag heap of art. Also, he is too loud. His main interest often seems to be in piling up decibels as though he were jealous of the sonic boom."

1 9 6 1

October 31

Cairo. Our route to the pyramids is blocked this morning by a band of wailing women in black cerements, squatting in the street in front of a hospital. This open-air requiem intrigues I.S., the idea of professional mourners, I think, as much as the exotic din they produce, but there is a leper-like pall about them, as if they themselves were from the kingdom of death.

At the pyramid of Cheops (now with television aerial) progress is obstructed for a moment by a second female mob, but this time the ladies are from transatlantis and a little hinterland. They cling for dear life to the saddles of kneeling camels, bravely trying to look happy for a barrage of tripod cameras (their own cameras, inactive for once, leaning against their middles like umbilical tumors). This is an ancient routine for the camels, of course, but in spite of that and though their thin shanks and shaggy skins show them to be unfit for less humiliating service, they yawp and whine most ungraciously. When the head drover shouts the order to rise, the animals dip backward and kick their forelegs out like dancers, while the air is rent with a chorus of Ohio-accented screams. A few seconds later the ladies are dismounted, and feeling pleased with themselves and exhilarated by the experience, as well as immensely relieved, they no doubt tip accordingly. But I.S. does not like the pyramids. *"Francmaçonnerie,"* he says, and back we go across the Nile.

Each street or alley in the Bazaar is a stage on which hundreds of absorbing small events take place, but we cannot watch any of them for long because of the squalor and overpowering stercoral stench. Brass founders and ironmongers, goldsmiths and silversmiths, cosmeticists and dyers, potters and treadle-loom weavers, jewelers with loupes, leather-makers with awls: all work *en plein air*. But the shopkeepers far outnumber the craftsmen, and the ineluctable interlopers, the unshakable cadgers and baksheesh-crying beggars are by a thousand percent the largest populace of all.

We enter the "Nile Vally Perfumes" shop, having been steered there by our driver about as casually as a tracer bullet; a preliminary parley between him and the proprietor seems to have ended in the promise of a mutually satisfying "deal." Soon other people are invading the shop—a team, as we eventually deduce—some to show us the commodities (sandalwood and musk, attars and sachet powders, mascara, antimony, kohl), some to wheedle us into buying and some merely to pose as other and extremely contented customers. The preliminary salesmanship leans heavily on the flattering of our taste and on the implication that "Nile Vally Perfumes" runs a secret pipeline to Rochas or Chanel. The proprietor himself stands apart during this phase, watching us shrewdly and silently chewing cachous. Then when V. orders a hundred ambar cigarettes (at at least four times list price, I suspect, if there *were* any list) he glides into action. Like a gambler confident of recovering an ante, he switches on the electric lights—we had not realized until now that there could be any—and displays a dozen resistible but very specialized products including an "aphrodisiac ambarpaste" for I.S.: "A

blood-warming concoction, very good, sir, for elderly gentlemen who wish to re-enter the portals of youth; yes, sir, an
open-sesame." When we finally escape—though it is not as
easy as that—a booklet is thrust into our pockets warning
us that, "owing to the great number of designing merchants
who vainly try to imitate my wares—an impossibility owing
to their excellence—and, furthermore, use a name similar to
mine in order to deceive, I have registered in the Courts of
Law to obviate entirely. I therefore advise my clients to take
great care that my FULL name is printed on each article that
comes out of my store NILE VALLY PERFUMES." Some vain
imitator probably gave himself away by spelling it "Valley."

At a street-side café, still in the Bazaar, we drink arrack
and ﻻﺱ ﺱﺱ (Coca-Cola). Within a few feet of our table a
man is tooling a piece of metal, a boy is honing a knife on
a whetstone, and a woman is suckling a baby from her mud-
caked bosom. At the next table, two turbaned Arabs smoke
a hookah, handing the stem back and forth without wiping
the mouthpiece. Soon peddlers are besieging us with pome-
granates and yellow guavas, with nougat and sesame-seed
cakes, with sandals (a load of at least a hundred draped
around a man's neck with cords), and even with birds: one
man has a cage on his back like Papageno. "O.K.?, O.K.?"
they say, as who in Cairo does not? They are not easily dis-
couraged, and when they realize that we cannot refuse them
a few piastres (so many of them are blind or suffering from
trachoma and the dread bilharzia), are quite undiscourageable.
They are a scratching lot, too, with very itchy pubic regions,
evidently, in which they are also regularly feeling for assur-
ance that their procreative organs are still there.

None of the objectives on our after-dinner taxi itinerary is
as interesting as the driver himself. He is dressed in an Arab
gallabiya, but instead of a turban he wears a bevel-brimmed
fedora at a menacing tilt, like a Chicago gangster in the twen-

ties (though the most bonhomous gangster imaginable). Like all Cairo cabbies he aims to deliver us to one of the nightclubs from which he will receive a commission, and to obtain my compliance in this aim he talks luringly of the favors of a houri. "We go Arabi Hasha. Egyptian place. Lovely." Everything Egyptian is "lovely," however, as everything American —pronounced as two words, "Emery Cain"—is "verygoodverynice" (one word). Thus, would we like to go to the Hilton Hotel and hear Emery Cain music? Is verygoodverynice. We go in search not of American music, but of halvah, though in spite of the fact that the recommended store, Aly Hassan El Hati, is "Egyptian" and "lovely," as well as very far away, it stocks nothing even remotely in that line. Each of these brief excursions into English is followed first by an explosion of what seems to be self-appreciative laughter, and second by a long soliloquy in Arabic. As a guide and source of information about Cairo, though, Mr. Verygoodverynice has shortcomings. For one thing, he will not allow us to see, and is snobbishly reproving of our interest in, neighborhoods he calls "very cheap parts, only for wogs." And for another, he cannot read. "Who is that?" I.S. inquires, pointing to an inscription at the base of a statue of Rameses the Second. "A statue," he says. "Of whom?" "Famous man." "What man, what is his name?" "Oh, Egyptians never put names." But he *is* a very good, very nice fellah, nevertheless, and we almost swallow his parting bait: "Bye. See you tomorrow. What time?"

At midnight the Cairo streets look as though a Shriners' convention had been aroused from its sleep and only had time, perhaps because of a fire, to put on its pajamas and fezzes. Some of the pajamas are striped, as though there had been a prison break, and some are sleeveless, like chasubles. A few of the men wear colored Kufayah scarves and a lace skullcap that looks distinctly to be a part of bedroom apparel. But the street noise, especially of radios blaring from the cafés, and of automobile horns, which are sounded without let-up, as they are after weddings in America, is in no wise nocturnal. And neither is the tempo of street life. The waiters hustle their hookahs and coffee trays far faster than they do in the daytime, and a group of men actually hurries out of the path of the murderous Mr. Verygoodverynice, holding up their nighties as they run, like Carpaccio's monks fleeing the lion of St. Jerome.

November 1

The Nile at sunup is flagged with sails, the upstream traffic barely moving, and the downstream racing out of sight as if by nuclear power. One lone felucca, with the legend "FLY TWA" on its sail, travels up and down the stretch of hotel-fronted river like a picket.

We are three hours at the Museum of Egyptian Art, not including the time it takes to get by the dragomen at the entrance. The building itself is hideous, and the crowding of the contents is suffocating. So much of it is macabre, too. The whole first floor is a mummy morgue, and the other floors are well-endowed with such items as mummies' rope-wigs (they look like clumps of discolored seaweed) and eviscerated organs, the which are shown with their original resin-soaked wrappings and their canopic jars. But this should be no surprise. The civilization is known almost entirely from its tombs, after all, and the Museum *is* little else but a repository of funerary artifacts. Death is the meaning of it all, and death the provenance, and though the eschatology of it may not have been so terrible for the Egyptian who believed in a Happy Nilotic Hunting Ground, we do not believe, certainly not in *his* form of it. Even so, the mortuary aspect of the

Museum is less stultifying than the sameness. The same deities, the same postures and patterns, repeat themselves through dozens of dynasties and thousands of years, and the tradition is iron-clad; anyone who feels the need to "escape from free-dom" and from more and more fragmentation and individualizing, should spend a month here contemplating the other extreme. And in addition to the gruesomeness and the monotony, there is still another complaint. Many of the objects are badly mutilated and defaced, and at least half of the limbs of the statuary are missing and the other parts are held together by plaster filler and a kind of orthopedic appliances like models at a surgical college. Every fractured Pharaoh in the building deserves the Purple Heart ten times over.

What, then, as we are unable to take Pharaonic art as a whole, what delights us and what, at the end of the long trek, do we delight to recall? *My* answer is each representation of the bird and fish and animal kingdoms, especially the lions, leopards, monkeys, anubises, rams, horses, and dappled cows. And we delight in the Nubian rooms where uniquely the statues of women and men are the same height. There is much beautiful jewelry, too—among the acres of turquoise and coralline amulets, scarab seals, and signet rings—though every attractive piece has long since been copied and put into commercial production; and some beautiful furniture, though not, to my taste, the *nouveau riche* rococo of the Tutankhamen tomb, that Eighteenth Dynasty "Forest Lawn." But many of the objects are interesting only by virtue of their modernity—a Las Vegas-type gaming board, for instance, and a carpenter's kit with T-squares, levelers, plumb lines, rules. But enough. Or too much: we hobble out of the Museum at one o'clock on wooden legs, and then, stepping out of the gates, are nearly run over by the "Nefertiti Laundry Service."

Leaving for Sakkara in the cooler part of the afternoon, we pass a flock of sheep being driven into a slaughterhouse, each doomed animal daubed on its neck with a bloodlike dye. We pass a wedding procession, too, though the sight of the bride enthroned on a tall wagon and surrounded by her maids is not very arresting, probably for the reason that a male Arab's dress is so much like a bride's anyway. The road is clogged with donkey carts, no two of the same size, but the wheels of most of them are so large that the linchpins are higher than the donkeys. They carry copra, fruit, tuns of water, palm baskets, and loads of men, the latter like prisoners in tumbrils on the way to the guillotine.

A canal flows on the right side of the road, and however polluted and uninviting, it is bathtub and laundry, fish pond and sewage system to a million human beings. On the other side, but at a distance, is the Nile, and though it is not always in view, masts of feluccas and dhows rise above the levee, reminders that it is there. The land between the road and the river grows tall stalks of maize and sugar cane made taller by millions of ibises; the plants hardly seem to bend under the birds except at landings, when the birds look like ski-jumpers, then at the last moment, like airplanes, as they tuck in their legs. But how biblically beautiful the landscape is, and what an infinite pleasure to behold the fertile fields and the carriage of the women with tall amphorae on their heads, and the buffaloes turning the water wheels, goaded by officious overseer dogs. It is, in fact, one's childhood picture of Joseph's Genesis, except for an occasional automobile.

At Memphis we wait as a trainload of apparently disconnected dromedary heads and humps passes by, those features alone surrealistically protruding above the frames of the flatcars. "Modern" Memphis is a cluster of mud huts in upper and lower layers, like Amerindian cliff dwellings, and the super-stratum is connected by ladders. The beggars here are proportionately even more numerous and more impudent than in Cairo. They ambush our car while it is still moving, and try to force us off the road, demanding to be photographed for money. For money, too, they climb the tallest palm trees, barefoot but as fast as monkeys. I hope to be forgiven for saying it, but they wear very beautiful rags.

At Sakkara, I.S. remarks that a black goat tethered on a hillside "is a color sounding board; just as an orchestra tunes to 'A,' so here, to a painter, the whole landscape must tune to this black." We walk by a row of feet of otherwise demolished statues (more surrealism) to the tomb of Mera, which for its low-reliefs of wildlife—gazelles, mongooses, ibexes, porcupines, hippos, crocodiles, birds, and fish—is worth all the pyramids of Egypt or other countries in which that dullest of forms has flourished. Mera himself is portrayed in various guises: dressed for a hunt, in leopard skin, claws, and tail; wrapped in a robe and listening to his wife perform on the harp; reclining on a high divan while his musical spouse sniffs a lotus. The colors are very vivid, even through the fine patina of blown sand.

The inland road back to Cairo is now congested with men and animals returning from the fields, the men carrying flails and hoes exactly like those in the Mera friezes. We come shortly to a Bedouin camp, over which the blue smoke of cooking fires has begun to settle. Along the road are files of Bedouin women carrying jugs to and from a well. They all wear the same black robes, and every face is curtained by a bangled or sequined veil, but some have amber necklaces and silver ankle bracelets as well. The evening air is of a silky softness, and the only sound in the villages is the murmuration of nesting birds.

❈ ❈ ❈

In the Kumais Restaurant, with our new Copt friend Fares Sarapheem, we sit on low leather cushions around a center cushion set with a round brass tray; the walls are covered with silks and damascenes, all epigraphically bordered with texts

from the Koran. As soon as we are seated, a waiter brings
a platter of bullet-shaped pellets of incense, with the same
speed with which icewater is served in American restaurants.
He is a dusky Nubian, with embossed tattoo marks on his
forehead, but the headwaiter is a light-bronze Arab; a hier-
archy of color seems to obtain here (and everywhere in
Egypt, judging by hotels and private houses) according to
which the whitest skins belong to the masters, the blackest
skins to the servants; we hear again tonight, from brown- or
khaki-colored people (or, at any rate, not conspicuously pale
ones), the remark that So-and-so "works like a nigger." The
meal begins with prawns and stuffed grape leaves (Warak-
Enap), and moves on to dorad, Karouss (no description possible), and Fateh, which is the main dish, a spicy stew of rice
and boiled meat. The Western palate—this one, anyway—is
quicker to fancy oriental sweetmeats, though, and tonight's
is the delicious *puri* (shredded wheat cooked in honey). As we
eat, Fares Sarapheem tells us that the Copts are the "true
Egyptians, the Christian inheritors of Pharaonic Egypt," and
he explains that the Coptic language, now a dead dialect sur-
viving only in the Mass, "is a rendering of hieroglyphic
Egyptian in the Greek alphabet, with seven additional letters
to signify sounds that do not exist in Greek." Fares Sarapheem
also tells us that Nasser's dissolution of the latifundia system
has deprived the Copts of their wealth and supremacy, but
that in spite of this they vigorously support his foreign policy
in so far as it keeps Egypt free from foreign intervention and
commercial domination: the bogey of the British cotton-
wallah. "Egypt was a subject country from the time of Cleopatra until 1917," he says, "and for six hundred years our
Khedive was the puppet of Istanbul." But I am summarizing
and therefore deflavoring some highly original English. Each
of Fares Sarapheem's sentences begins with a little introduction: "Perhaps it would be interesting to mention . . ." From

the restaurant we walk in the Kasr el Nil, where we come upon a blind man in the street singing for alms the most beautifully floriated song I have ever heard.

November 2

The delta road to Alexandria is dual carriage most of the way and it is all of the way in good condition. There are frequent police checkpoints, like toll booths on American turnpikes, and we are obliged to stop at each one of them— they are invariably decorated with toothpaste ads of Colonel Nasser—evidently for no other reason than to be counted. Of the beasts of burden on the road, women outnumber both the donkeys and the camels, and *no* woman is empty-handed. Sometimes they carry babes-in-arms in addition to the bales on their heads or the flat head-trays with round loaves of *rayesh*. Woman's uniform is black, of course (otherwise how in this transvestite society should we distinguish the men?), but closer to Alexandria some of the women wear washed blues and even pink and orange.

The donkey and camel traffic is marvelous to watch, though some of it seems almost equally cruel. There is a steady parade of very tiny donkeys with huge sacks on their backs and fat passengers like garnishings on the sacks. When a donkey carries no other freight, the rider jogs along with his legs straight out in a wide "V," his sandals dangling from the big toes. No load seems to make the camel less supercilious, but the animals' long, knock-kneed, foreleg amble so reminds us of Aldous Huxley that on his account alone we are bound to regard them with fondness and respect. Never again, though, will we use the expression camel-colored. They are a thousand shades of white, pink, puce, fawn, bister, black.

On the south side of each village is a cemetery, elevated because of the lowness of the land so that the chimney-like nodules of the tombs are visible above the walls. There are small mosques from time to time, and we see two domed marabouts (at least I think that is what they are). Scarecrows, dressed in *gallabiya* and turbans, are everywhere, but no bird is scared and the millions of them now in the fields must consume as great a share of the crops as the farming fellaheen. The latter are naked except for turbans, dhotis, and the seed sacks they carry on their shoulders. Some of them work the Archimedean water screw or supervise the circle of blind-folded oxen turning the water wheels.

The mast tips of otherwise unseen feluccas in altogether unseen canals move across the flat land like periscopes, but the boats themselves are visible only from bridges. Road re-pairing is women's work, of course, and it seems to be a privilege of the oldest and weakest to carry the heavy scuttle-shaped head trays heaped with gravel and stones. We see a man dressed in a clean white jibbah with brass buttons and riding a neatly groomed Arabian horse shade himself from a squad of these laboring women with a white parasol. A girl with a purple veil, daughter or wife, follows him several paces behind on a donkey.

By noon the roadside world is asleep; even the chickens stop their incessant earth-scratching, while men sprawl on the ground, in doorways, on mule carts, in rope nets under mule carts, and even possibly in the houses, which are prettier and more prosperous the deeper we go into the Delta. At Tanta, capital of Lower Egypt, the yashmaks are much smaller and less concealing—like bikinis—covering the face to the nose only (is this a mark of emancipation?). At Daman-hur, the next village, a skinned and decapitated water buffalo hangs by the tail in the middle of the main street.

Suddenly the air is fresher, cooler, more moist, and the

vegetation changes abruptly to banyan trees and date palms, the latter now pregnant with yellow and red udder-shaped fruit. We enter Alexandria by a teeming canal for which the road is also the quay. As the men unloading the feluccas are bent so low under the huge sacks that they are unable to see, old men are employed to lead them by the hand from the boats to the street side.

On the seaward side of the city the dress of the majority of Alexandrians is European, and so, too, are many of the names. Along with the "Ali Ibrahams" and the "Fawzis" are the "Banco Donizetto," the "Rosenthal Brothers," and "Socrates and Co." French seems to be Alexandria's first European language (it is the only one on postal boxes) and French is spoken in the Union Restaurant, where we find our most delectable meal in Egypt: grilled *crevettes, loup de mer*, a compote of dates in buffalo milk, a "*Clos de Pharaoh*." Afterward we hire a Hantur to see the Column of Pompey, but stop instead at the gates of a cemetery to watch a band of wailing women, professional *pleureuses* who as they squat on the sidewalk with black shawls over their heads look like a flock of ravens.

In the early hours of the afternoon the city is emptied as if by a plague, and so are the beaches except for a few fishermen painting or caulking their caiques. Our driver here is English-speaking and he is very indignant about "Durrell's misrepresentations of Alexandria," though it seems to us that the novelist's only crime was in making the city so much more interesting than it is. We take the beach road to the royal palace, now a museum, and Samalek, the royal harem, now a hotel, both of them the crowning exhibits in anybody's collection of *art nouveau* freaks. The palace is a masterpiece of Boca Raton Gothic complete with crenellations and even gargoyles. Each new king has added a new monstrosity, and it is possible to regret the fall of the monarchy simply out of

architectural curiosity. But the lawns are greener than anything else in Egypt, and the gardens, though they smell like
hair tonic, are better kept.

The sun is low when we re-enter the city, and life has
returned to the streets; and not only life: in the Greek quarter
we pass an eight-horse, cherub-gilded hearse. The Moslems
are spreading prayer mats on the sidewalks, or already praying, in the foetal position and turned as though magnetically
to Mecca (as white ants are magnetically sensitized to the
north). The rim of the sun remains afloat while we cross the
salt flats of Maryot, then disappears in a sudden dive, like
the keel of a sinking boat. In the dense reeds men are fishing
from knifelike, pole-propelled boats (the *tarada*). The profusion of ducks and birds reminds us of the Mera friezes, but
the water buffaloes oozing to their necks in the mud are like
overweight bankers in Turkish baths.

> *O what a sweetness strayed*
> *By the Mareotic sea*
> *When that exultant Anthony*
> *And twice a thousand more*
> *Starved upon the shore*
> *And withered to a bag of bones*
> *What had the Caesars but their thrones?*

Liberation Province, south of the lake, begins hopefully,
for us (well not *very* hopefully), with new houses and newly
irrigated patches of land. In the scrub desert, thereafter, we
come to nomad encampments, villages of flat tents with cooking fires in front of them and huddles of men, and with camel
herds, some of them foddering, some sitting on the ground
like domed oriental cities. The only buildings all the way to
Ghizeh are a gas station at the halfway point, and some tattered British barracks from 1940 to 1942. All through the
black night our headlights flash on Arabs walking along the
road, their white robes blowing in the rising wind like ghosts.

November 4

Cairo. On our way to the Coptic Museum this morning we count nine chandelier stores (one of them called the "El Ismail Youssef Mohammed Chandelier Company"); chandeliers seem to be the city's second major industry (next to tourists), and every large home must have at least four or five.

The Museum lies within a Roman redoubt whose walls are three thicknesses of brick and five of stone. The interior is cool, clean, well-organized, and in general agreeably unlike the Museum of Egyptian Art. Our difficulty here is one of identification: what in fact *is* Copt when there are no obvious iconographic clues such as camels, black-faced saints, Angk talismans, or the Cross with supporting standard of three steps to represent the three days before the Resurrection? So much of the earlier art, especially the animal portraiture, the rabbits, lions, donkeys, eagles, and doves, might be Byzantine as well; and many of the later objects are distinguishable from Islam only in that they have been stamped somewhere with Christian symbols: the forms appear to have been borrowed whole. The Gospels themselves are shown in Cufic copies, and there are parchment lectionaries with Coptic and beautiful right-angular Cufic script on facing sides. And finally, the Museum itself, with its one-way, inside-to-out, balcony ventilators and light-tempering honeycomb window grilles, looks Muslimite. Perhaps only the Ethiopian treasures, especially a barbaric crown of Menelik II, and the loom arts with wonderfully animated figures in many-colored threads are uniquely (that is, identifiable to me) Coptic.

A monk with a sextant-shaped beard like Tintoretto's *Nicolas Priuli* shows us through the adjoining Church of St. Sergius, which is so Moorish in *décors* that without our guide we would soon forget it *is* a church. A spidery old woman in black rags sits in the doorway nibbling nettles.

We ourselves eat immeasurably better than that at the home of Victor Simaika, a cousin of Fares Sarapheem, and the son of the founder of the Coptic Museum; a very *mondain* cousin, too, as it appears from the photograph with Barbara Hutton on the wall, the references to polo games with the Duke of Edinburgh, and the blizzard of so many other famous names that there are hardly any gaps between. Mr. Simaika has just returned from the airport, whence he dispatched his favorite Persian cat to Switzerland for medical treatments (no doubt by Niehans and Jung). But Mr. Simaika is a charmer; indeed, a great deal more, for he confesses, and without dropping his monocle, to his reputation of a "big ladies' killer" (which leaves one wondering as much about the large mysterious females as about Mr. Simaika's methods—whether routine strangulations or what). Conversation, otherwise, touches on Evelyn White's *The Curse of the Copts* (in which, we are told, Copts still devoutly believe); the Sothic Cycle; the discoveries in Coptic painting at Faras, on the Nubian Nile, by the expedition of the Polish Academy of Sciences; the monachism of Cairo's Bektashi Moslem sect; the Coptic addition of "love" to Pauline Faith, Hope, and Charity. Here V. remarks that it will be necessary to explain to another generation that charity the virtue and charity the tax deduction are not the same, "otherwise the Basic-English Bibles of the future will have emended the trinity to faith, hope and tax deduction." Mr. Simaika's apartment faces the Nile over a garden of sycamores and jasmine, and throughout the lunch sails glide by the window like giant moths.

My smallpox certificate having been filched yesterday, along with an otherwise valueless wallet, I go from Mr. Simaika's to a hospital to be revaccinated. The operation is performed in a malodorous and forbiddingly dirty room, and I roll up my sleeve with no confidence and receive no cleaning

daub of alcohol. Has the needle itself been sterilized? Too late
to think about that now, or to pray to my American gods
of hygiene, but the nurse (no odalisque) who jabs me seems
to be holding me personally responsible for Suez. By dinner
time I have a fever and my arm is a festering mump.

Though Ibn Tulun is one of the most famous and beautiful mosques in the world, our Copt driver has no idea how
to find it. When we are within three blocks of it, according
to my map, he stops to take soundings from pedestrians, but
of course no one has ever heard of it (though everyone knows
about us: "American?" "Money, please?" "O.K."). Eventually an urchin offers to guide us to it and he has climbed
aboard and directed us over a considerable area before we
realize that he has merely chosen us to be the sponsors of
what is doubtless his first automobile ride. Another waif, this
time with a book under his arm, offers the same service; and
this time it is fulfilled, though when we reach the dun-colored
walls he reviles us rudely because of the size of our—extra-
large, as it happens—baksheesh. We cross the ambulatory,
swaddle our feet in felt, and enter a court as large as the
piazza of an Italian town. In the right portico a congregation
of women kneel, in purdah, behind a wall of rugs suspended
on a wire; and in the *liwan*, to the left, as many men are praying, but in groups of six with one in each group slightly to
the fore. Nowhere is there any sign of a clergy or, as I.S. says,
"sacramental middlemen."

November 5

To infidel and untrained eyes a day in the Museum of Islamic
Art is both several hours too long and several years too short.
"Taste" is an imperative, in the absence of cultural and his-
torical blinkers, and we therefore force our simple prejudices

for things Persian to the point at which we begin actively to dislike most things Egyptian, polychrome lusters and brassware above all. But Islamic art, that of Persia included, is an art of ambages, and the meshing, the fretting, the filigreeing, foliating, interlacing, lobing, and lozenging are too much for our unaccustomed eyes. Even the water jets in the fountains are coiled like cobras.

Because of its minaret mustaches the Mohammed Ali Mosque suggests a great crustacean from the outside, but a laboratory from the inside, where the colored lamps are shaped like retorts, alembics, test tubes. We walk from it to Saladin's Citadel, on which pennants fly as on a medieval city, and around the tallest tower of which three ravens are now wheeling like a propeller. Here Cairo is a reek of urine and filth, and a nauseating stench of the *abattoirs;* and it is smoke and dust and flies (halos of circumvolant flies crown us the moment we leave the car); and beggars and children who swarm about us *like* flies; and it is a city of sickness and disease, of the hobbled and maimed, of eyes covered with white film, or red and vitreous, of faces pitted and scrobiculated, of rasping catacomb coughs. And it is a city of death, of vast necropolitan suburbs in which hutches are built over the tombs so that relatives may spend the holy days in ghoulish proximity to the departed. Funerals are held in the streets, too, in large furnished tents, and it is almost impossible to traverse the city without encountering several of them.

November 6

It appears to be both market day and wash day in the villages on the way to Fayum, judging from the spread of food and wares on the bridges, and the copper ewers and drying laun-

dry on the canal banks. South of Aiyat, the road signs are in
Arabic only and the life is abruptly more primitive; we de-
tour around two men who are dismembering a still-bleeding
buffalo carcass in the middle of the road, and going about
their grisly work as nonchalantly as if they were chopping
a log. But appalled as we are by the *condition humaine* in the
villages, the pastoral life and the life of toil in the fields do
not repel us, I think because of the romanticizing notion that
these modes of existence are "natural"—by which we probably mean that we see no barrier and little difference between
a man and his animals, though I had better not pursue the
thought lest I reveal that my own prejudices are to be traced
back to the illustrations on date boxes, so romance-inducing
to me as a child. During Kayf, the noon siesta, the roadside is
strewn with an array of exanimate bodies, and as the Arabs
cover their faces with their burnous, they really do look
like cadavers.

The temperature leaps fifteen degrees when we turn from
the river to the desert, leaving the parasols of eucalyptus and
Australian pines for the sand and the open sun. The world of
"Mobil Oil" is left behind, too, and we depend on a nomad
gas station, a mule cart with a tank like a puncheon or a Porto
wine barrel, and a siphon hanging from the bunghole like an
umbilical chord. At a police guard-post in the desert we
receive Nazi-type salutes and the greeting "Nasser"; the
police camels are white, like patrol cars of American state
troopers. A few miles later we come to a walled city with a
single gate and a domed dovecot on every roof. We wait
for a caravan to cross the road here; each camel is heavily
loaded with hay, in spite of which the humps show through
like partly camouflaged tanks.

The denizens of the desert road are evidently accustomed
to great privacy. Men, certainly naked except for their turbans, are cooling themselves in the roadside culvert, and we

surprise a Bedouin woman without her veil; she has evidently failed to gauge the speed of our approaching car, perhaps never having seen any vehicle move so fast.

A few minutes later, however, a thirty-year-old Packard, carrying at least a dozen Arabs, nearly collides with us, automobiles being so rare that each confrontation involves a crisis as to who shall pass on which side of the road. And at El Fayum, a new red Cadillac convertible, an oil millionaire's bauble, we suppose, shines in the restaurant parking lot as though specially minted and flown in from Michigan this morning. A Bedouin woman with a ring through her nose stands staring at the car, but she gives us a savage look and struts off like a peahen when she becomes aware of our attention to her. We eat water-buffalo scaloppine in the restaurant under a plaque commemorating Mr. Churchill's banquet here for King Ibn Saud, February 17, 1945. Outside, a snow of ibises has settled on the shore of the lake.

1962

August 29

Lod Airport, Tel Aviv. As we leave the airplane, a chorus of schoolgirls welcomes us with songs—or at least that is what, by their open mouths and thrusting bosoms, we suppose them to be doing, but a jet is threatening to take off and we hear nothing. The girls pelt us with carnations when we move within range, and I.S., gathering them from the ground into a bouquet, waves a return salute with it. This is the warmest reception ever, from people, photographers' bulbs, and the setting but still sweltering sun. *"Shalom, shalom!"* everyone is saying, and the cordiality flows around us like a warm bath.

The room clerk at the Dan Hotel speaks Russian, the receptionist Greek, Spanish, and Italian, the *maître d'hotel* German, the telephone operator English, the chambermaid French, the elevator boy—a *sabra,* I think—Hebrew only. We shake hands with all of them, and they greet us like long-lost relatives. "Welcome home," the room waiter says, as though I were the *juif errant,* but his confidence in me has waned by the end of the meal, I fear, for he illicitly procures cream for my coffee (forbidden after meat). The delicacy of the dinner is a kosher red caviar on unleavened bread.

Tel Aviv, from our rooms, is a cliff of balconied apartment houses, like dressers with the drawers opened. On the other side is the sea, now under a sky like a planetarium, and sprinkled with lights from fishing boats. The only sound beside the surf is an oriental wail in a café somewhere down the beach.

August 31

Awakened by shouting, I hurry to the window and see a group of women, sufferers from nothing more serious than overadequate adiposity (I think), drilling on the beach like a squad of recruits in the Marines. The instructor shouts and the ladies salaam; or twist and bend their trunks, arms akimbo, then folded behind their fleshy backs; or roll on the ground, apparently trying to bounce; or lie as nice ladies should not, kicking their legs like overturned beetles. They droop a bit after the workout, but no one is noticeably more svelte. Perhaps the simpler solution would be to reduce the curds and whey.

I begin the morning rehearsal in Mann Auditorium with misgivings, having been advised that everyone in the orchestra once was, and in many cases still considers himself to be, a conductor. In fact, they are as cooperative and adult a group of musicians—orchestras generally being very childish—as I have worked with. They are quick, too, which is not surprising except that we had anticipated a show of polite resistance to our all-modern program; the stalwarts are reputedly not only conservative, but Viennese conservative, and as the mold of their style is the sentimental tradition—which we see from the first beat—Old Vienna (but not old enough Vienna) is clearly the orchestra's first love. Their musical performance, though good indeed, is less remarkable than their linguistic one. I.S. addresses them in Russian, French, and English, and no translation is required in any of the three cases. After hearing their own exchanges in a dozen other tongues as well, one feels that any language would be understood, if not by the triangle player, then by the harpist or the trumpeter. In fact, the only missing language ingredient is that loveliest of brogues, Brooklynese. Nobody says "Khau do you do?" and "Don't be noivez."

A joke is told during intermission, one of many sparked by the recent visit of the Mayor of Berlin, Willy Brandt. The launching pad for this one was the Mann Auditorium. It seems that Herr Brandt had expressed pleasure in the fact that it was named for a "great German writer" (author of *Buddenbrooks*). "But it is named for an American writer," Mr. Ben-Gurion rejoined. And Herr Brandt: "Really? I don't remember having heard of him. What did he write?" "A check," said Mr. Ben-Gurion, and one visualizes this sample of the patriarchal powers of repartee touring the country and leaving great family pride in its wake.

We go from the rehearsal to Jaffa, "for purposes of sightseeing," as the driver explains. The impressive "sights" are people, most memorably an ancient rabbi wearing the corkscrew side curls, the gabardine coat, and the black hat over his *yarmilke* (skull cap); a small boy leads him by the hand, and with his free arm he taps his way with the white cane of the blind. In the same neighborhood, the narrow streets near the harbor, we see another religious venerable in the Daniel Boone cap of twelve fox tails—for the twelve tribes. It seems impractical and even cruel, however, that these people have transplanted themselves from Chagall's Vitebsk to a Miami climate with no modification of wardrobe. Our friend the Haganah veteran, Ahron Propes, remarks that "such costumes are survivals from a mystic way of life, and they should be

modified." But no one will say how—or venture to introduce
a rabbinical summer style—and the ambivalence toward religious orthodoxy and indeed every kind of hereditary religious
dispensation must be one of the government's profoundest
problems. "I do not believe," an American acquaintance tells
us, "but I take my hat and go to the synagogue, nevertheless,
and though I have drifted away from all but the semblance
of the dietary observances, I follow them strictly here." And
the statement is typical. Now, however, when rigid traditions
are no longer needed to preserve the identity, one wonders
how long they will last.

Our driver on this excursion is a refugee from Germany
(though Israel is home, and "refugee" is not used here; today's
refugees are "newcomers"). He had served with the British
Army during the war and acquired therefrom a somewhat
critical approach to English, as we see when he refers to the
"crucification." As one who lives in and by the Book, he
has a ready biblical reference for practically everything, and
he could probably recite the dramatis personae of the entire
Bible. Fortunately, for relief, he has another, newer lore, a
bag of stories about the 1956 Suez campaign. "The Arabs
removed their footgear when they ran," he says, "and as
they were always running, the Sinai desert, when we got
there, was a harvest of shoes."

It is the eve of the Sabbath, and as we enter the hotel dining
room a waiter points to a table with two candles and two
loaves of bread wrapped in a napkin, asking us at the same
time not to smoke. Then, thinking that we must be "newcomers," he bids us "welcome home"; and rightly, I am beginning to think, for I feel at home here, and as though to
convert feeling to fact, a letter awaits me in my room from
a woman in a kibbutz who has seen my name in a newspaper
and who claims kinship, substantiating the connection with
a long list of wrong relatives. So much, at any rate, for "Jewish names."

September 1

"*Shabbat Shalom*," says the room waiter this morning, and the greeting is also an explanation for the frugality of the breakfast: fire must not be created on the Sabbath. Another effect of holy writ is the suspension of rehearsals, and this is welcome for the reason that our basic mechanisms are still functioning on California time, an eleven-hour difference that has left us with a diagonal feeling. (A time-pill ought to be invented for a more rapid adjustment in the change of hours.) As the weekly examination of I.S.'s blood is due today, we have asked the laboratory to send one of its less devout nurses. In spite of this a doctor comes, and though punctiliously fulfilling his scientific duty, he will not sign a report of it in I.S.'s medical log book and defile himself with a pen.

Public transportation services, including some international airplane flights, are halted until sundown, and automobile traffic is thin indeed, and in some areas virtually at a standstill; the expression "Sabbath driver" would have no meaning here; we wonder, in the car en route to the Weizmann Institute, whether we are not being thought of as flagrantly sacrilegious. Remarking that the interdiction of travel on the Sabbath did not apply to journeys on water, I.S. recalls how the younger Jews of Ustilug rode in railway coaches seated on water bottles. I.S. has been reminded of Ustilug, incidentally, since his arrival in Israel, especially by scraps of conversation with elderly settlers from Russia, but also by a kind of coziness which, he claims, is peculiar to Russian Jews. Yesterday he was given a history of the Ustilug community compiled by descendants of families who had lived in that part of Russia, and I have rarely seen him so moved.

Dr. Weisgall, Director of the Weizmann Institute, is delightfully unorthodox as an academic dignitary. His imagery

is refreshingly earthy—"bald as a camel's ass" is the way he
describes a colleague's tonsorial situation—and his favorite
expletive seems to be "Jesus Christ." We dine with him and
the Israeli Minister of Education, Aba Eban, who is there with
his famously beautiful wife. A discussion develops about anti-
Semitism in the Soviet Union and recent Soviet newspaper
attacks on "the philosophy of the Bible," though it would
appear on evidence that few Soviet writers have read the Book,
which, indeed, has been on their *index librorum prohibitorum*
these forty years. The Minister also attributes to policy
(fear of defection?) the Soviet failure to arrange concerts
in Israel for Russian-Jewish violinists and pianists. The I.S.'s,
meaning only to keep the discussion afloat, nearly sink it with
some testimony of exactly the wrong kind. A room waiter
at the Dan, a newcomer from the Soviet Union, has told them
that there was no racism whatever in the Red Army,
"whereas every linguistic group in Israel is waging a faction
dispute."

We return to Tel Aviv via Ashquelon, birthplace of Herod
the paranoid. Sections of pipeline for the rerouting of the
River Jordan have been rolled to the side of one stretch of
the road. They are as large in diameter as an automobile.
Near Ashquelon we pass a kibbutz of exotically dressed newcomers from Algeria.

September 2

Caesarea. Our *cicerone*, a French-speaking archaeologist, is
a fluent quoter of Josephus and a learned expositor on such
subjects as Roman castrametation and the origins of the
cunei, the *diazoma*, and the *skene*. A stone has been uncovered
in the amphitheater, incised with the name of the Procurator
Pontius Pilate, on whom, incidentally, and on all Romans,

local Christianity took iconoclastic revenge. Nearly every Roman image in the country has been decapitated, and the exception, a remarkable statue of a woman in Ashquelon, proves the rule. It may have escaped, such is the theory of our archaeologist, by its resemblance to an early representation of the Madonna.

Reaching Haifa at dusk, we drive to an eminence near the gold dome of the B'Hai-ists and from there watch Acre lighting up across the harbor. Scores of Druses are in the streets tonight, mysterious people in white turbans with trailing veils.

Haifa being without concert hall, we appear in a cinema palace, as an entr'acte between screenings of *A Streetcar Named Desire*. It is the hottest room in the world; to move is to provoke a flash flood of perspiration. My clothes swaddle me as though I had fallen into a pool when I conduct, and my spectacles steam like frosted glass. After the first movement of the Symphony, I remove my tie and unbutton the upper part of my shirt, and at the end of the third movement I peel my jacket as well. The audience is greatly amused by this, and I suspect the prolonged applause may be less an expression of enthusiasm for the music, which they may now suspect of having been the *Istar Variations*, than one of curiosity to see what will come off next. At the end of the first movement of the Violin Concerto, I pull a bath towel from under my score and lend it to Zvi Zeitlin, the soloist, whose handkerchiefs are water-logged. He mops and then I mop, and this humid scene wins a thundering ovation.

September 3

Life along the road to Nazareth and Tiberias is mainly pastoral, but some Arab husbandry exists in the valleys. In Nazareth itself, a remarkably hideous city, almost everyone seems to be selling souvenirs; and as business is being done with the water of "Mary's Well"—"Where Jesus Drank"—no doubt the air and the earth have been bottled, too. A church "as large as St. Peter's" has been promised a few years hence and, indeed, size is the only attribute in which it is possible to have any confidence. An hour beyond Nazareth the Sea of Galilee comes into view, and the purple-beige mountains of Syria. Our ears crackle as we descend.

A stone village with iron balconies, Tiberias is forlorn and oppressive. At this noon hour, the only life is in the sea; there are bathers, both human and goat, and many leaping fish. At Capernaum we wait for a tribe of long-eared goats to cross the road, then are admitted by a Franciscan friar who is as lonely as a lighthouse keeper and so delighted to have visitors to whom he can speak his native Italian that he will probably never be able to stop; and, of course, he wants to talk about us rather than the quarry of old stones—Roman olive-oil presses, mostly—of which he is custodian. For the I.S.'s, however, the dereliction of Capernaum, after the tawdriness of Nazareth, is a shock. No church marks this site of Christ's first miracles, but only a dingy chapel which might have been dumped here as surplus goods even by the city fathers of Nazareth; and instead of an honor guard of a holy brotherhood there is only this garrulous monk who falls on us like the last defender of the fort in *Under Two Flags*, the sole survivor, now gone mad from the solitude and the heat; or in this case, Capernaum being some 600 feet below sea level, the solitude, the heat, and the bends. But how much of the shock is owing to conditioning by art, to the fact that the Holy Land of our imaginations is partly the Umbrian landscapes of *quattrocento* painters?

September 4

Prejudices of art raise no obstacles on the road to Jerusalem, in any case, and this in spite of the wrecked trucks and tanks which have been left by the roadside as monuments to the blockade-runners of 1948. On the contrary, the Judean hills conjure biblical mirages at every turn; a man on a ladder picking a fruit tree becomes Absalom himself, hanging by his hair. At times the territory of Israel narrows to a defile hardly larger than the road itself, and at times we are no more than a bull's-eye from barbed-wired Jordan. The higher the climb, the more barren the brown, terraced hills, until suddenly the city of the mellifluous name looms before us like a white crown.

From our rooms, Jerusalem is a white wall, turreted in front, machicolated to the west. Before it is the gulch of Gehenna, a dry moat, and beyond it are round Turkish towers, square Gothic towers, the Tower of David, cross-capped cupolas of Eastern churches, Moslem orbs. The border is marked by a row of carrot-shaped cypresses and by the shrubberies of the hotel gardens which are hollowed like bagels. Beyond them is a no-man's-land of desert and rubble. From the angle of another hill we are able to see the Mount of Olives, Gethsemane, the Valley of Moloch, Golgotha, and at sunset we follow the border as far as Manhat, which lies directly on the line and has therefore been evacuated, a dead city under the eye of a ghostly Turkish tower. The desert is now violet, and the cities of the desert—Moab, Gilead, and Bethlehem—are salt white. Back in Jerusalem, in the blue evening, we leave for the concert under a barrage of church bells as discordant as the several versions of the Only Veracity they advertise.

President Ben-Zvi's presence at the concert obliges I.S. to lead the national anthem. This, the "Hatikva," a dreadful dirge in D minor ("the Sanhedrin Blues," I.S. calls it later) which sounds like an excerpt from *Ma Vlast*, has frightened I.S. more than anything else on the program. Whereupon, after an uncertain first beat he finds the orchestra able to sustain the mournful melody on its own, the relief is so great that he swerves into the conducting with blood, *schmaltz*, and tears, even giving a Bernstein thrust at the end.[1]

September 5

We tour the city in the morning, starting at the Mandelbaum Gate to Jordan. Buildings are sandbagged here, judging from which the two countries appear to be as far as ever from a *détente*. But there is another, less belligerent but hardly less troublesome, border, and that within the Israeli zone. This is the ghetto of the Me'a She'Arim, home of the Orthodox extremist Neturi Karta sect. These zealots live only for the Sabbath, measuring all time in terms of distance to it, and they are rabidly opposed to the Erastian state of the Zionists, on the unarguable grounds that it was created not by Messiah but by man. They are a considerable nuisance to the state, of course, and they refuse to pay its taxes or serve in its defense; but they are more than that, too—are, in fact, the atavistic conscience of the whole country. What most impresses us about them, however, is that their gnostic way of life—way of waiting, rather, waiting for God—has been able to maroon itself so successfully in the heart of a modern city. The men

[1] Next day's newspaper notices cited the discernment of the interpretation, but what was said about the other music led I.S. to remark that "the Talmudic tradition is still active in music criticism."

go about in sackcloth, covering their wives and daughters in long dresses, coarse black stockings, woolen wigs, so that these chattels shall not attract other men—while only half a block away *Lolita* is playing at the cinema.

The Dead Sea Scrolls, in Hebrew University, look disappointingly new. The black script on the clean white parchments—sewn together like frames in a spool of film—is clearly legible and in fact can be read, without difficulty, by a school child, though saying so makes one aware that the state of preservation of the scrolls is a less remarkable fact than that in two thousand years the language has not changed. A commentary on Habakkuk is on exhibit, a copy of the Book of Isaiah, and the Essene text, "The Sons of Darkness and the Sons of Light." With each scroll is the jar in which it was found, and photographs of the jars in the caves at the time of their discovery.

At noon we are received in the presidential "Log Cabin," which, along with the incumbents, is a national symbol of pioneer Israel. An adjutant reads citations, after which Mr. Ben-Zvi presents I.S. with an antique vase, myself with a medal and standard. The ceremony over, the President switches from Hebrew to Russian, which appears to be the domestic language of elderly officials, white-haired cabinet ministers as well as octogenarian social planners. The President and I.S. had known Poltava at the same time in their youth. They exchange recollections of it, then play a game of renaming the Russian writers, had they been Jews ("Pushkinson, Gogolman, Lermontovich"). As we depart, Mrs. Ben-Zvi beseeches I.S. to "say a good word for Israel when you are in Russia."

We dine in Tel Aviv with Theodore Kollek, who is a representative of the Prime Minister and who typifies the new Israel. Being largely home-grown, he presents a striking contrast to the—for comparison—Russian refugees of the morning meeting. A scholar and a man of versatile intellect, he is also husky, hard-drinking, cigar-smoking. His private passion is archaeology, and he gives me a Luristan chariot ornament which he had found on a dig and which I have too much admired.

September 7

The morning is spent in packing and receiving visitors. One woman, proud mother of a six-months-old Mozart—she says —is proof that the glorious tradition of *chutzpah* is not dead. She plainly implies that it is time for I.S. to renounce his own footless activities and to devote himself full scale to her son's certain-to-be-world-changing genius. Another caller, this one a *meshuganah*, wants to commission I.S. to compose a concerto for shofar and orchestra.

We leave early for the airport, allowing time for the Haaretz Glass Museum, an attractive new circular building in Ramat Aviv. The director escorts us through, discoursing the while on glass-making techniques—the discovery of the sand-core method, of coloring by the oxides of cobalt and manganese, of the marvering and crizzling of the parison, which is the glass in its bubble-gum state. Like many chronologically arranged museums, the Haaretz is an argument for the decline of culture. In glass manufacture, the downgrade is already noticeable after the Late Bronze Age. The gradient is not always even, of course, and beautiful objects are found in all periods, but the direction of the slope as it courses ever lower through the Persian, Phoenician, Sidonian, Hellenistic, Roman, Byzantine, and Islamic periods is unmistakable. The decline, moreover, is characterized in every culture by the same process. It is a matter of more incrustation, more gilding, more bulk, more volume, MORE; and it is marked by a turning away from the functional in favor of the baroque, and by a final stage which is merely bizarre. It follows, then, that the Haaretz is an argument for old bottles (leaving aside the question of wines), and that the oldest—a cosmetic phial, a finger bowl, a tiny aryballus—are very small and very simple in form and color. In the Roman period, which is a long way downhill, the stock of utilities has increased to include such an implement as the strigil, but the old forms have been vulgarized, and pure colors have given way to color effects, especially to iridescences and rainbow patinas like the curtain lights at Radio City. Ancient Hebrew glass is identified by representatons of ashtaroths, menoras, corn sheaves, clusters of grapes.

Leave-taking at the airport is misty-eyed and smothering. Another departing passenger, seeing the fuss that surrounds I.S., asks me if I know "who the old guy is," but without waiting for a reply he goes on to remark that "whoever it is must be a *goy* or they wouldn't pay that much attention."

In the air en route to Rome, I.S. is wondering what it is in Israel that has given us such rare elation. "I think," he says, "that it is because Israel lives in hope for the future—unlike most other nations, which only fear the future—and that we have breathed some of the contagion of that hope. And," he continues, expressing all of our sentiments as well, "though Israel is a democratic country, the people of Israel are the most aristocratic in the world."

1963

April 20

Hamburg. *Mahagonny* at the Staatsoper, our first evening in a two-week "Theater Cure." The staging, by a Brecht pupil, is admirably severe, especially in the groupings of the chorus. After applauding the director, however, one hurries to credit the composer. Though I.S. will say no more than that "there are good things everywhere in the score, but it is not everywhere good," the wonder of *Mahagonny* is that so prodigal a musical substance was given to so flimsy a play. (Berg must have been impressed by *Mahagonny*, incidentally, and it seems to me there is a touch of Jenny in Lulu and more than a touch of the athlete in Berg's own funambulist. Perhaps, too, the sax and banjo in the jazz band and the zither in the glutton scene helped to influence the choice of instruments for the "Garderobe" scene in *Lulu*.) But however good Weill's music may be, what a dispiriting work is *Mahagonny*. After a gay beginning, it plunges unswervingly downward for three far too long hours, until at the end one leaves the theater quite literally in the dumps. And the long decline has a correspondingly deleterious effect on one's judgment, so that most of what is remembered as "good" seems to have occurred comparatively near the beginning: the boxer's death, for example, and the glutton's, with an *"Er ist tod,"* a "hats off," and a that's that; or in the brothel scene, the *"Erst wasch die hände"* and *"Jungens mach rascher."* But Hamburg is no Berlin-in-the-twenties. Risqué lines and situations meet with uncertain titters, and Herr and Frau Schmidt in the fifth row can be seen exchanging whispers and knowing nudges. The reception as a whole is exactly the opposite of the author's intent, too, for the audience sits back to enjoy it like an operetta or "musical," albeit a strangely depressing example of either one.

The Vier Jahreszeiten restaurant, after the performance, could be a continuation of the last scene of the opera. There, the final abasement of society is indicated by pickets whose placards carry slogans of *FÜR GELD!* Here, bellhops in floor-length aprons march about with the same kind of signs summoning people to telephones: *BITTE HERR STOLZ!*

April 25

The Gründgens production of Schlegel's *Hamlet* at the Deutsches Schauspielhaus is a language lesson if nothing else: the English lines leap into the mind like subtitles in a foreign film, providing, of course, that one catches the German trigger words which release the spring. But with me there is a curious side effect of this involuntary translation mechanism. It makes many of the German phrases sound disturbingly comic—*"Ein Meisterwerk ist der Mensch,"* for example, and *"Hat der Kerl kein gefühl für seine Arbeit?"* and *"Gnädiger Herr"* this and *"Gnädige Frau"* that. The vocabulary of the German seems so much smaller, too—the I.S.'s say that it is as simple as Lamb's Shakespeare in comparison—and we are aware of the repetitions of phrasing. (But what can anyone do with the richness of, for example, the Ghost's "unhousel'd, disappointed, unanel'd"?) Another impression is that the language, though German only, is actually softer than the English combination of Latin and Germanic. How exact it is as translation, though, I am unable to say, except that at times the action seems to indicate that any connection is tenuous.

"Who is there?," says Marcellus and the guard replies, "Nay, stand and unfold thyself," but Marcellus is long since unfolded and, even allowing for poor visibility, less than a foot away. Hamlet himself takes hardly any pains to act in reasonable conformity with what he is saying, or what one remembers him saying in English. He has absolutely no intellectual temperament, but is a great one for leaping and somersaulting, for playfully knocking Rosencrantz about, for half-throttling his mother, for wrestling Laertes—the loudest Laertes, incidentally, in the history of the theater. Hamlet is faster-moving than anyone on the stage, in fact, which contradicts not only the general picture of the character but also the specific suggestion in his mother's speech during the duel that, like Aeneas, he has a cyclothymic build. The way he comes tearing into the *prie-dieu* scene—like a professional sprinter—one suspects him of having followed a canine interpretation of the phrase "a Great Dane"; and in another scene he is continually rolling and squatting as though rehearsing for a performance somewhere else as Puck. In short, no indecision, no pale cast of thought, but a great deal of roistering and rapidly translated action. And this is a large part of the reason why the play feels so prosaic.

The decorative aspects of the staging are no less odd. A succession of Abstract Expressionist panels is imposed as backdrops. Like subliminal advertisements, however, they become less "abstract" and more specifically "expressionist" with each successive scene, until finally they form a close and, of course, intolerable "symbolic" accompaniment to the play. Thus, a great deal of gray appears when the outlook for Hamlet takes that complexion, and of red when we feel that blood may soon be shed. In the graveyard scene, the panels are smeared in such a way that they seem to be posing a riddle, and attention focuses on the solution of the visual conundrum rather than on what otherwise is the most successful scene of the evening, a masterpiece of *Schadenfreude,* in fact, which the diggers play like Berlin wits. But whatever *do* those panels mean? Dirty laundry? That the cemetery is located in a shabby neighborhood?

As for the costumes, Horatio is a *maître d'hotel,* Polonius an idiot cousin of Wilhelm II, the King an Edward VII, Fortinbras a space-traffic policeman, and the Norwegian army— green leather uniforms and crash helmets—Storm Troopers of the near future. Still another period is suggested by the music: the usual rancid sackbut sennets are replaced with spurts of pseudo-Handel on the organ; and the dance for the dumb show (during which Hamlet never so much as slyly glances at the King) is a modern ballet. It remains to be said that this action thriller takes place in two dramatically shapeless divisions, the one intermission being just long enough for philosophers to read Karl Jaspers's program notes, *"Hamlets Wissen."*

I.S., after the performance: *"Hamlet* the play is like a great turkey which nobody knows how to cut because Hamlet the character is developed so far out of proportion to everyone else. . . . Tonight, the play seemed above all to be saying important things about belief, belief beyond appearances and sciences, as, for example, in the line 'there is a special providence in the fall of a sparrow' . . . and, perhaps because of the German, the 'philosophical' passages seemed to stand out; Ophelia's 'We know what we are but not what we may be,' for instance, which rather neatly makes off with the cake of existentialism. . . . Another thing, too: I had never noticed before that Polonius's boringness is a family disease, but both children are afflicted with it as well."

April 28

Don Carlos at the Staatsoper. The staging lacks action, and some of the little there is goes wrong; in the sword-drawing street scene, for instance, though this is a breakdown of credibility in the work itself, and a weak curtain in any performance. Nor is there any compensation in the *décors,* which include a row of overgrown asparagus possibly meant to represent trees. In any case, the opera falls off so badly after the Grand Inquisitor scene that the end is hardly more than a costume concert. Tonight's Inquisitor is miscast, a feeble elder rather than a holy terror; and the orchestra does the casting, implacably setting the scene for a person and a voice both more powerful than Philip's. I.S. is rapturous, nevertheless. "Verdi could give such grand scale to his people only because his own scope and vitality were unmatched; how I would like to have known him! His was the true spirit of *libertà,* too, and he, not Wagner, was the true progressive, not the *man* Verdi of the Risorgimento and Cavour's parliament, but the composer of the *Don Carlos* duet:

which is more likable, you must admit, than that other *Blutbruderschaft* music which fat people in horns and hides howl at by the hour."

May 2

The audience applauds I.S. as he takes his seat in the first row of the Staatsoper a moment before the lights dim for *Der Rosenkavalier*. He acknowledges this with a bow while whispering to me that "It is only because everybody is very happy to see me obliged to sit through four hours without syncopation." But he doesn't sit or, at any rate, doesn't sit still. "How long can this false counterpoint go on?" he says, and "How can anybody swallow all of that *Schlagsahne?* . . . Prurience is intolerable even in Mozart. The music has no highs or lows except too locally; it is too even, and Strauss always holds his breath too long . . . How well they go together, bad taste and vigor . . . It is an operetta—and as 'if Richard then Wagner,' so 'if Strauss then Johann.'" And the defamation keeps up after the performance: "Perhaps Strauss can charm and delight, but he cannot move. That may be because he had no commitment; he didn't give a damn. . . . But I have a terrible thought. What if I am sentenced to Strauss in Purgatory?"

May 5–8

KERJÜKAZÖVEKET BECSATOLNI! DOHANYOZNI TILOS! (No smoking, fasten seat belts.) This is in an Ilyushin turbo-prop carrying us from Amsterdam to Prague and Budapest, and as if deliberately chosen as a contrast to so many letters, two of the shortest words in English have been painted on the door of the W.C.; they advise prospective occupants to PU SH. The Prague airport is empty and ominous: just before the take-off, policemen enter the cabin and check every face against a

photograph. That of Budapest, a half hour later, is totally
dark and, except for our welcoming party—a photographer,
a tape-recorder, and three Italian-speaking women from a
concert agency—equally deserted. As we step down, the photographer seems very intent to tell V. something about choco-
lates—"*csokolom, csokolom*," he says—but, at length, the
Italians explain that "*Kezet csokolom*" merely means "kiss the
hand." The city, on our way to a hotel on the Danube Island,
might be under a wartime curfew. There is no traffic, vehicu-
lar or pedestrian, and the streets are dimly lighted, even in
the center of town. Shell holes and other damage from the
fighting of seven years ago can be seen on one street, nevertheless, and even in the gloom.

The Grand Hotel on Margits Ziget (Margaret Island) sits
behind a levee in a forest of chestnut trees, now in full blos-
som. Apparently—all too apparently—the Grand has not been
disturbed by renovations since the good old days of Hapsburg decay. The bedroom furniture—there are short eider-
down dumplings on the beds themselves—is imitation
rosewood, and the paintings are framed in gold guilloche.
Each window is skirted with a velvet curtain ample enough
to cover the modesty of a small operatic stage. Less charming
to non-antiquarians (or, depending on one's tastes, *even* less
charming) is the plumbing. All water, both "cold" and "hot,"
dribbles out equally lukewarm and sulphurous, and the toilet
gurgles vindictively for an hour or so after each use. (So does
the neighbors': a high transom permanently open to the
adjoining apartment keeps us informed as to all activities
there.) But the only clue that some ill may have befallen the
old Empire is found here in the W.C. Each morning a dirty
paper band is wrapped around the toilet seats. It says "sterile"
in Russian!

The contrast between the faded Franz Joseph appointments
and the clientele is extremely bizarre. Almost all of the guests

appear to be political missionaries, a description that includes four different delegations of Africans, a party of Frenchmen who when we pass them are always muttering against General de Gaulle, and a surprisingly large number of Chinese, dressed in tunics with stiff collars, who speak correct Russian (I.S. says) to the Hungarian officials with whom they share endless speech-making dinners. The entertainments of this extraordinary company are no less odd than its appearance. At about five o'clock every afternoon, a five-man jazz combo starts through a repertory composed largely of American hit tunes of the thirties, the favorites being "Stars Fell on Alabama" and "Smoke Gets in Your Eyes." The dance floor of the restaurant is then rapidly filled and color-integrated—except by the Chinese, who do not participate, seeming to regard their western and southern allies as puerile offenders against intellectual dignity. It is a vivacious crowd, however, and the Hungarian girls all wear their hair like nests, in the American way (or is it the Thracian way? *cf.* Archilochus: ". . . the ungodly Thracians with their hair done up in a fright on the top of their heads . . .").

The hotel food, except for *caffè espresso*—café bars in Budapest are two and three to the block—is ostentatiously bad. A few imports are available, however, including Scotch whisky, English gin, French sardines, French champagne ($40 a bottle), French wines (I.S. finds that most Hungarian wines taste "like shellac"), Icelandic caviar (*sic*, not "outlandish," though it is that, too). The U.S.S.R. being at the same time the world's largest producer of caviar and Hungary's biggest brother, the fact of this Icelandic brand strikes us as spectacularly eccentric. Is it protest or penance, or both? Surely no one could *prefer* it to the Russian, as the I.S.'s rather too openly indicate, clamping their noses against the strong ichthyoid smell. I.S., watching four crapulous creatures bolt and guzzle at the next table, remarks that "in spite of rumors of famine, everyone looks remarkably fat," but V. thinks the evidence of so much appetite is "a sign of deprivation, and surely the fat is emotional."

The Hungarian National Radio Orchestra is an excellent ensemble, rich in tone, and precise and fluent in rhythm. The performances are the best of our entire tour and they are the most warmly and discriminatingly (I think) received, but the rehearsals, which take place in the small but acoustically perfect Franz Liszt Hall, are more gratifying than the concert. The orchestra's first foreign language is a grudging German, but English is a close second and far more common than French. Few people appear to speak Russian, and in spite of the parity with Hungarian on toilet seats, it is certainly not popular. The few Hungarians who talk to us about Russia are not enthusiastic, in any case, and those who have actually traveled there are openly disparaging.

The dress rehearsal is followed with a reception by the Union of Composers, a multilingual and well-informed group, one of whom is a very pretty girl who, it is said (though that is beside the point), has written a highly successful opera. Representatives from the Union of Soviet Composers are present, too, and they give us recordings of our concerts in Moscow last year. Zoltán Kodály has also promised to attend, but as he is I.S.'s age and has only recently taken a bride of twenty—after a first wife some thirty years *his* senior—his absence is accountable.

Le Sacre du printemps at the Hungarian National Ballet is musically accurate though the director of the theater apologizes for "the very tired orchestra"; and it is well danced, though the choreography looks like group calisthenics. According to the director, this season's repertory contains some sixty operas: "In a city as small as Budapest many operas have to be given a few times, whereas in New York a few operas can be played again and again. Our ballet has done

Le Sacre forty times this year, however, which I think is as good a record as New York."

After the performance, we go to a restaurant in Buda to hear an orchestra of cymbalom, clarinet, and strings. Most of the pieces begin with moody cadenzas, but eventually all of them turn into rhapsodies. During their first vodka break, the players, who wear muzhiks' blouses, stand, click their heels, and raise their glasses to I.S.

May 9

As we leave the hotel to drive to Zagreb, I.S. receives a note:

> Dear Mister Stravinszki! I please one
> autogram because I very like *Petruska*
> and you,
> > Podmaniczky Judith

and he signs in the Hungarian manner, "Stravinszki Igor." Travel fever shows deeply in the eyes of all the people who come to see us off.

A long avenue with ocher churches and trams leads to black fields in which stooks of straw are stacked like tepees. Here, and all the way, the majority of workers are women. From time to time the motorist is reminded of who is in authority by a Red Star on the gate of a collective farm, but roadside crucifixes are far more numerous. In Martorvásár, a plaque on one of the low, thatched-roof houses commemorates Beethoven's visit there in 1808; at least, that is what it seems to say, but when I read it, or try to pronounce any Hungarian aloud, our driver gives way to such violent laughter that I fear we may land in a ditch. A catastrophe of the sort is only narrowly averted, in fact, when we come to Székesfehervár (say-cash-fe-hair-var), a city with Roman and Byzantine ruins and a turquoise and marigold rococo square, but by Nagykanizsa (nadj-caneezha) I have learned to hold my tongue. We eat at Siofok, in a "bisztro" on Fö-ut street, a name, as we now know from experience, that will sound less Chinese than it looks.

Lake Balaton is half hidden by a blizzard of dandelion fluff. South of the lake the fields and forests are wider, but the people farm with primitive hand implements and still seed the earth from aprons as their ancestors did a thousand years ago. At the frontier, the barbed wire, the gun-toting guards, and the doubly barricaded bridge help to explain the look of claustral fear in the friends who came this morning to say good-bye.

On the Yugoslav side the road is unpaved as far as Čakovec, and thereafter, in the mountains of Illyria, worse than anything the word unpaved can suggest. The land is poor, too, and the few plowed strips on the steep hills are as thin as toboggan slides. Without exception the people are dressed in gray or black, as though in mourning for some national disaster—which, indeed, seems to be the case. Many of the houses in Čakovec have TV antennae, but the fact hardly inspires confidence in the local prosperity, and a crew of workmen sitting in the yard of a derelict factory looks as if waiting to be fed intravenously. Our Hungarian driver pronounces Čakovec as "Ka-ko-kek," like an Aristophanic chorus, but the Yugoslavs to whom he appeals for directions fail to recognize any area of their geography in this version; and the "aids to pronunciation" in our guide book are no help in this case—or indeed in any case but the most desperate. The Croatian for "Where is the nearest restaurant?" ("nearest"?, is it a question of starvation?) is *"Gdje je najbliži restorán?"* And "Could you recommend me to a good hotel?" is *"Možete li mi preporučiti jedan dobar hotel?"* The Croat for "restaurant" and "hotel" will be remembered, to be sure, however we manage the anterior matter.

At Zagreb we drive by the Strossmajer Gardens and the vined and turreted old city, then enter the megalithic new city through the "Square of the Victims of Fascism." Hundreds of vanguard musicians, here for the Biennale of Contemporary Music, are billeted in our hotel, and posses of electronic and aleatoric composers are milling about in the lobby and bars.

May 9–14

(Zagreb). One immediately likes and admires, as well as sympathizes with, the Yugoslavs. I do, anyway, though I could not live in their East-West, North-South, Latin-Slav, Catholic-Orthodox cruciform culture. After having been criminally underrated by the Allied governments in the war —many more German divisions were held down in Yugoslavia than in Italy—these brave people are still patronized and neglected, in spite of which they are full of good will even now. I have noted one idiosyncrasy, though, which is that they can be relied upon to follow instructions to the letter, but seem not to understand the purpose of them and therefore the need to extend them to unspecified eventualities. Thus the guards at the late-night far-out concerts are careful to keep people from standing in the doorways or entering the hall during a performance, but when a young man jumps to the stage like John Wilkes Booth, and begins to strangle another young man tootling on a clarinet mouthpiece, they do nothing about *him*. Or am I wrong, and are they really far more subtle than I think?

The Zagreb "Musziči" learn to play I.S.'s *Movements* more

quickly than any orchestra heretofore, and their performance of it with the excellent local pianist, Jurica Murai, is music-making of a high order. After the concert I.S. remarks of his Gesualdo *Monumentum* that "the harmonic tension is short-changed in transferring the music from voices to instruments, and the most radical progressions to sing sound tame and archaic when played." As we re-enter the hotel lobby, an American newspaperman corners I.S. with the question "Is John Cage's stuff music?" I.S.: "And where did you get all of that optimism?"

May 16

Paris. A journalist calls asking I.S. to record a get-well message to Cocteau, as Braque and Picasso have already done. I.S. refuses, however, and so firmly that parts of the telephone fly off as he cradles the receiver. Then at lunch, with all ears to him, he says that *"Cocteau ne peut pas mourir sans faire réclame."* Though part of this remark is to be taken merely as a sign of reversion to type—as I.S. became more Russian in Russia, so in Paris he always returns to that between-the-wars society which lived for the clever remark—there is nevertheless a change of feelings. Only two weeks ago the news of Cocteau's heart attack (or the thought of the sub-traction and the narrowing circle) deeply upset him. Then, when a few days ago he heard that Cocteau had begun to recover, little signs of annoyance began to appear, as though having already written off an account, he disliked reopening the books. But I.S.'s feelings toward Cocteau have always puzzled me and though V. attributes them to Diaghilev's influence, surely at the time of *Oedipus*, I.S. must have known

Cocteau on independent terms. I have heard only sharp remarks about him in all my fifteen years with I.S., in any case ("talented, yes," preluding the devastation) and the last time the two were together, in Paris a year ago, I.S. jibbed at keeping the appointment. At about that time, too, and after repeatedly saying that "I should put something about Cocteau in one of my books," I.S. produced for that purpose a thousand or so mostly unprintable words later to be edulcorated under pressure from V. to the two paragraphs in *Dialogues and a Diary* which I.S. considers high praise.

One of the luncheon guests is a biologist who talks about a possible life on other planets based on non-carbon elements. How I wish I could follow even the half of what he says concerning the chemistry of carbon compounds and the Red Shift, but in fact I am a scientific illiterate, understanding as little of the world around me as a three-year-old Eskimo.

Dinner with Eugène Ionesco. As he enters the room, I have an impression of a Chinese actor: a slightly slant-eyed mask with remnants of hair tucked about the ears and lower cranium by a skillful make-up artist. Behind the mask is a permanently worried face with a deep frown and sulky eye sockets. No smile escapes it all evening, but after watching it pan through some jokes (someone refers to a book by Jean Genet as "a sort of Posterior Analytics"), one doubts that the zygomatic muscles are any longer capable of pulling out of the pout and into such unfamiliar directions. Would he be less cross if his striped serge suit and checkered shirt were in less violent conflict? I think not, for with a second look one sees that this is the actor's costume, exactly what the well-dressed Béranger would wear; and, after all, sharp clothes can be used to mortify one's shyness and punish one's self-consciousness as well as to shield the man who wishes to be well guarded. And that, certainly, he does want. "*Ça depend*" is his phrase again and again as he fiddles with his fork and molds and unmolds breadcrumbs, and for a long time the conversation is not allowed to stray from inhibited artificialities.

At length someone refers to the New York production of *Rhinoceros*, but Ionesco condemns it, "except for the freak virtuoso performance of Zero Mostel." But he dislikes New York, too, and not only *"le Broadway."* New York is a *chien ville*. "Most cities are either dogs or cats, though Paris is both. Naples and Venice are cat cities, of course, and London and New York are dogs." (Though such sexual identification games are old sport to Auden, I think of how he would enjoy this feline-canine form, and with what *a priori* certainty and relish he would set about classifying the cities of central Asia; nor, of course, would Auden miss the point of Ionesco's preference for a Paris he considers ambiguous.) We switch from the United States to the Soviet Union, but it, too, is unloved—in fact hated so strongly that he swings blindly, like a boxer stung to the quick. The Russians buy more books than any other people, V. asserts, and read more: "You see them reading in buses, on benches, in queues, even at intermissions of concerts." "Yes, but such bad literature," says Ionesco. V. mews back at this with, "True, it *is* likely to be only Pushkin or Gogol, and no one would claim sophistication such as ours for the Russians; nevertheless, masses of people do read poetry there, as masses of people in, for example, Paris and Romania do not." Ionesco: "Yes, but such bad poetry. Evtushenko." A form of remonstrance comes this time from Nathalie Sarraute, who has just been to Moscow and who has been conversing with the I.S.'s about it in Russian, but the subject gets out of hand and Ionesco is soon shelving the whole Soviet achievement as a *"revolution tech-nocratique."* He is somewhat guiltily talkative about a visit of his own to General de Gaulle, though, calling it an act of courage on his part, "for the reason that French intellectuals

are a hundred percent against De Gaulle, and I am what people call a Saint-Germain-des-Prés intellectual." Whether he
feels that "courage" does not quite have the right ring, or
that his motives may seem shaky, he tries to cover the tracks
of his visit by implying that it was an anti-conformist gesture
—which is like Cocteau's attempt to justify *his* standing for
the Academy on grounds that as the honor is no longer
honorable, to receive it is an act of rebellion.

We come away from the dinner railing against French
insularity and the Parisians' pretense, because of past primacy,
to be the planet's acutest critics; and I.S. claims to yearn for
"the raw technocratic materialism of the *chiens villes*." But
later, on the way to the hotel, Michel Butor tells us that
Ionesco must have felt intimidated because "he is not really
like that." (I.S.: "Fewer and fewer people are what they
seem.") "He can be five different characters in an afternoon,"
Butor continues, "and the whole gamut from gay to morbid.
His mixed-up politics are due to the fact that he has suffered
both from failure and success, and fears both the avant-garde
and the reaction." I.S.: "How interesting to be five different
people! And if you have the talent to create a variety of
personnages for the stage, I see no reason why you shouldn't
create them for yourself, too."

May 25

Bergen. I go with Brigitta Lieberson to a lunch by H.M. King
Olav V in the Royal Lodge at Gamlehaugen. All week long
the hotel maids have been squealing *"Kongen, Kongen"* at
the sight of the invitation on my dressing table, and since
yesterday, when H.M. actually appeared at the concert—

because of which I have had to conduct the Norwegian anthem and "God Save the Kong"—their service has improved to a point where they actually re-mop the floor every ten minutes. The Gamlehaugen village is a thirty-minute drive from Bergen, by forest and fjord. The royal colors are flying when we arrive, and all approaches to the lodge (Rube Goldberg Toonerville Gothic) are guarded.

A protocol officer meets us at the door and ushers us to the main room where we are presented to H.M. He is pleasant and ruddy (alcoholically florid, in fact), and his gracious smile betrays no hint of the intense boredom he is reputed to suffer at all concerts and therefore no less at ours. (When the audience began to applaud in rhythmic unison after the Beethoven Concerto, H.M. rose to leave, which meant that the audience had to rise, too, and that the applause froze in mid-reverberation.) From H.M. we are handed along to admirals and generals with ever-diminishing clusters of medals and braid, and to high clergymen, M.P.'s, millionaire shipbuilders, Miss Sonja Henie. At table Brigitta is seated next to the King, and I sit between a bishop and a knight where, until receiving my neighbors' toasts, I feel like a pawn. One cannot drink solitarily here, but only by fixing a partner's eyes in one's own during the whole draught as though practicing hypnotic fascination. As the guest is naturally inclined to fortify himself at such an event, as the vintages are excellent, and as he may never again succeed in drawing the attention of another free pair of eyes, glasses are drained at each opportunity. The Kong himself drinks the health of each guest individually, clockwise around the three-pronged table from his position at meridian. We watch for the royal nod as our turns approach, then hoist ourselves and our glasses, locking H.M. in the eye to eye embrace but this time omitting the "*sköl*." None of this is as formal as I am making it sound, however, and the excellent "*Lunsj*" of "*Sprøsteke Kylling*"— spring chicken—is served expeditiously and without interruptions, as I had feared, for testimonials. Somewhat teetering from the toasts, we move to a veranda for cognac and liqueurs. It is furnished with the kind of *Jugendstil* which has lately become interesting: tasseled cushions, frilled armchairs, chintzes, and paintings and tapestries of Norse mythology—blond goddesses, lilies and swans, Yggdrasill.

Conversation among shipbuilders touches on the stave churches but settles on Edvard Munch. One of the collectors tells how it has been determined that, say, 66½ F. and not 67 F. is the optimum room temperature for Munch's oils—this is for the Munch Museum which opens in Oslo next week. "But I remember Munch's studio when the paintings were lying on the floor," the same gentleman says, "and if they were in his way Munch would walk on them, or stack them up outside in the snow. Now, too, we pay fifty thousand dollars for the kind of picture he would give a tradesman in payment of a bill. In fact, those very tradesmen are now sitting on their Munchs so to speak, and waiting for us, just as unprosperous American farmers wait for the builders of turnpikes to buy paths through their lands."

Back in Bergen with nothing to do (having avoided today's installment of the perpetual Grieg concert), we walk by the quay and the steep gable houses. A more vigorous promenader than ourselves is Björnsen—or rather, the statue of Björnsen at the head of Ole Bull Street. Its stride is the most powerful, living or graven, I have ever seen.

May 29

Oxford. Professor Gilbert Ryle for lunch, a big-boned, robust, major-in-mufti type with a bald, brindled cranium and thrusting "intellectual" jaw and brow; one feels that he could take to the stage, and without further make-up—he arrives in a parka, tweeds, specs, pipe (now let's get our teeth into the problem)—in the role of a private eye (Bulldog Drummond). The Professor is a purely British phenomenon, as a minute or so of his conversation makes clear. He is deeply suspicious of "continental intellectuals," or indeed of anyone from "abroad," and though an exception could probably be made for a lean-looking outdoor-type Australian pragmatist, one feels that no exchange whatever is possible with a pasty-faced Central European logical positivist even if his ideas of how to "do" philosophy were similar to the Professor's. "Why are your chaps always bringing up Dewey and James?" he asks. "The world would have been much better off without either of those Great American Bores." No defense is expected, of course, and the impossibility of expostulating with him on any subject is already conceded; and besides, more seriously offending countries have yet to be dealt with. (When they have been, incidentally, one sees to what extent Philosophy is a national and school bias; "steeped in port and prejudice among the monks of Oxford," said Gibbon, escaping that fate.) Non-competitive philosophers, those of the U.S.S.R., for example, rate only indulgent amusement, and for laughs a Soviet philosophical journal is quoted on the Professor himself; it calls him a "creeping empiricist" as well as a "bashful materialist." The stronger medicine is reserved for closer trans-Channel targets. "Almost my greatest satisfaction as an editor was in printing a review of the works of one Teilhard de Chardin, then rumored to be a biologist. What a lot of lemon juice we poured on that old teleological pancake." Merleau-Ponty fares hardly any better: "French *clarté*, indeed! And by the way, have you noticed how many French intellectuals seem to be retroactive heroes of the *maquis?*" At the mention of a contemporary German philosopher, the Professor remarks that "the first person pronoun,

found twice in all Aristotle, occurs seventeen times in one
of Herr P.'s footnotes. He can hardly bear to use any other
words." Two Israeli philosophers are dismissed with the comment that "neither of them is actually very good at listening,"
while a too-enterprising British colleague is swept out of the
way for being a literary civil servant. "One wonders about
these people who try to take the pulse of every new movement. Where do they get all the fingers?" But the acid tickles
more than it burns, especially on the subject of philosophers'
"jamborees." "The best philosophers are the translators. Picture two thousand of us in a Brussels auditorium with Professor Gorgonzola at the rostrum being translated line for
line: 'The ontological postulate of the, and . . . oh, pardon
me, Professor, but I didn't get the last sentence.' *I* got it,
though. Rubbish, of course." He goes on to tell us of an
invitation to a similar convention "somewhere in the American West. They wanted me to express my 'views on philosophy,' as they put it, in a five-minute televised interview, to
which I replied that I doubted I could make anything clear
to anyone out there in less than five years."

Discussing the problem of how to find time to keep up
with new publications, I.S. cites the case of a friend who has
learned to read while he walks: "though he looks like the
absent-minded professor, or the last eccentric." The idea of
crossing the quad with a book to his nose delights Ryle—
"Oh jolly good, oh very impressive, splendid, splendid"—
but he does not agree that eccentrics are disappearing, "at
least, not when I look about at my colleagues in the common
room." He uncorks an aroma unmistakably of that location,
and of classrooms in general, by replying to one of our
queries with "That's a further question which I will answer
when you've answered mine," and by illustrating a limitation
of the word "correct" in the sense of behavior, with the example of Lord So-and-so, "who when told that his wife had

been killed, responded with 'What a pity.' This, you see, is perfectly correct, though you would no doubt agree that something is missing." But the best of his *aperçus* appear somewhat too readily ("Every generation or so, philosophical progress receives a big setback by the discoveries of an alleged 'genius' "), and one begins not only to lose confidence in their hundred-percent spontaneity, but even to suspect that they have been collected and are being worked off in the manner of Tchichikov or Mr. Jingle. At the termination of the meal a bowl of cherries is handed round. (The Professor's appetite is commensurate with his frame, and he resists three attempts by the waiter to remove his bread plate after the main course has been cleared.) He has his own cherry tree, he tells us (I have until now pictured him as inhabiting landless bachelor's "digs") but he has never eaten any of the fruit because "the birds get there first." With this, V. tells him that protective nets are purchasable now, but he replies that "the tree is thirty feet tall and I'm not," which is an empirically verifiable answer, to be sure, and an example, one sometimes fears, of not a little philosophical activity.

The only mishap of the meeting occurs when the word "music" slips out of I.S. Thereafter the Professor becomes glum, and he is soon beating a retreat "back to academe," as he says on the way out. (But when did he leave it? Can he have regarded the visit as an excursion into "real life" as the concept is defined in his new lecture "A Rational Animal"?) "He is like a very brilliant schoolboy who, without meaning to, makes us feel like very dull schoolboys," says I.S., but, in fact, the Professor has enlightened and exhilarated us all, whereas we have failed even to give him good cutting matter for his wit.

Back in London we split the evening between *Figaro* at Covent Garden and the fiftieth anniversary performance of *Le Sacre du printemps* at Albert Hall. The *Figaro* is a Gala Performance in the presence of the Queen Mother, who, as we see during the national anthem when the audience faces her loge, has great allure. The audience is bedizened and glittering, too, and is therefore something of a contrast to the set for Act I, which looks like a suite in the Dorchester Hotel and which is vigorously applauded, I suppose because recognition is gratifying. As for the performance, I.S. thinks it "overmolded, souped-up, too pushed and high-powered, with a scale of dynamics appropriate to Varèse. Mozart is poorer than that. Conducting should be midwifery, but this *chic* nonsense has nothing to do with obstetrics."

We arrive at Albert Hall during the *Danse de la terre* to find half of the orchestra following Monteux's actual beat and half what they, and probably *le maître*, too, know the beat should be. At the end, *le maître* comes to our loge and the two tiny gentlemen pose together like an advertisement on the longevity value of modern music ("Why we didn't retire at sixty"). Afterward I.S. remarks that Monteux is shrinking. "I saw him last at another *Sacre* blowout a decade ago," he says, "and now he seems only half as large," and the question of the old maestro's dissolution continues to disquiet I.S. in spite of V.'s attempts to reassure him by quoting *multum in parvo*. But I.S. has not been touched in the least by the sentiments of the occasion. On the contrary, it has incited him to loud criticism, and only late at night as we are re-entering the hotel does he cool off about the wrong *tempi* long enough to call *le maître* a "*très brave homme*."

May 31

We drive to Canterbury in the morning, then to Saltwood Castle and luncheon with Sir Kenneth and Lady Clark. Pink hydrangeas are blooming in the country gardens all the way,

and there are carpets of bluebells in the Kentish woods. Near
Canterbury the fields of hops are honey-colored, and the
sandstone Cathedral itself has been newly scrubbed to a pale
gold.

   To go from Canterbury to Saltwood is to retrace the murder of Beckett: the plot was hatched, or pledged to, at Saltwood, and it is there that Tennyson's best scene takes place,
the villainous knights extinguishing their candles to avoid
each other's eyes. Approaching the castle, one thinks not only
of Beckett, however, but of more recent stories, as well. One
visitor is reported to have been told, after rapping at the port-
cullis, that "Lady Clark is busy weeding the battlements."
According to another anecdote, the chatelaine is supposed to
have reproved a serving maid for "fingering the tulips just
before the Kents come to dinner." But in the best of this
Firbank collection, a gathering of distinguished Ladies complains of the nuisance of having to send to the bank twice a
year or so to fetch their tiaras for Royal receptions, whereupon Lady C. is reported to have informed them that *her*
tiara has become terribly worn. But to visit Saltwood is to
see that the battlements *are* real as well as weedy.

   With the removal of only two properties, the picture of
the castle could be called "Saltwood as Beckett knew it" (and
the two, a TV aerial on the parapet and a flivver parked by
the moat, belong without doubt to varlets and scullions).
As we arrive, Sir K. is reading under a chestnut tree—with
a pencil and pad instead of a halberd and shield. We follow
him to the entrance hall, which houses a collection of nar-
whals' horns second only to that of the Musée Cluny, and
which is the introduction to one of the great private museums
of the world. In every room and corridor are masterpieces, a
list of which would tally to the hundreds, and all in impec-
cable taste and perfect pedigree. Even in the "loo" the wall-
paper pattern is by William Morris. (The plumbing, though,

is less *chic.* "Only the Queen Mother knows how to use our W.C.," says Lady C., innocently adding a new anecdote to Saltwood lore, "and that is because she is Scotch.")

From the battlements Sir K. can survey his demesnes, looking over the milky haze of the downs to the sea. It is the sea of Turner's *Storm at Folkestone,* which hangs in Sir K.'s library and about which he talks to us with great eloquence of which, alas, I remember only the gist: "Turner was always living in houses on bends in the River Thames, you see, and he was always getting up at dawn to study morning light on water. Now look at that light. . . . And at this circular movement . . . he thought in circles, you see; I doubt that his hand could move at all if he had had to do classical symmetries. . . . In fact, I would call him the arch anti-classicist. . . ."

At lunch someone says that "real gourmets always take red wine with salmon" (and in rapid succession I feel that I am (a) an unreal gourmet, (b) no gourmet, (c) an anti-gourmet). Sir K.'s table talk is devoted largely to a discussion of Russian painting. He suggests that "instead of trying to suppress modern painting, the Russians might have claimed to be its discoverers, what with Malevitch, Gabo, Archipenko, Soutine, Chagall, Kandinsky, De Staël, Poliakov, Tchelichev, Berman, Larionov. The difficulty for the Soviet Union in this, of course, is that everyone on my list is a refugee. Kandinsky is the most interesting case. He was a *great* painter during the last years before he went back to Russia and became a commissar (he liked that, I'm sure, for a time, anyway), but after his political experience, reality went underground and he painted only squares, circles, abstractions. There you have a clue to modern art."[1]

Back in London we dine at the Garrick Club with Henry

[1] When I.S. realizes that Sir K. is counting exiles as Russians, he demurs from this interesting idea. The description "Russian composer"—instead of Russian-*born* composer—used to set off tantrums a few years ago.

Moore, an open and immediately likable man with clarion opinions and a delightful debonair giggle. At one point the talk drifts toward the quagmires of "taste." "Taste is for pederasts," says I.S., "and beyond that it is mostly a question of familiarity. Other people's toes are ugly, but not our own because we grew up with them and were fond of them in the piggly-wiggly stage." Here Moore supervenes wonderfully with, "But there is something much greater than 'taste' and that is the sense of a terrible importance." Which sculptors have this sense, or in other words, who are the real sculptors? Moore's responses to the names we propose are immediate and certain: "Rodin was a great sculptor, Degas was a sculptor, Brancusi was only and totally a sculptor, Matisse was a sculptor, Picasso is a sculptor, Wotruba is a sculptor, Giacometti is a great *artist*, Marini is a bit of a sculptor, Manzù is a sculptor, but a bad one." While he is excitedly telling us about a Cycladic vase he has just purchased, words fail him and he takes a pen and draws it for us with a few fast strokes. "Well, as you can see, it's not a ceramic at all," he says, "but a sculpture."

June 1

A visit to David Jones, in his bed-sitting room on the second floor of a lodging house in Harrow-on-the-Hill. It is less a room, though, than a cocoon, and the tenant, even as silk-worms go, is delicate and withdrawn. His face is boyish, an impression owing in part to his bangs and glabrous skin. But he has a boyish grin, too, though it breaks and vanishes in a way that makes one aware of how deeply troubled his expression is, and was before. His extreme shyness and lack of animal confidence retreats, just perceptibly, with each link in a chain of cigarettes, but our presence must be a terrible burden at best (the cocoon clings so close) and we feel like intruders in a self-willed solitary confinement.

Paintings, drawings, manuscripts, and a thousand books are scattered everywhere about the room; one wonders whether Mr. Jones has ever willingly parted with any of his works, and when he shows us a lion drawn at the age of six, we realize that a mere request to him to sell a drawing or water-color would be enough to shock him "traumatically." Mr. Jones tells us that he is obliged to "unpile the bed every night, then pile it up again in the morning." It is now strewn with sheets of foolscap, each one partly covered with a calligraphic script that trails off to the lower right of the page as though the author were unable to confine his thoughts there.

The most potent pictorial image in the room is a colored drawing of a woman's head, faintly reminiscent of Henry Moore. A more recent picture, of Tristram and Yseult aboard ship ("I know only a little about ships, enough for a little ship, perhaps, but you must know a lot to do a big ship") is pre-Raphaelite, and more than faintly. The latest picture of all, a labyrinthine though still unfinished "Annunciation" suggests Blake both in shape and color, but comparisons to Blake can be made elsewhere in David Jones's work, and at the deepest level. I.S. likes this "Annunciation," and he gently confesses that it seems already complete to him, and that it is in danger of becoming too complex. Mr. Jones agrees about the danger, but says that he wants to add a little more color, "if, at the same time, I can keep it a drawing. . . . Of course, I don't mostly like *anything* I do," he subjoins, and in a more cheerful voice. At one point he is deeply distressed trying to remember the word "wire," the which broke on one of his pictures, he says; and at another moment, eyes closed, he counts on his fingers struggling to recall whether he was born under Capricorn or Scorpio, until we wonder whether in fact he has any quotidian count of time. A sudden, mercurial, change of mood occurs when he exhibits one of his plaques of Latin lettering *à la* Eric Gill. "I posted it to a convent in Wales from which it was returned, after a great time, with an explanation that no one has any use for Welsh in Wales anymore; and evidently even fewer people have any use for Latin." The smile is seraphic this time and it disappears more slowly.

And so we turn about the room, examining a long-undusted book, or a cross of palm, or a majolica angel. But why have we come? In homage and admiration for a writer of genius, the greatest living in English imaginative prose (as I think, and if it *is* prose). Have we disturbed his world? Yes, I fear, like one of those glass paperweights in which, because of abnormal gravity, the "snow" inside takes a long time to settle. But the effect on us will be more disturbing simply because most people (myself included) lead lives of pastiche, and David Jones's is a life of purity.

Mr. Jones offers us "China tea"; a kettle hangs from an andiron by the fireplace, and a clearing has been made on one of the tables for a small mound of sugar, a punctured can of milk, and a few other comestibles. Slowly and with frequent interruptions of silence, Mr. Jones tells us that he has been ordered to pay back-taxes on some American Foundation Award money, and he is obviously terrified, obviously penniless, and obviously incapable even of formulating an answer.

After leaving him, we are haunted for the remainder of the day by his aloneness—or the possibility of our own. At what point does the self-consciousness of the solitary man, and the pedantry and overdeveloped sensibilities which are his forms of hypochondria—at what point do they begin dangerously to shut him off from his "super-ego" and the outside? When, to put it bluntly, does he sink into celibacy and solipsism? ("Sisyphus was a bachelor," Kafka wrote somewhere.) When did David Jones begin to believe in his illness (agoraphobia, a too-perfect typological disease for the inward-turning), or is he a *malade imaginaire?* Can one trace the malady to the war, to experiences and emotions that could not be shared afterward with women, and that therefore in some cases resulted in a withdrawal from women? The great dramatic monologue *In Parenthesis* is no withdrawal, of course, but an affirmation of this world. But the *Anathemata* is a retreat, I think, behind the windowpane of this room, behind symbols, behind language; and to me it is a breakdown in communication in some of the same ways that *Finnegans Wake* is a breakdown after *Ulysses.* "To me," I repeat, which does not excuse the Philistinism of the judgment, but which at least puts the onus of it on my own ignorance—and that, indeed, is doubtless the only fault with the *Anathemata,* just as the "breakdown in communication" is no doubt purely on my end.

June 2–9

Áth Cliath: the "center of paralysis," Joyce called it, and more indulgently—for it is far dirtier than Chicago—"dear dirty Dublin." We are surrounded at the airport by parties of sunburned and freckled priests, and by Sisters of St. Vincent de Paul wearing swan-like *chapeaux à corné.* What strikes us about these people is their musical voices, so different from the flat, pinched, and unvaried vowel sounds of Londoners. Nor is there any reluctance to speak. "Now would that be Mr. Eyegore Strawinsky, the musician?" a bystander asks me, almost singing the question. There is only a little of this Hibernian lilt in our driver, but he quotes Yeats in his descriptions of some parts of the Ould Sod he thinks we should visit. This itinerary does not include North Ireland, incidentally, for the reason, as he says, that it is "still occupied."

* * *

The Joyceana on exhibit in Sandycove martello, now "James Joyce Tower," is more modest than that of many a Midwest American university, but at least *Ulysses* is on sale here, as it is nowhere else in Dublin. We climb to the small bleak room on a spiral fire escape and in an appropriately spinning wind, and though we freeze in our topcoats, the beaches to the west of the tower are dotted with purple-blue bathers.

In rich and poor neighborhoods alike, residential Dublin is composed of rows of identical brick houses, each with clusters of small chimneys like upside-down sows' teats. The richer homes, among them Yeats's, Wilde *père's*, Sheridan Le Fanu's, all in Merrion Square, are distinguished by elaborate portals with rounded arches, white pilasters, brass knobs and knockers. Fewer and cheaper bricks form the birthplace, on Synge Street, of G. B. Shaw, but at least a plaque identifies the site and describes Shaw as an "author of many plays," whereas nothing marks the no less brick birthplace of James Joyce in the more bourgeois purlieu of Rathmines. On our way there, V. remarks that no other modern city of the size has spawned so many writers, whereupon the driver says that "to be a writer here all you have to do is keep your ears open," and as if to prove the assertion, he is soon giving us a vivid account in steep b'jayses brogue of how Brendan Behan, having had too many noggins, started to brawl with some famous bowsies and how all of them ended up in the pokey.

After hearing this story, I.S. wonders why it is that so many writers have been Dublin born and bred but so few have been buttered here. (Paronomasia is a Dublin disease, and we have caught it too, I think because the speech is musically so contagious. Puns *are* music first, it seems to me, musical accidents and then contraption and adjustment. The words bump together by their similarity of sound, and only then does the punster discover the coincidence with which to connect them in a new context, the success of which depends on how far-fetched it may be.) But the driver is unbudgeably certain that Joyce and the others evacuated the homeland for no other reason than to escape the climate.

❅ ❅ ❅

The illuminated books in Trinity College Library are a Celtic fantasy world of magic birds and beasts, but the Mandala-like mazes of the ornamented borders, and even the script itself, especially the minuscules of the Book of Armagh which look like Cufic because of the flags over the syllables (accents? ligature signs?), are at least as beautiful. But color is the books' first attraction, and the color not only in a green, yellow, or miniated illumination, but of the vellum itself and even of the binding (madder-stained pigskin, commonly, with linen cord and iron hasps). The library's oldest but comparatively drab paleographic treasure is a Ptolemaic stone with a text in hieroglyphs, enchorials, Greek.

The National Museum is equally rich in spoliation of the monasteries, but of another kind; here are jeweled missal cases, crucifixes, croziers, pricket candlesticks, and a thousand other ecclesiastical utilities and adornments. But we have come to see the Bronze Age gold collection in which the lunular and penannular forms are strikingly similar to Nigerian art. The most common objects are torques, gorgets (for wimples), and posy rings with the bezels carved like clasped hands.

We drive afterward to "Howth [Hoath] Castle and Environs," where the seaward slopes are covered with golden gorse, and return through Phoenix Park, Chapelizoid (Chapel-iś-id), and the slum neighborhood of Summer Hill, where one sees a good many Unsmiling Irish Eyes. The tide is out and the swans in the Liffey lie like symbols of soiled virtue in the sulphurous mud.

✳ ✳ ✳

A drive to Athlone and Clonmacnoise, returning by ivy-covered Clonony Castle and Kildare. The road from Dublin is shaded for a way by beeches and elms, and all the way are stone bridges, stone-walled lanes, hems of stone fence enclosing each field and dell. The roadside cottages are always stuck together and repeated in rows, as though by a hall of mirrors, but they are individualized by their flowers, trailing clematis, lilacs, or whitethorn. In the main street of Mullingar, in a traffic of mule carts loaded with pigs, four men accompanied by a fiddle and surrounded by a hand-clapping circle of on-lookers are dancing a reel. South of Athlone we enter the peat bogs, which have been shaved of the scutch grass and are now being prepared for cutting. Huge machines do most of this work, but on the road near Clonmacnoise we overtake a mob of farmers carrying sleans, the old double-edged peat shovel, and they look like a rabble army on the way to the revolution of 1789.

At Clonmacnoise, seven ruined churches and a cemetery of old Celtic crosses sleep on a small hill by a bend in the Shannon. The smaller churches are mere walls slanted corbelwise together, but the one they call "Ui Ceallaigh" (O'Kelly's) has a vaulted roof. The best-preserved building is a crannog tower with a cap like the nose cone of an ICBM. Hand querns and other stone implements of the monasteries lie scattered in the grass, where we wander in the spring-sweet air thinking that Clonmacnoise is one of the haunted places of the earth.

June 23

Milan. A custodian harries us in the Church of St. Ambrose by jangling his keys like the sacristan in *Tosca* and every few steps insinuating the need for a fresh boost in his economy. Ambrose's skeleton lies in a glass catafalque in the crypt, with the skeletons of Saints Protasius and Gervase lying on either side and at a lower elevation, like lieutenants. A miter has been fitted to Ambrose's skull, while those of his escort saints carry gold crowns. The tightly clamped teeth of all three are deeply stained, as though they had been habitual chewers of betel. But the accoutrements—Ambrose's royal purpure, jeweled slippers, branch of silver palm, and the brocaded scapulars of the flanking saints—are a dramatic contrast to the skeletons, and the picture seems more like an allegory, a triptych of medieval kings in an illustration of the temporality of earthly treasures, than a picture of three Christian martyrs. A gold phoenix perches on the catafalque like a vane, ready to crow the Resurrection.

The exhibition of Iranian Art in the Palazzo Reale offers a rich representation of Islamic Luristan, but a disappointing one of the Hittites, except for two gold tablets covered with thorn-shaped script, and a pair of gold *mitènes*, fingerless gloves with a gauze of gold chains fastened across the back of the hand to a gold ring at the hilt of each finger.

❋ ❋ ❋

We go to the Certosa di Pavia in the drowsy afternoon, under soft, foamy summer clouds. Wild poppies and wild sweet peas are growing by fields of bronzed wheat, and the air is scented with lime trees by the Pavia canal, by the perfume of privet (sweet, but mintlike) in the Certosa, and everywhere by new-mown grass.

The cold breath of the church extends twenty feet outside the open door, but apart from this natural air-conditioning I do not like the interior. It is crowded, for one thing (an angel in every archivolt, a portrait squeezed into every squinch); and, for another, the colors of the marble and lumachella, especially in the altar table, a garish, Fabergesque bauble, are overripe. A party of tourists is marauding the silence, too, among them a woman whose persistent "What?" in response to anything the guide says so resembles the bark of a dog that we are tempted to offer her a biscuit.

But the only sounds in the cloister are the buzzing of flies as they pursue their matrimonial activities and a shovel turning gravel, an agreeable, old-fashioned scrape that defines the surrounding peace. (How dependent on such definitions—simplifications and refuges—we are, and like chimpanzees what euphoria our laterally symmetrical bodies feel, for a moment, at least, in the cloister's symmetrically balanced space.) The cloister is defined by a fence of twenty-four Gothic chimneys, each rising from a duplex cell. The cells are equipped with a revolving dumbwaiter for the meal tray, a strapontine table and bed, a garden and well, and a leafy pergola in the community vineyards. From appearances the Certosa would seem to have been a kind of meditators' co-op, rather than a strict Christian order ruled by ascetic disciplines, yet it kept its inmates, all of whom were noblemen, in trim condition for *this* life (in fact, records for longevity were established), whatever it did for them in the next. Why then do *I* shudder at it? Because I doubt my power to summon the positive and favorable images necessary for prolonged solitude? Because, though my life is a chaos of distractions, I do not believe I can resist them by the method of prayer reading, of the Hindu endlessly reciting his *japa?*

❉ ❉ ❉

At the late night rehearsal in La Scala of the Hamburg Staatsoper's *Oedipus Rex* and *The Flood*, the collaboration of German and Italian technical personnel affords a good insight as to how the Axis must have worked. The German stagehands march to their tasks like an army on the Blitzkrieg, and a Panzer army, to boot, for they are equipped with two-way radios and closed-circuit television. In fact, the evening's most efficient and impressive performance is that of the German work crew. This occurs when the director, Herr Dr. Rennert, exasperated with the misfocused lighting, orders the entire *Oedipus* set to be dismantled and rebuilt to the reach of the beams, an operation that takes the "Huns," as I.S. calls them, a mere eighteen minutes, but that would defeat the Italians for a season or two. The Italians are in charge of the lighting, of course, and they do about as well with it as they did with other matters in North Africa. All during the rehearsal a *"maestro direttore"* shouts and begs through his telephone: *"Luigi . . . la luce . . . per piacere, Luigi, pronto la luce . . . si, la luce, ma adesso, adesso . . . la luce . . . L-U-I-G-I,"* and the impatience of the Germans becomes more open each minute, until at last we expect them to seize the apparatus as they once took over the Italian army and Italy itself. And, whereas the Italians merely fawn and crumble before their superiors, the Germans click their heels and respond smartly to Herr Rennert's commands with a *"Jawohl, Herr Doktor."* (I.S.: "People are born '*Herr Doktor*' in Germany; it's an hereditary title, I think, like '*Prinz.*' ") The

Italian stagehands squat on the floor, too, and huddle together like prisoners of war, and with the same bewildered expressions. In fact, the only apparent difference from 1945 is that they are able to desert their German masters and disappear for long *espresso* breaks.

Oedipus Rex is creditably staged, except that Oedipus' gorily gouged eyes at the end would be more appropriate to *The Cabinet of Dr. Caligari;* and that the cardboard effigies —like photographers' dummies—behind which the chorus stands, exposing heads only, make each individual appear as though he were in a mud bath. Musically the only criticism is that the Shepherd is vocally too heavy—"he should be more of a Bo-Peep," says I.S.—and he bleats as though he had been too long removed from his fellow Greeks and had picked up the language of his flock.

Greater credit is due to this first attempt to stage I.S.'s latest problem opus. *The Flood*, in Herr Rennert's view, is a potpourri of I.S.'s characteristic theatrical media. Thus, the element of pure opera is represented by the arias of Lucifer-Satan and God, and the element of pure dance by *The Building of the Ark*. Thus, too, the narration, a Stravinsky dimension as old as the *Soldat* Faust-play; and the pantomime, for which the typology is again found in the *Histoire du soldat* or in *Renard*. Herr Rennert's musical-play approach to *The Flood* is consistent, and his staging is distinguished by sound ideas. God's voice, for example, is broadcast *in* the audience, like a concert of electronic "music," while onstage, at the same time, His words are lowered from Heaven on plaques, like the Tables of the Law. The difficulties with this in such a large theater as La Scala are that the electronic God becomes too portentous for the frame of the music, and that the plaques either do not appear in time or disappear too quickly, before anyone has read them through, apparently for no other reason than to prove that the hand is quicker than the eye. Add to this the fact that the lighting during the bass-drum[2] introductions to God's speeches is invariably late (*"Luigi . . . L-U-I-G-1 . . ."*). Another attractive idea in Herr Rennert's conception is that of keeping Satan on hand and in evidence at all times, and especially during the actual flood. But the Lucifer must move. He must, as the music tells him to, dance and caper as he sings, and not attempt to plant himself as this one does. The failure of the scene can be charged to this paralysis, in fact, as well as to the absence of any transformation in Satan after the Fall beyond a mere switch of masks; the new mask bears an unfortunate resemblance to Papa Katzenjammer, moreover, and the comic touch at this point is disastrous. Then, too, the *Melodrama* must be treated as an inset, separated from the action before and after by lighting. The Satan must do *something* to indicate a change of scene, even if only to step into a telephone booth and say "Eve."

The curtains part in Herr Rennert's production, revealing a solitary bench, stage-right, and behind it a cloakroom rack containing the masks of Satan and the Noah family. The actors, wearing shawls over their street clothes, enter stage-left, followed by the chorus, uncostumed but carrying helmets at their sides like a football team—though even to hint at anything athletic is misleading; in fact, they look like members of Local 27 leaving the factory at rush hour. At stage center they halt and don their helmets, which is the signal for the music to begin. They sing the *Te Deum* in this position, then fan out to stage aprons on either side of the orchestra pit, watching the play from there like spectators, and singing the final *Te Deum* there, after which they exeunt severally in the worst sense. Though this at least solves the problem of dis-

[2] I.S. says that the drummer should use a wooden stick, press the center of the head with the flat of his left hand, and strike close to the taut edge of the vellum.

posing of the chorus, the interruption of the music required to ferry them across the proscenium and into position is fatal.

This tonight-we-improvise beginning suffers from another mortal disadvantage in that it contradicts the music. The *Prelude* must be played without visual associations—*viz.*, before a closed curtain and in darkness—and it is essential that the opening of the curtain be synchronized with the twelve-note harp ladder.[3] So should all four twelve-note ladders accompany a curtain, whether of material or of light. The bassoon version of it, the dissolve from Eden, should be coordinated with a *crescendo* of light from the deepest darkness, though at the high point the stage should remain shadowed, in correspondence with the new, minatory note in God's music, that master stroke which adds a cloud of *ponticello* violins and violas over God's voice while the voice itself is doubled with piano and harp.[4] The third ladder should support a small ray of colored light leading from the blackout to the Devil,[5] and the fourth ladder a very slow closing curtain, which could start as early as the cello-bass chord. In the Hamburg production no visual exploitation or connection is made of any of these musical staircases.

I think, too, that the *Te Deum* cannot be sung as a concert piece for the reason that the music is the least active (and, incidentally, the least new) in the score; or if it is to be a concert piece, then the angels (Local 27 angels, in any case) would

---

[3] Which requires an expressive *ritenuto* not included in the score.

[4] The change of color in God's music at the end of the score, and the restoration of the octave at this point, are equally remarkable touches though the most effective and economical of them all is in the accretion of the few magical celesta, flute, and harp notes during Noah's speech, "The Earth is overflowed with flood."

[5] After the first stage performance in Hamburg, an astute French critic described the work (which he retitled "*The Drouth*") as "anticlerical." In fact, the music associated with the idea of sin, or with those who have made it their business to preserve the idea of sin, is unaccountably nasty compared to the innocent *pater familias* music of Noah; though accountable, all the same, in certain religious ambiguities in the composer.

be better heard and not seen. I should note, too, that in the Hamburg staging the music stops before the return of the *Te Deum,* to give more time for the narration, which is yet another fatal pause, but here the fault is at least partly I.S.'s, for the music *is* perilously short, and because of it the bridge is too slick. (I remember I.S., stopwatch in hand, asking me to "read the narration in a brisk tempo," and his relief, after I had done so, in announcing that he would "only have to compose ten seconds of music.") But is the whole of *The Flood* too short? Not for the film I.S. had in mind, certainly, though he cut the text to a third and the ballets to a half of what originally had been calculated as minimum timings even for television. In the theater, too, the impression of scrappiness (at least) can be overcome by, among other remedies, not pausing between every bit and piece.

The narrator is wrong, too, but narrators always are; they have a way of standing about like "natural" children, reminders of weakness. For the *Catalogue of the Animals,* Herr Rennert's narrator becomes an on-the-spot television reporter. Microphone in hand, and swiveling from Ark to audience, he reels off the arrivals as if he were doing a newscast. The idea is sound, but the person is wrong and distracting as, again, narrators usually are. And this complaint must be repeated more emphatically when the narrator, who in principle is *only* a voice, receives the full burden of attention during his *Genesis* speech, where cinematography alone can lift the fatally non-dramatic strain.

Still, in the Hamburg production the *Comedy* is the gravest failure—or unfunniest failure. The music has been cut, the lines are bawled in dead earnest, a half minute of silence is intruded to get the Noahs aboard, and though the music calls for action, running, slapstick, no one moves. And, once aboard, they stand in their deadpan masks looking as tragic and frozen as ever anybody in *Oedipus Rex.*

Nor are the ballets notable successes. The Ark is built by

male dancers (hammer and nail sex symbolism, of course) dressed and helmeted like space cadets, but the ship they build is an ancient galleon suspiciously like the titular vessel in last week's *Flying Dutchman*. The aqueduct is supplied by female dancers (waterdrop shapes suggesting female sex symbolism, of course), which is a curious reversal of Balanchine's notion as to the identity of the beleaguering and beleaguered sexes. At the first lightning bolt, a pretty solo waterdrop splashes in from the wings, followed in a trice by a cloudburst of equally thirst-inspiring colleagues, who then join in washing around the enchaféd Ark. The *Bild*, at this point, of the eighty animals riding out the storm—super-numeraries in street clothes but wearing papier-mâché animal heads, antlers, trunks, tusks, bills, manes—is a thing of beauty that redeems the whole performance. And the animals are a touching sight as they look back from the Ark, which is as crowded as any refugee boat.

August 30

Rio de Janeiro. The afternoon sun turns the fog to mica, then during an eery twilight moment, the Corcovado Christ looms apocalyptically through the dispelling vapors like the beginning of *La Dolce Vita*.

I have acquired ten new words of Portuguese today, jumping my total to eleven. But progress even on this scale is a questionable asset. For one thing, our driver takes too much heart from it. Supposing us to have been shamming until now, he fires away with such speed that I am at a loss to insert even a punctuational *"sim?"* (yes) or *"espere um instante"* (wait a minute), and as nothing else in my vocabulary will turn him off, I switch in desperation to an equally un-resourceful Spanish (*"caramba"*). Searching for a store in which to buy whisky for I.S., we discover that sign language will eventually reduce even the most garrulous direction-giver to the same means. But when the address is found, after sev-eral tryingly Trappist scenes, we happily rehearse our pro-nunciations of *"não"*—a less nasally feline noise than the one Brazilians make—until at last the clerk holds up a bottle of one of I.S.'s brands (*"sim"*).

In the evening all Rio seems to be holding hands; and more than hands as the dark deepens, when the Copacabana beach becomes the vast public bed of innumerable twining couples. V., surveying this sabulous Agapemone, wonders why the course of love is so fluent here, and attributes it to the effects of climate and topography, "the giant sugar-loaf phalloi, and the continual caress, the sensual sound and scent, the loneliness and timelessness of the sea." But I.S. thinks the human topography is the more actively conducive landscape, the dark and, though blowsy and uncorseted, still lissome Brazilian women (and not only the Copacabana professionals with their thrusting *labia majora*), so different from the slen-der, squint-eyed vixen of our Anglo-Saxon North.

Later at night the city's large mendicant population seeks cubby holes and crevasses, though some, the most feeble and destitute, coil up on the open ground protected only by news-papers or rags. While we are parked for a moment on a hill above the bay, a bundle in the gutter shifts position—an old woman, as we find when the poor crone raises her blanket of sacking as though to ask us why we have disturbed her sleep. But she disturbs mine, too, appearing again and again in the procession of remembered people: the Negro laborers, barebacked and barefooted but with fanciful folded news-paper hats; the Negro belles with percale and dimity dresses and orange-rust hair; the girls in a street-side lace factory

manipulating their bobbins with, for Rio, unwonted dexterity
and speed; the cariocas in stand-up street bars drinking round
after round of coffee (when do they work?); the near-naked
waifs stealing precarious, one-arm rides from the running
boards of the *bondes,* or open trolleys.

August 31

All Rio is rebuilding, which means that the regional and
the characteristic are being replaced by the international; and
the few doomed remnants of colonialism still extant are always found side by threatening side with the newest opus
Niemeyer; thus, little laundry-blueing Santa Luzia, hedged
by a fence of skyscrapers, and thus the old frame houses with
tall shutters, wrought-iron railings, walls of pellagrous paint.
One notes, not necessarily with insinuation, that the Casa de
Saudi, the most graceful structure we have seen, was until
recently an asylum for lunatics.

But colonial church architecture is disappointing. The ele-
gantly simple exteriors are merely decoys for the tropical
tangles inside. In San Bento, for example—which is also sinister because of a pyramid of coffins on the altar—the walls
crawl with *rocaille* and creep with vegetal ornaments; only
leaving it do we discover human figures in the lush carvings,
as one suddenly discovers a hidden face in an Henri Rousseau
jungle. The exceptional church, with the interior as pretty
as the outside promises, is the white octagonal Outeiro da
Gloria, which sits like a coronet on one of the older city's
highest hills.

September 1

The Zoological Gardens are also, though only incidentally, a *jardin des plantes*, the walks shaded by banyans and colored by hibiscus and bougainvillea. V. does not enjoy the visit because of the sight of animals from northern habitats suffering, as she supposes, from the heat. With uncharacteristic compatriotism she talks Russian to an old bruin *"Ve govorite po Russki?"*—though she will not speak German to a seal who looks like Bismarck and seems even unhappier than the bear. I.S., fascinated as always by the anthropoids, wonders "what it would be like to go about on all fours with one's behind in the air, and with a plaque on one's cage identifying one with a Latin binomial and a paragraph of false information like program notes at a concert . . . but I suppose that nowadays the chimpanzees all have kinky sexual attachments with the keepers." Near the exit a flock of flamingoes stand in a pool of pea-green scum, like fixtures for middle-class lawns.

A rehearsal in the Igreja da Candelaria, in which our concert of sacred music is to take place. Though we have been told to come at two o'clock, the doors are not unlocked until two-thirty and none of the musicians arrives before three, at which time it is discovered that the librarian has failed to bring the parts. But more than half of the players never turn up at all, while those who do eventually present themselves allow us only thirty minutes' working time: the union foreman has decreed that no matter how late-starting, the rehearsal must end punctually. Our complaints are received with amiable shrugs and bluff counter-protests that this is no factory, as if anyone could believe in the rule of stop watches in Rio even in factories. But the rehearsal, such as it is, pleases nevertheless, because of the Latin of the chorus. The Brazilian pronunciation, a squall of sibilants, softens all edges (*genite*, for example, becomes *zhenite*) and smooths out all "k" or "ch" sounds with gently hissing cedillas (as in the *pacem* of the Mass).

Returning to the hotel, we visit a *favela*, a hillside Casbah smelling powerfully of *merde*, carrion, cooking-in-oil. We are told that as a political unit it is virtually outside the jurisdiction of the Rio police; the physical density of the place, but also its secret codes, customs, kangaroo courts, are well-nigh impenetrable. The path, thick with pullets, is barricaded at the first turn by a sow and her farrow; but we do not wish to go farther. Later, discussing the experience with Brazilian acquaintances, we are surprised not so much by the absence of a moralizing tone—of the sort affluent North Americans employ in berating *their* slum dwellers for laziness and lack of aspiration—as by a disapproval of V.'s readiness with a *cruzeiro* for every beggar and a lack of sympathy with her remark that "the only possible question is 'Do *I* deserve to have anything to give?'" At the same time, though, neither V. nor I.S. would ever question or protest the social conditions responsible for the *favela* (or perhaps, more fairly, one should say that it would never occur to them to protest); and they are sufficiently detached to regard its Cubistic superimpositions of basketwork huts as "beautiful," whereas I am unable to behold such sights scenically or, indeed, to see the "view" in any picture that contains a prominent display of misery, though this is also an admission that my idea of social structure is material first of all and doubtless much less profound than theirs.

The C—— restaurant. Tall mirrors and high ceilings, old prints, liveried and gaitered waiters, *cachaça* (cane-sugar alcohol) cocktails, coconut *entremets*. To the *maître d'hotel* taking our salad orders I.S. explains that a "paregoric dressing" would be the only safe kind for him, and he goes on to give the full intestinal news of the day. I do not record this unsavory description, but it is typical, nevertheless, and, in its variants, a regular and major part of I.S.'s conversation. During fifteen years his standard matutinal greetings to me have taken a form of inquiry about W.C. behavior, and though I have usually been able to devise acceptably evasive answers myself, I have never escaped detailed descriptions of his own morning fears, allayed (flushed) as they might have been, hours before. It is also characteristic of I.S. that when bowel movements are concerned, total strangers are chosen for the frankest confidences, and if these people are attentive to him on such favorite topics as pyloric spasms, diverticulitis, enema dreams (or log-jam nightmares)—as tonight's *maître d'hotel* is, though he, fortunately, understands very little—I.S. always finds them, as he does this waiter, "*muito simpatico.*" The preferred setting is always the dining room, too, where the mere mention of, say, prunes, will lead to the most alarming intestinal intimacies; all of which and the identification of "pre-napkin" and "prelapsarian," indicates what I suppose would be called a traumatic toilet training.

September 2

Not surprisingly, our concert at the Teatro Municipal begins an hour late, a time passed in a sweltering Green Room under a portrait of Gomes, the composer of *Il Guarany*. The audience is loudly, even vocally, appreciative and the performances are good, my usual failure of nerves when sharing concerts with I.S. (which I explain to myself in terms of a psychological block, as if to do so were a stroke of self-insight or a feat of intellectual honesty) not having "frozen me up" and destroyed my part of the program. A large contingent of admirers including Governor Carlos Lacerda besieges I.S. backstage afterward. Then, at a reception following the concert, a young American doctor fills me with sleep-destroying information about the local forms of filariasis (did Darwin have this?), the "snail vectors" of which are the first subject on the agenda of the current International Congress on Tropical Medicine.

September 3

A drive to Tijuca to visit the family of Machado de Assis. Their home is at the base of a steep mountain which, as we arrive, is being climbed by a safari of black women with head loads like those of African porters. "They live in the 'favel of the ants,' " explains Machado's niece, but whether the name derives from the metaphor of the safaris or from actual entomological activity we never learn. At this point, hearing that I.S. is American, her husband hustles us off to show us the "Order of Merit" awarded him by President Roosevelt in 1944 and a photograph of himself in San Francisco among his country's signatories to the Charter of the United Nations.

The descendants of, as they pronounce it, "Machadasi," seem hardly to have read the founder of their fame, and they are apparently worried by the fact that the spread of his reputation may soon oblige them to do so: one of Machado's books has been published in Russia, they tell us with a mixture of pride and alarm. Their store of literary leftovers is small, Machado's injunction to burn having been less ambiguous than Kafka's, but a few family letters survive. Showing us one of these, in which Machado addresses his fiancée in a clear, clerkly hand, the niece blurts out that her uncle was not "white" and that the family was against him "*parce qu'il avait de couleur*," and this is said with evident concern for our reaction. Some photographs have been preserved, and a chessboard and chess pieces; but only one item is worth the mention: a portrait of a too-sweet, young-but-motherly woman, which picture seems to have held Machado in a state of trance—onanistic trance, I would say, judging by the poem he addressed to her with its fixation on her gloves, and by associating these verses with the similar sentiments of his classic of onanism, *A Woman's Arms*.

After we have seen the relics, a parade of children and grandchildren brings whisky and salvers of sandwiches. I now find myself with an unmarried and obviously too father-devoted daughter of the niece. Lighting a cigarette for her, I notice that she stares at my matchbook—from a Hollywood restaurant—as a Conquistador might have regarded a gold ornament on a savage. Her collection of these folders exceeds three thousand, she tells us, and her satisfaction with this addition is inordinate. (Later, V., analyzing this match-hoarding malady, concludes that it is "the perfect expression of the unmarried woman's vengeance on the men who did not take her, matches symbolizing penises by flaring into flames in the same way and by being similarly consumed.")

September 6

Shortly before midnight we drive to a secret rendezvous in the hills where a Macumba ceremony is to take place. The route to this eyrie is marked at strategic turnings in the road by candles, and at major intersections by piles of poultry

eviscerations as well. The actual entrance is designated by a
whole galaxy of candles and a portable shrine. Here we mount
a flight of about sixty steep stairs and are received by two
women, white-robed like Sisters of Father Divine. They lead
us first to a grotto of holy images—St. Sebastians, St. Georges,
Josephs and Marys, all black-faced—chalking crosses on the
ground in front of us every few feet of the way; and then
to the Hairoo—or heiru?—a rolled-dirt compound roughly
the size of a tennis court, where we sit on a bench near the
center sidelines; and sit not uncomfortably until the exceptionally rich insect life (the stridulations of which are like a
whole percussion orchestra) has found our bearings; V. is
afraid of "fat, velvety caterpillars," she says, but I.S., hearing
the snort of an unseen creature in the woods, hopes only that
"nothing larger than insects decides to fraternize."

One end of the heiru is formed by a candle-decked altar
and a painted backcloth of the moon and stars. At the other end
is the stone circle of the dead, to which everyone gives wide
berth; it encloses a cairnlike pile of stones and a wooden cross
marcelled with white ribbons. Beyond the fenced sides of
the heiru stand two hundred or more spectators, men and
women segregated as are the white-robed celebrants now
gathering inside; V. is led to the women's side, too. Presently
a man in a white suit darkened on the sleeves with mysterious
insignia comes to warn us not to cross our legs or arms—lest
the spell be broken and ourselves disclosed as enemy warlocks.
This is said in solemn earnest, but when I.S. asks him whether
a group of women in white organdy dresses and silver neck-
crosses are "the virgins," he explodes in unmistakably profli-
gate laughter, assuring us, when he catches his breath, that
"*Ça n'existe pas ici.*" But these necklaced women *are* matronly
proportioned, or at any rate far from wraithlike, which fact,
I find, reduces one's faith (never bounteous) in them as spiritual agents. (Are they perhaps the exact opposite of I.S.'s sus-

picions, in fact, the instruments of what anthropologists call "sexual hospitality"?) Most men among the spectators and many women are smoking cigars, and everyone except ourselves is "black."

Tonight's ritual is to be that of *ubanda*, or white magic, but how this has been determined, by the phases of the moon or contemplation of the eviscerations along the road, we never learn. It is for this reason, though, that the celebrants are continually touching the ground: the gesture is intended to signify the burial of black magic. Tonight's principal participant is a kind of black, bearded, and turbaned Billy Graham—though this estimate of his importance is measured only by the time he consumes; it is in no wise suggested by the stingy drum roll which greets him as he walks to the center of the heiru. The tone of his address is partly evangelical, partly heart-to-heart sex talk, and though the matter is incomprehensible to us, the argument, judging by the many repetitions of words, seems to favor the "spiritual" over the "material." It fills an hour, in any case, and survives as many false endings as Beethoven's Fifth, but because of the audience, especially the animal audience, we are never bored. The flocks of doves that have fluttered noisily about the heiru before the sermon are now settled in the surrounding sapodillas like baseball fans in the bleachers, except that they listen with Sunday attention and quiet. When one of them perches on the Billy Graham's head at about the halfway point in his discourse, we are certain that a message has been exchanged and are ready to believe in metempsychosis. Preternatural agencies are also suggested by the perfect timing of a chanticleer's bugle notes at every major pause in the prolix speech, by the transfixed expressions and maudlin nuzzling of a pair of previously ferocious mastiffs, and, above all, by the performance of two geese—I.S.: "One spiritual goose and one material, I suppose." The geese have claxoned

excitedly before the sermon, but now lie silent and rapt before
the Billy Graham's feet. The moment he finishes—with a
sign of the cross touching forehead and heart only—they
waddle a yard or so from him and, as though at his bidding,
consecrate the matrimonial rite, the gander rowing his wings
atop the goose like a *premier danseur* in a ballet about a boat.
One naturally attributes this priapic activity to the Billy
Graham, who watches conspiratorially as a plangent *cri de
coeur* heralds the climax and as prolonged flapping and post-
coital cooing confirm it. "ESP stands for 'Extra-Sexual Per-
ception,'" says I.S., and that is his only comment on this
D. H. Lawrence parody scene, but I know that the picture of
the trees full of mesmerized doves will continue to haunt him
as it will me.

One of the Father Divine girls now takes the place of the
Billy Graham (whose retiring tattoo, incidentally, is no less
niggling). Three men join her, ceremoniously dressing each
other in scarlet mantles and nightcaps, like the tasseled nup-
tial hats of Mohammedan brides in the *nichau* ceremony. They
light cigars—the incense and lustral smoke from which, elsewhere in the heiru, nearly asphyxiates us, though it is a great
tonic for the mosquitos. The men in scarlet then plant candles in the ground at the center of the heiru and the whole
assembly kneels to sing a litany

which clots with passion as it grows louder. A chant, "*Jesus,
Mary*," comes next and is accompanied by clapping, drum-
ming, and intensified earth-touching until at long last the

Father Divine girl rings a large dinner bell. This is a cue to a hag, thickly strung about with beads, to become possessed, though it also sets the now becalmed geese honking loud enough to save Rome. The beaded hag promptly releases a feral yell with a wind-up like whooping-cough, throwing herself to the ground afterward where she pants "ya, ya, ya, ya, ya" and puffs her cigar to a blaze. It is a most unconvincing performance, though, and when colleagues follow, venting eldritch screams and flinging themselves to the ground by her side, we prepare to depart. These seizures occur against the background of a chant that settles on the word "Negro"— *"Nay-gro"*—repeating it monotonously over and over, but as we stumble along the candle path back down the mountain (it is 3 A.M.) another litany has begun, and I go to bed still humming the fading responses:

and

September 7

Brazilian Independence Day. Another midnight drive, this time to a Samba, which is also alleged to be clandestine, though one wonders how a secret is kept by three thousand or more people making all that noise. As at Macumba, we are again the only "whites," but unlike Macumba, tonight's tumult portends "B-Day" (the Black Revolution). To penetrate the crowd, we link hands like mountain climbers, but are therefore unable to hold our noses against the sickening acridity; every sebaceous gland in the steaming room must be hyperactive. And what a room! At one end is a platform with a backdrop representing the black-and-white mosaic waves of the Copacabana sidewalk. Here a band of about twenty musicians is playing both standard and native instruments, though the percussion section, throbbing like a migraine at the core of every piece, is by far the largest; even the brick walls vibrate. Nor do the dances bring relief, for although one naturally expects so much sizzling flesh to ignite into something saturnalian, nothing happens but the weaving and swaying of the Samba line—the memory of the coffle— always the same and always repeated. Then, pulling each other outside again, to the comparative ozone of the street, we stop to ask a direction to Rio, and hear an old man on a curb alternately piping on a penny fife and singing a melancholy *saudade*. It is almost compensation for the Samba.

November 16

Palermo. So many bombed buildings are still unrestored and even uncleared that some areas of the city look as though the war had just ended. In one narrow street near the market, struts and wooden soffits have been erected between the buildings on either side, as though to keep them from caving in. The market itself was heavily damaged, but is thriving now and is the liveliest center on the island; and the most deafening. The drivers of the fiacres which wait in a long queue at the exit, solicit their fares by cracking whips as loud as the revolvers of on-the-town cowboys making Saturday-night whoopee. And the market itself is powerfully vocal. Every booth, table, trundle, costermonger's barrow is in possession of at least one pair of bellow-lungs, and we hold our ears against the rapscallions who cry their produce two feet away from us in great high-to-low arcs of incredible resonance and duration. We enter by the fruit-and-vegetable stalls, by strings of red peppers, pyramids of melons, piles of tomatoes, prickly pears, purple egg plants, persimmons, lemons, grapes, figs, and squash displayed in pendant, testicular pairs. There are towers of tangerines, too, and the tangerine perfume saturates even this stew of odors. Each booth has a Madonna image framed with a tiara of candles, a photo of the proprietor's wedding or of a deceased loved one, and a painted oilcloth backdrop, usually a scene of fruit-picking and loading the mule carts against a background of churches and angels. But the fruit displays are less remarkable than those of the spongelike *funghi*, and of the *finocchi*, and the artichokes, and the purple and green cauliflower, and the loaves of *mortadella*, and the piles of polenta, and the spherical cheeses, and the grains in turned-down bags. Toward the center of the market are butchers' shops, with black ropes of sausages, and poultry plucked and red as though flayed, and hares and lambs still in their skins; and in the center, by the Church of St. Eulalia of the Catalans, are the fish markets, the heaps of sardines, wet and glistening like tinfoil, and the tubs of blue, gold, and bronze glazed-eyed fish, and the pink langoustines, and the black mussels, and the turtle claws and clams and squid and calamari. We watch a fishwife as she flips a mullet on the scales and lets go with a great Santuzza cry of passion which, however, does not accomplish its purpose of distracting the customer, who follows the dip of the beam with distrust and begins to haggle as a matter of course.

We go from the markets to the Oratorio of the Knights of Malta, which is in Baroque buttock-style; and to the Oratorio of San Lorenzo, a wedding-white confection said to be

Serpotta's masterpiece. The I.S.'s come to San Lorenzo to see Caravaggio's *Nativity*, but the sight of a donkey with mountainous bales tied to its sides, and shackled to the curbstone (all Sicily depends on a cruel system of donkey slavery) makes them forget about Caravaggio, and they buy lumps of sugar and fetch a pan of water for the overburdened beast.

No performance is scheduled in Maestro Giacomo Cuticchio's marionette theater today, but we go there anyway, hoping to persuade the puppeteer to give us a private one. He himself comes to the door of the theater (which is in a bomb-made alley in the heart of the old city and which resembles a chicken coop both in size and squalor), but he is only half-dressed and not prepared for a performance. We are invited to come inside, though, and as soon as we have done so he begins to demonstrate how the marionettes work and is in fact soon giving us a show. We sit on the last of four backless benches, while a dark and doe-eyed little girl with large earrings cranks a mechanical piano in a corner by the stage. The area of the latter is a frame of about five feet by four, covered by an oilcloth on which Maestro Giacomo's motto and formula is advertised in large letters:

ARTE   *   MORALE   *   DILETTO

Though the scale is deceiving, the marionettes are from one to two feet tall, I think, rather than, as D. H. Lawrence wrote, two-thirds of human height. They are controlled by wires rather than directly, digitally, a fact that accounts for their jaunty, hip-swinging movements and bowling walk. Before beginning a play, Maestro Giacomo exposes them to us in their backstage cupboards where they are gibbeted on racks like the poultry in the market. All have shining armature, silver in the case of Rinaldo, Tancred, Orlando, and other heroes, but bronze for "Papa Leone" and the several noble ladies whose cuirasses, incidentally, are proportionately bosomy. The traitor knight is in black, of course, and as, reversing David and Goliath, he and all villains are small men (the generous hearts reside in the burliest brutes), a black plume attempts to compensate for a diminutive stature. The Saracens are black, too—their turbans, coats of mail, Stalin mustaches, swarthy skins—but the Spanish knights, who are also dark and also, though to a lesser degree, unsympathetic, are allowed red kirtles and boleros. But these descriptions are unnecessary. Painted likenesses still decorate peasants' carts everywhere in Sicily, and on the way here this very afternoon we have followed a cauliflower wagon covered with scenes from the *Chanson de Roland*.

At first, Maestro Giacomo demurs from the strenuous work of a battle scene, but he gives way at the appearance of some small children (all the girls have pearls in their ears) and favors us with a fierce fracas. The story seems to have confused an episode from the Crusades with one from Charlemagne, and exactly what it is about and who is involved I cannot say; nor is Giacomo's thundering dialect narration any help. We identify St. George only because of the dragon, and Carlo Magna by the combination of a scepter, crown, and red, Frankish beard. The devil, a horned, cloven-hoofed, but very human creature, is armed like the Saracens; he is brought to book at the end, fettered like a felon, then haled away by angels who are armed like the hero knights, though less heavily, as befitting an aerial force. There are four changes of scene, each unrolling a deeper interior stage. The final one is a plain before Jerusalem, or so I think, but whatever the geography, an Armageddon gets underway there beginning with solo combats and ending in a carnage from which the severed parts—the puppets are built in sections like meat cuts on butchers' charts—pile to the height of the stage itself. The clash of arms and shields and the grunts and groans are louder than a Japanese movie, and the stomping, the shouting,

the neighing of the knights' steeds are as *fortissimo,* one imagines, as ever could have been the real thing. When it is over,
the tinny piano stops its death rattle, a light goes on, and
Maestro Giacomo emerges like a conductor from a hidden
orchestra pit, vigorously mopping perspiration and bowing
to our applause. He then begins to piece the sautéed Paladins
together again and to rack them up in their closet.

We dine at the Circolo Unione, which is a kind of Jockey
Club; the meal concludes, but might better have begun with,
a great green *cassata siciliana.* Our hosts are the Barone Ag-
nello, the principal patron of the Palermo orchestra, who is
more renowned for having been kidnaped by brigands a few
years ago and held two months in a mountain fastness; and his
sister, a beauty who might have modeled for a Laurana queen.
As represented in the Circolo, Palermitan society is insular
and separatist; Rome seems to be a distant city to them, and a
trip there appears to be something of an undertaking. Like
Bogotà's, the society is literary-minded; " 'they read much,' "
says V., " 'and go *north* in the winter' "; and the table talk is
in French, albeit not very fluent French. Their brand of
Italian is difficult to follow, in spite of a few helpfully exaggerated pronunciations (the word *"contento,"* for instance,
which rolls out of the Barone as *"cone-taint-toe,"* like a speech
lesson), and their speech seems to me faster than anywhere
on the peninsula. But, in any case, they prefer to converse in
their parody dialect, which, they hasten to explain, is distinct
from the parody dialect of the *"borghese."* Their speaking
voices are musical but weary, and one feels the oppressiveness
in them of the surfeits and depredations of all those successive
cultures as they reel off the catalogue of this or that Greek,
Roman, Carthaginian, Byzantine, Saracen, Norman, Cata-
lonian, Hohenstauffen, or Hapsburg pile of stones; and the
Barone himself positively drones through a word like *quattro-
centesco.* Later I.S. remarks, "They are less lively than

Neapolitans," and he adds that "the flies have all the energy," but his only comment to his hosts is that there are "too many monuments."

November 17

The long corridors of the Villa Igiea, our hotel on the bay beneath Mount Pellegrino, are useful for photographic tricks in movies like *L'Avventura* (parts of which were, in fact, filmed here), but the real talent of the hotel, as background for a ghost or murder story, has yet to be exploited. (There have been some celebrated suicides, though, including that of Raymond Roussel.) It is possible to get permanently lost between the lobby and the bar, and at least momentarily lost in one's own room. But nearly all is forgiven for the view, especially of the first slot of morning sun on the perfectly still and metallic sea, and for the soft morning air broken only by the lonely vascular put-put of a fishing boat.

The Villas Valguarnera and Palagonia, in Bagheria, are dying of deturpation and indifference, endemic Sicilian diseases, and though Valguarnera is a sumptuous ruin still, Palagonia will soon disintegrate altogether unless a rescue squad is formed in a hurry. It is a late-seventeenth-century cousin to Bomarzo, but odder even than Bomarzo because, like the Rodia Towers in Los Angeles, surrounded by ordinary buildings. No wonder Goethe, whose august wholeness left no room for unwholesomeness, was so exasperated by it,[6] and

---

[6] "The cornices slant this way and that so that our sense of hydrostatic balance and the perpendicular, which is primarily what makes us human beings . . . is upset." Later, writing of a monastery, he claims that "a celibate group can create the greatest of works . . . but one old bachelor—witness the case of Palagonia—has rarely produced anything sensible."

how shocked he would be if he knew to what extent it has delighted our own age. One would like to know more about the Prince,[7] its owner, in any case—all those thousands of mirrors, and all that perverse statuary, on the garden walls, of goblins, dwarfs, animals with human heads, hunchbacks, moors, winged fauns, griffins, misshapen classical divinities, obscene goats: an all-hallows-eve, in fact, except for the musical instruments (cymbals, zithers, flutes, guitars, long-necked cellos and basses all faithfully carved in black tufa), which the strange company is playing.

We drive from Bagheria to Cefalù, stopping in a spooky *trattoria* on the way, where we are serenaded by a fiddler whose fanglike teeth make his mouth look like a mousetrap. Near Cefalù we pass a funeral procession in which the coffin comes first, borne on the shoulders of four men, whereas the hearse carries only the flowers. The widow walks alone behind the coffin, and a group of girls in convent uniform follow her, praying aloud. Next comes a team of glistening black horses with black pompoms and black panaches that draw the hearse. Behind the hearse is a gathering of solitary mourners, a curious company because of the fact that it is *cacciatore* season, and many of the men are dressed in buskins and carry guns slung on their backs, while dogs chase at their heels. The road as it passes the next village is lined with people silently awaiting the procession, and all automobile headlamps are lighted as a sign of respect. Bunting and quilts have been draped from the second-floor windows of every house, too, and they are as brightly colored as Joseph's coat.

[7] And Goethe had seen him! One regrets that he was unable to put aside his passion for progress and good works for a moment and give his powers of observation to the service of abnormal psychology. The Prince was obviously a bimetalist with interesting complications.

November 18

The Capuchin catacombs, which we brave this morning, contain eight thousand skeletons; or, rather, if skeletons were what they are we would not be quite so horrified, but in fact, many of them are still quite fleshy and (I suppose because of limestone walls) only slightly decomposed. Some have very long hair, some are an off-putting pistachio color, and some are, for my comfort, far too recently deceased (1929). These corpses hang from the wall in a most macabre way, too, and we can fairly hear the rustle of dried intestines as we walk by. At one moment the lights falter, as no doubt they are made to do for every tourist, and after this we make for the exit in haste. But we are still obliged to pass by "The Children's Corner" and to see a score or more of infants clothed in their burial best, a sight so strongly lacking in appeal that when at last we emerge into the daylight, we are looking very green ourselves.

The *Trionfo della Morte*, in the Palazzo Abatellis, is a kind of fifteenth-century *Guernica*, and one of the most impressive frescoes in the world. Riding a huge half-skeletal horse, Death the Archer, his mouth in an oval rictus as though he were hoarsely screaming, shoots his arrows through every lord of wealth and power in the picture, which is a kind of "death strikes high society," the victims being not peasants, for a change, but princes and popes.

Minutes after leaving this picture we are suddenly confronted by a brutal reality. Only a few feet ahead of us, an old woman starts across a street without looking and she is instantly hit by and crushed beneath a bus. It is a shocking, a sickening sight, the carcass lying under the bus like a crushed animal, in spite of which a crowd is soon pushing and fighting for a look, so that the police are obliged to hack their way through. They cover the old lady with a newspaper winding sheet, but the gutter is her *chapelle ardente.*

Why does this experience shock me more than any of the others with me? I cannot say, but I do know that there is too much cruel and careless and unnecessary death in Sicily, and that the feeling that death is always near is largely brought on by the sight of so much misery and poverty, a sight that is only mocked by beautiful buildings and noble landscapes. In fact, it is not only indecent but impossible to try to entertain "aesthetic emotions" in view of the ragged *ragazzi* of Palermo (at least in my case, and though D. H. Lawrence would call me lily-livered); or, indeed, any kind of emotions except pity and indignation; and to address the misery of these people to such complacencies as "democratic progress," "Christian charity," and the philosophies of "not by bread alone" (as if anyone had the right to say that until everyone at least has "bread") is nothing less than criminal negligence, American as well as Italian, for our own government does not yet see that there can no longer be any "standards of living" to be protected for the reason that there is no longer any place to hide.

November 19

On the way to Segesta and Selinunte this morning the driver regales us with stories of the Mafia, Cosa Nostra, and Salvatore Giuliano. Giuliano was shot not in Castelvetrano, he says, no matter what history may have established, but in Monreale, and he points out the sacred site. We hear from him, too, that when the film of Giuliano's life was shown in Monte

Lepre, its subject's native village, the *contadini* pelted the screen with eggs, the point of view having been insufficiently epic. But going from Monte Lepre to Partinico—from the illegal to the legal social reformer—the driver's arguments are loaded the other way, and he does his best to prick Danilo Dolce's balloon. "Foreigners have been duped," he says, when I tell him about an evening with Dolce at Auden's in New York. "Dolce is only *molto filibustero*, and furthermore he has a dozen illegitimate children and lives with a married woman who has a lot more children of her own; in fact, he seems to want to populate Partinico all by himself." But from what he says next we see that Dolce's real fault has been in offending the Sicilian pride. "He has exposed our poverty abroad with great success, but he hasn't made any of the rich Sicilians aware of it, and there are more millionaire *principi* now than ever."

The only sounds during the steep climb to Segesta are the glitter of distant goats' bells, but as we reach the level of the temple, a flock of surprised swallows scuds noisily away from it. From fifty yards the texture and color are like cork, but at a few feet the surfaces prove to be as deeply pitted and eroded as the barks of very old olive or camphor trees. The colors change inside, too, and in the full sun the columns are iridescent, with lustrous veins of red, gold, and orange. Goethe was not impressed by the temple, incidentally, and he felt the countryside to be brooding in a "melancholy fertility"; and just as he found a natural moral metaphor in the friability of the tufa at Palagonia, so here he discovers more matter for contemplation in the structure of the wild fennel than in the dead temple—but I must not criticize the great man, for I am not elated by ruins myself. The higher hill of the amphitheater is tufted with clouds like pieces of lint, but the view from there exposes the sea.

South of Segesta the trees are turning autumn colors, muted

as yet in the yellowing aspens, but flaming red in the pear orchards. But though every arable ell has been plowed, the land is poor and pock-marked with cacti. In the town called Vita, the "life" seems to refer to chickens and mules, some of the latter plumed like Theda Bara. Santa Ninfa, which sits on a knoll and is an agglomeration of angles like a cubist picture, is livelier.

Whereas at Segesta the skeleton of the temple, though gnawed, still stands, every bone of Selinunte has been violently and as though systematically broken. Discobolus-shaped capitals and huge salami slices of columns are embedded in the earth like flying saucers that have crashed; and one is obsessed here imagining the noise that must have followed the exertions of the sundering Samson.

"Psst, Psst." That is *not* an imagined sound, I think, and on repetition we trace it to a man of unprepossessing aspect partly concealed behind a cracked stylobate. He waves something in his cupped hands for us to see—lubricious photographs, one would imagine from his manner, but it turns out to be a female figurine, which he claims to have excavated today and which he wishes to sell. And his story is very likely true: nowadays the expert tomb robber is employed for his skill, despite the risk to the petty cash; it is difficult for these poor scavengers to find receivers any more, and quite unlikely in any case that they will be able to make off with anything as major as a metope. But the scamp will not give up and he pops out at us from every fallen rock along the path—"Pssst, pssst, *professore*"—later even following our car for a way on a bicycle.

We return to Palermo via Gibellina, where the land is the color and texture of elephant hide; and Alcamo, which is the "heart" of Mafia country, according to the driver, though "arsenal" would probably be a better word.

We call on the Principessa Lampedusa in the evening after

nearly being turned back by the built-in look of disapproval in her concierge, and then after narrowly escaping dismemberment by a cerberus at the *Porte-Cochère*. The Principessa, a big, vehement, coronary type of woman, receives us on the *piano nobile* attired like a Doge, in a coif, mink shoulder-rug, black robe, velvet slippers, richly jeweled hoops on several of the fingers. The daughter of a famous soprano, the Principessa has a round, uvular, bass-clarinet voice, and she vocalizes her vowels so that a word like *"vuole"* comes out in three warbled syllables: *"voo-oh-lay."* She is an impressive linguist, too, speaking Russian with V., as well as French, English, Italian, German, or, as she loftily implies, what one wills. She is more Doge-like still in her salon, plumping herself in a thronelike curule and distributing ourselves to left and right as though at a court. The room, which was Lampedusa's library, is book-lined from floor to ceiling, but, save for one dim lamp, there is no concession in it to the last hundred years; nor does it seem to have been disturbed in as long a time by the vulgar enterprise of dustcloth or mop. On a table in front of the Principessa is a pile of foreign editions of the *Gattopardo*, and on a console to her right is a framed photograph of the author, her late spouse. Conversation is restricted to the world represented by these objects, and on the topic of her husband's novel the Principessa is a formidable monologist. *"Ah, Lampedusa, quel homme. Il avait des sentiments si fin. Comme je suis triste et seul sans lui. Imaginez-vous comme c'était de vivre à côter d'un tel homme."* And with this she launches an account of the writing and publication of *The Leopard* which is as good a story as the novel itself and one, if it were filmed with the Principessa herself as a character, destined for an equally successful cinematographic career.

But the Principessa is autocratic, and with her servants even more than that, in fact despotic. The only interruptions in the *Gattopardo* monologue are her commands to a rheumy-eyed old codger standing slump-shouldered in the doorway in a long-unlaundered white jacket, and to a still more brow-beaten footman who from time to time is ruthlessly told to fetch another cognac, or admonished for failing to pass the *hors d'oeuvres*. But I have overlooked one other and frequent interruption, as one might term the digressions that occur whenever an imperceptive critic has to be disposed of, or anyone else who may have stood in the way of her husband's book, and here one cannot but admire the fast, clean strokes of her ax as "whish" goes the head of Donnafugato, whose criticism is *"tutto falso,"* and "wham" goes Orlando, who was incompetent simply because "he did not know Lampedusa."

November 20

Smoking is permitted in Palermitan audiences, and therefore by intermission of our concert tonight the air is as blue and dense as the club car on the Super Chief. *"Agnus Dei,"* the chorus sings, and "scratch" goes someone lighting up in the tenth row. I.S. remarks that the fault with his *"Vom Himmel Hoch"* variations is in the fact that the chorale melody should be unobtrusive, but that doubled in so many octaves it tends to overbalance the whole, and so far from being the *point d'appui* for the ensemble, it is a clumsy contrast to the light-footed artifices of the variations. But the main difficulty to-night is in the lack of articulation, the unwillingness or inability to play "off the string." Left to themselves, the violists would perform every line not merely *legato*, but also *porta-mento*, for *"tone,"* and the harpist, instead of using a *smorzato* attack, would glue every note together.

November 22

We drive to Agrigento by way of the Castello Diana ("an impregnable fortress," says the driver, though it seems reasonably pregnable to me), where hollowed, tentlike loaves of hay are pitched between the wheat-soil black hills. At Mussomeli the men wear long archiepiscopal purple capes that cover their heads like cowls and flow over the flanks of their mules; though the coastal cities of Sicily may be Italian, the harsh and half-savage interior is another land altogether.

The interior of the Agrigento Cathedral, except for the columns quarried from temples of older religions, might be Mexican. Some workmen are repairing the coffered ceiling, held up to it on a giant wheeled tower like a Leonardo da Vinci siege engine or mangonel, and as we watch, a cataract of wood and plaster crashes around our feet.

The Museum of Archaeology is safer. Judging by the profusion of Demeters with breasts like *brioches*, infertility was a serious problem locally, but the fault, on the Museum's evidence, may have been a corrupt bachelordom: the penises of many of the demons are curled like anchovies on *hors d'oeuvres*. There is a Silenus here that looks exactly like Cyril Connolly.

The temples of Agrigento have not suffered as much violence as those of Selinunte, but the Juno ruin looks as though its roof had been swept off in a tornado, and Concordia has been made to swallow, though it has not digested, a church, "St. Gregory of the Turnips." (The discovery that "Selinunte" means "celery" deflates most tourists' sense of romance, but to me, names like "Our Lady of the Asparagus" are definite gastronomic stimuli.) But personal violence seems to have befallen the statue of "Il Telamone," which lies on the ground fractured into layers, like the *pneu* figure of the *Guide Michelin*.

The country around the Lampedusa town of Palma di Montecchiaro is parched and white, and thereafter the land flattens until the dunes of Gela, where we count twenty German "pillboxes." At the sight of these, the driver recalls how the news of the landing here affected him as a small boy in Palermo: "The Germans would kick us if we came anywhere near them, and they behaved as though *we* had betrayed *them*. The Americans were friendly and generous when they arrived, but the first soldier I saw gave me chewing gum when I asked for *caramella*, and not knowing what it was I swallowed it." (I remember this day myself, or at any rate easily funnel back to the day dead and buried in time; or remember another self, though I cannot enter the other mind —"*je suis un autre*"—wearing a dog tag and on it the number 32748830. "I" am standing in an endless line in the New Orleans Staging Area, as newsboys on bicycles ride by shouting "*Times-Picayune, Times-Picayune:* Landing in Sicily.")

A half hour north of Gela, Etna is in view with a plume of smoke like a *bersagliere*'s feather. And soon more smoke is appearing, though nearer home, and, in fact, as I discover after removing my glasses, from the hood of the car. The driver stops halfway up a hill, steps out, looks, listens, waits, listens and looks, but nothing happens, and on a second and third and more tries the motor does not "turn over." Instead, *we* turn the car around, aim it downhill, push and jump aboard but the bottom of the incline is soon reached without so much as a mild tracheal cough from the engine. Now for the first time we notice the loneliness of the surroundings and the rapidly descending dark. The looking and listening are much more agitated now, and thanks to that we attract the attention of two passing motorcycle policemen. What is the trouble with the car, they ask, and don't we know that it is dangerous to stop in these bandit-infested hills? But, *mirabile dictu,* they have heard a radio announcement of our coming Catania concert, and because of that they requisition the next automobile to carry our driver to a nearby town to find a certain mechanic. Some forty minutes later, during which time a number of other drivers have stopped to investigate our accident (hoping, no doubt, to get a view of some spilled *sanguine*), the said mechanic appears, a short, dark, excitable man in a beret and roomy overalls who begins by looking, listening, pushing, waiting, then finally inclining his ear to the hood as a doctor might do to a man whose heart has stopped beating. The result is a decision to operate—a grave step, calling for much shrugging and arm-waving. The car is actually opened up at long last, and a large and frightening array of tools is flourished, among them a giant monkey wrench that accidentally precipitated anywhere in the now exposed viscera *would* no doubt justify several months in a garage. The beret and upper half of the overalls now disappear into the unhooded nether regions, accompanied by, to some extent, *la polizia*. And a long time later the beret-and-overalls emerge, rather blacker than before, and enter the car, the knobs and gears and clutches of which are then poked, pressed, pulled, pushed, pedaled, though nothing happens, not even a churr. And at last the submerged *polizia* surface also, and they also enter the car, and perform there in the same way and with the same result. A decision is now taken to commission one of the kibitzing bystanders to tow us to the next town, for which eventuality, miracle of miracles, beret-and-overalls has brought a rope. When the towline is "secured," the exchange of "*ciaòs*" and "*grazies*" and "*pregos*" and hand-wavings at the break-up of the party would befit a departure for the moon. A debate ensues as to a system of signaling to be adopted during the trip, as though some monumental engineering feat were, in fact, about to be essayed. Then, off we go; or, rather, off *they* go, for the rope slips loose at the first tug by the other car. Tremendous oaths and accusations now hurtle between beret-and-overalls and the indentured other driver, and a fifteen-minute *pausa* occurs while new knots are tied, this time of Gordian complication and durability. And at last, and strange to tell, there is no mishap. Our new (indentured) driver is delighted to have us, and he proclaims himself *molto contento* with the whole adventure. In fact, he speaks some Inglis, having been captured on the second day of the war and transferred to Cairo and later Palestine, where he married. And, *certo*, those were the times. And what do we think of it all now, of *la Roosia* and the *cinese?* At Caltagirone we rent another car whose driver also speek some Inglesia, having spent the war (ah, those were the times) in Glasgow after managing to be captured in Algeria. "*E molto bello Glazgo, ma fredda, fredda.*" And what do we think of Mussolini? He wasn't so bad, you know? And the Americans, they have all the money, and America is a better country than *la Roosia* anyway, because of *la democrazia*.

We enter the hotel in Catania at ten o'clock and hear the thunderclap "*il presidente Kennedy e morto assassinato!*" and sit, stunned by radios most of the night.

November 23

Siracusa. Every flag is at half-mast and black-bordered pictures of the late President have been pasted on walls all over the city. We wander in museums and churches, climbing a wobbly ladder for a close-up of Caravaggio's *Death of Santa Lucia*, burrowing in "The Ear of Dionysius," a cave with remarkable acoustics in which the tearing of a Kleenex in a certain location sounds like an express train; but we see and hear only "John F. Kennedy," and even a taxi line of empty *carozze* is like a train of hearses. Back in Catania, I.S. composes a cablegram to Mrs. Kennedy, but after dictating the message he instructs me to "send it as a 'night letter.'" V. intervenes, arguing that "at a time of personal and national tragedy you cannot show that you have thought of saving money," but I.S. says it is not parsimony on his part but good sense. "Furthermore, I do not see why I shouldn't always use good sense, especially during national disasters." And I.S. prevails.

November 24

Rome. During our train stop at Naples this morning we learn from a newspaper headline that "*È morte il piccolo maestro Aldous Huxley.*" And so it has happened, and in the time the doctors predicted. Poor Laura. My thoughts are with you, though they will not help; and I am already thinking more of my own loss, for I mourn him, too: his death is the death of part of myself. For five years we met regularly at least once a week. Then, after Maria's death our travels and his remarriage separated us until, recently, Aldous seemed to have become part of an already completed past. But are past feelings also complete in themselves? And if we attempt to interpret or articulate them today can we escape today's pictorial edition of them? Is it possible to revive a memory without memorializing it, or deny that essential part of the form of all valedictions, the need to mourn? And how shall we tell the story of the "he" except within the intruding and irrelevant story of the "me"?

All recent memories of Aldous are vividly clear, in any

case, and the picture most of them help to form is heartbreaking. His last decade of life, from the discovery of Maria's cancer, was never free from the mental cruelty of incurable illness. Hardly had he watched the end of her struggle with it than he entered the same lists himself. It can be put down to "his way" that he did not complain; and ascribed to the desire to "guard his grief" that he kept others from touching his wounds. But he was a very brave man. Alone and blind, he went on working, supporting a host of dependents. He *had* to produce books at the rate of one and sometimes two a year; and he *had* to lecture, even until three months before his death, like *L'uomo dal fiore in bocca*, from cancer of the throat. Nor was mortal disease the only specter. The failure on Broadway of a play, the time and intelligence wasted on film projects, the often belittling reception of books: these were hard blows, more so to a man who was once a very fashionable writer. During McCarthyism, moreover, he was even subjected to an official indignity; and this makes *me* fighting mad. The danger of an Aldous Huxley to American society? Or the honor that such a man has lived in our midst? May a Dantean bootlicking punishment—Aldous's feet were large—await his inquisitor. "Would you, sir, refuse to take arms against an enemy of the United States?" How much more responsible to society (human as well as American) Aldous Huxley was than most of the U. S. citizenry he was never allowed to join because of the pacifist clause.[8]

As Maria's condition declined, Aldous appealed to every agency including hynotism, acupuncture, and the newly discovered psycho-pharmacological "expanders of consciousness." As a last hope he flew with her to Lebanon in search

---

[8] He took the trouble to testify in Sacramento against oppressive legislation, and the motive for one of his expeditions there—to defend against a business lobby a would-be manufacturer of automobiles powered by self-charging batteries—is too characteristically Huxleyan to go unmentioned.

of a miracle worker. But he did not tell us when the disease had entered its final stages, and consequently her death came as a shock. Aldous was an agonizing sight then, so miserable and so alone. I see him at the funeral with tears in his blind eyes (his intaglio head bowed but still a head taller than anyone else); he gropes his way but gives his arm to support Maria's strong and dry-eyed mother, who does not need it. Maria, who shared little of the world of Aldous's creative imagination, who cared little for his beloved music, who could read to him hours at a time without listening: this same Maria was his seeing eye, the only eye of all of his affections, and without her he was as helpless as an unfledged bird. In the lonely weeks after her death, we kept him company as much as he would permit. Painful slips would occur, the solecism of the present tense which shows delayed shock. "As Maria tells me . . . I mean, used to tell me," he would say, and because we tried to avoid her memory in our own remarks, conversation was both ghost-ridden and leadenly self-conscious. We worried about him continually. How could he bear to go on living in that empty, penumbral house? He would allow me, taking him home at night, to accompany him to the door and fit the key in the lock, but he resisted boy-scouting and would refuse my help in, for example, crossing streets—passages which I could only watch, or not watch, in terror. He trusted to his hearing and memory on his walks, but even those faculties were inadequate in Los Angeles traffic. There were accidents in the last years, including one very serious fall.

Now, as I scribble, memories of the early 1950's are beginning to return as well, though helter-skelter. A view of Aldous at the cinema comes first to mind, though why there I am unable to say: with the exception of science documentaries—*The Sex Life of Lobsters* was a favorite—he loathed films. Is it because he seemed so lonely sitting in the front

row? Or because of the comedy of the way he mumbled?—
"inconceivable tripe," "monstrous oafs," "semi minus epsi-
lons," I could hear as he wriggled and moaned. Ordinarily
he watched the screen through his Chinese perforations, but
he would switch to the magnifying glass when a pretty woman
appeared; at a revival of *The Blue Angel* I remember him
staring at Miss Dietrich's charms as intently as Emil Jannings
himself. But Aldous only braved the cinema to accompany
I.S. who, like Wittgenstein, would go to any movie, no matter
how bad, and as frequently as anyone could be found to take
him.

And now a sheaf of pictures returns of Aldous listening to
music, and these are all characteristic, for music was the
delight of his life. But here the "I" intrudes. From 1952,
Aldous attended rehearsals and concerts of pre-classical works
which I conducted: Monteverdi's *Vespers*, the *Sinfoniae
Sacrae* of Schütz, the Couperin *Tenebrae*, Bach cantatas; he
was interested in, but did not love, new music—or indeed,
any music after Beethoven, with the exception of *Falstaff*, as
much as most music before. In 1954 he fell under the spell
of Gesualdo da Venosa, whose score books I was then tran-
scribing: he came to rehearsals of our madrigal group, he
translated the texts for us, and he lectured at some of our
concerts, on madrigal verse and on the musical history of the
north Italian courts in the sixteenth century. I may indicate
the quality of his musical ear by testifying that he was able
to perform the speaker's part—though his voice was too subtle for it—in Schoenberg's *Ode to Napoleon*. We worked on
it for a time with a plan to record it.

Another no less characteristic picture now reappearing is
of Aldous the museum addict, his gracile and elastic-vertebrae
back bent to an object which he studies like a bacteriologist
through a pocket glass held to his left eye. The museum might
be the Huntington Library, in which I see him sloped over a

manuscript of Haydn's "London" Symphony in the hand of Richard Wagner; or the Museum of Modern Art, in which he hated most of the pictures[9] but to which he returned on every visit to New York, to see Monet's Water Lilies; the artist, being almost as blind as Aldous himself, had painted it to Aldous's scale, and here, uniquely, Aldous did not need his pocket glass. (We were ever astonished at the reading, writing, proofreading and manuscript-correcting accomplished with that glass, incidentally; not until the last years did he begin to use dictaphones and tape recorders.)

In another, but random, picture I see Aldous threading his way through the thick of a Hollywood party—at Glenn Ford's, the last one I remember. He would wince from the jazz and the party voices, but fasten like an anthropologist to the film moguls and actors with pink shirts and bare feet, and we could expect a lesson in the mores of these people at our next meeting, with a commentary of groans and comparisons to wilder New Guinea. But Aldous endured these affairs for other reasons, too, some of which, I suspect were the starlets; in finding and physiologically appraising *them*, his eyesight seemed to improve. In any case, he was surrounded at social events by adoring female flocks, in which elderly, non-Indian women in saris mixed with culture-struck nymphets for whom the strange charm of the English language (after the "beat" talk of their boy-friends) seemed to provide the initial attraction, but who must eventually have felt some other awe as well in the presence of this shy but charismatic man.

---

[9] "Why should we take Mondrian seriously?" he said to me one day. "After all, he was a bad academic painter before he did abstractions, and he certainly could not draw." I wanted to ask him if, by the same token, he would dismiss Cézanne, who also, though only by his own admission, could not draw; and to interpose the thought that we judge what a man has done, not what he could not do once; but I never contested with Aldous, either being stricken with verbal paresis or else garbling whatever I did try to say.

I should add that Aldous was anthropologically interested in other types of juvenile delinquents than the luminaries of filmdom. I remember how he described his rescue by a mafia of neighborhood boys from the fire that destroyed his house: "The gang warned me about fifteen minutes before the arrival of the TV camera trucks which, in turn, were half an hour ahead of the fire engines that could have saved the house. After the boys had guided me to safety by the one passable street, I noticed that some familiar faces among them were absent. I said I was concerned about them, but the leader told me not to worry, that they were merely out starting more fires."

❃ ❃ ❃

"*E morte il piccolo maestro Aldous Huxley*," says the Rome newspaper, and even before the long drawl of his body is cold, the reputation industry will have decided just how "*piccolo*" he was; will have attended to the summing up—which is obituarese for hatcheting down, the denigrating epithet being so much easier to find than the epithet for the value quality. How boringly predictable it is, being exactly in accordance with the birth dates of the clerks who practice it. Aldous Huxley, a man gentle and good and a writer better than any who will literarily bury him, dear Aldous will be patted on the head and put away as an "era."

And what of myself, for I too am a clerk with a birthday, and an even unholier obituarist than the others? I know only that the man and his work can never come unjoined for me, and that the joining place is not on the bookshelf but in the heart. And I know that I will never read him again, for I could not bear to hear his voice, though I hear only that voice now, and it is the measure of the void.

1964

January 21

New York. Wystan Auden for dinner. He drinks a jug of Gibsons before, a bottle of champagne during, a bottle (*sic*) of Cherry Heering (did he think it was Chianti?) after dinner, but the qualities for delectation in these fluids are less important than the fact of them as means of conveyance—supersonic jet, one would suppose—to the alcoholic Eden. But in spite of this liquid menu—or because of it, the alcohol acting as an intellectual ichor—he is more lucid and brilliant than ever, and remains so all evening. V. looks for a physiological explanation: "He must have multiple stomachs, like a cow," she says, "so that the gin goes to the omasum while the wine stays in the reticulum and the kerosene is just entering the rumen." I.S., being French-minded in these things, is more impressed by the liver power, "though livers learn, of course, and Wystan's is undoubtedly the most intelligent in town." My own fascination with *Homo bibulus* is in the capacity of its plumbing system: not a trip to the "loo" all evening. There are labial difficulties, to be sure, and the effort to overcome them involves a sort of isometric-exercise screwing up of the face; and there is a tendency to some sonorous singing of bits of *La Petite Messe Solennelle;* but nothing else, no other sign of tipsiness, and after a preliminary lurch or two at departure the locomotion is as well equilibrated as if it were governed by a gyroscope.

I.S. wants to compose a short piece to the memory of President Kennedy, and he asks Auden for a poem, "two long lines and a short, I think, and either six or nine stanzas. I have a low-*tessitura* choral piece in mind, and probably I will use a male chorus, though whether or not with instruments, I cannot say."[1] Auden is delighted to be given carpenters' measurements such as these ("I'm an old hand at this sort of thing"), and he decides then and there "to do a double octet and a quartet. I'll put in a bit of 'Grant Us They Peace,' of course, and I won't forget that 'his name was John.'" I.S., later: "Wystan doesn't care in the least about J.F.K., but he does care about the form, and it is the same with his Christianity: what interests him, what his intellect and his gifts require is the form of Christianity; or, to go a little deeper, the uniform."

As Auden is preparing an essay on Shakespeare's sonnets, we are treated to some of his opinions about the scholars. "Hotson is frightfully learned, but all wrong, of course," and Rowse is "good on the background, but quite dotty on Shakespeare." Dismissing the writings of another distinguished Shakespearean as "belles-lettres," he points out that "It won't do just yet to discover that the top bard belonged to the homintern or that in all probability Beethoven was queer." He mentions a public reading on his agenda, but forbids us to attend. "I never allow anyone I know to come. I want to keep my little tricks to myself, first of all, and second, I am afraid of someone in the back of the hall shouting 'We've heard all that before' or "Get her.'"

---

[1] This suggests the combination of the *Introitus* for T. S. Eliot. As soon as the *Elegy for J.F.K.* was received, March 3, 1963, Stravinsky decided that the words were best suited to a solo voice.

Auden says that the Hammarskjöld Diaries, which he is currently working on,[2] reveal the belief from a remarkably early age in a mission and a tragic end. Mention of Hammarskjöld's death leads to the story of the suicide of the Austrian poet whose house Auden now owns, and he says that this poet was "too late in seeing that Hitler wouldn't do." ("Won't do" is one of Auden's hardest-worked expressions.) Switching to English writers, he remarks of certain elderly ones that "the Lord should hurry and take them now that their time is up." One of those reprieved from this company is Compton Mackenzie, for the reason that "he still has to do his book on the great liars, T. E. Lawrence and so on." Auden thinks that a doctor who conceals from a patient the true gravity of his condition is guilty of great wickedness. "As the Psalm says, 'Lord, make me know the measure of my days'; and, after all, we need time to make peace with our competitive friends!" He tells us that, when called to his father's deathbed, he greeted his parent with, "Well, Dad, you're dying, you know," and he remarks: "Ideally one should die upstairs, like Falstaff, while a party is in progress below with people saying things like 'Now why doesn't the old boy get on with it?' "

When the conversation turns to music, he offers an estimation of "the influence of Max Bruch on Elgar," and then advances the opinion that a certain composer will never realize his talent "because he cannot bear to be long enough alone." Speaking of the opera *A Midsummer Night's Dream*, he suggests that "it is a mistake to conclude each act with people going to sleep"; and of the opera *Rasputin* he remarks that "the idea should have been rejected out of hand. It won't do because the true subject is hidden—a fact the audience is aware of and *quid pro quo*. Now obviously what *Rasputin* is *really* about is a quite prodigious penis."

The talk moves to historians, and we hear that if a certain professor "has missed the whole point of a small event like

---

[2] *Markings*, with a Foreword by W. H. Auden. New York, 1964.

the general strike—as, being a witness, I know he did—how are we to trust him with the Middle Ages or the Russian Revolution? The real reason for the strike, of course, was the desire of the middle-class English boy to drive buses and trains." Another historian's "attack" on Hannah Arendt's *Eichmann* is referred to as "the point of view of the disguised *goy*, of the Jew who has it made," and he says he would have defended the book except that "there is an automatic answer, that '*goys*' like it."

He complains of an obligation to attend a dinner party of a "social-register bluestocking who speaks to me either in words of six syllables or Greek and who is always quoting my poetry." He then claims the ability to recognize every line of verse he has ever written, though he admits he often fails to identify his prose. His favorite German quotations tonight —the Teutonic period is still at high tide—are from Qualtinger, but Rilke he declares to be "the greatest Lesbian poet since Sappho." He has little use for most of the younger Russians. "Yevtushenko," he says, is "the poor man's *Howl*."

September 23

Berlin. Auden for dinner, in great form, though he has suffered some ventral expansion since New York. He gives us of his best "unacknowledged legislator" manner all evening, and reconfirms my belief that he is the world's most delightfully gamboling wit. Though he has come to Berlin ostensibly for a congress of African and European writers, he professes himself "unable to follow nigritude," and he shares none of our enthusiasm for the tribal dances of Dahomey, which we have just seen in the old Berlin Opera House. (Did

nothing of all that beautiful bird mummery—for the dancers
are like grounded birds—move him? Not the way they climb
poles and flap like birds that have lost the magic secret of
flight, or run around like plucked birds, without their tail-
and head-feathers? And not the scene of the big male dancer
whose ruffs vibrate like a cock's, while the females, with hair
like willow trees, hover around him waiting for the cock to
regain his vigor, and while the young males challenge and
threaten to understudy him?) On the topic of today's meeting, the poet's loneliness, he holds that "poets are no lonelier
than anyone else, in spite of all that *einsam* rubbish. Poetry
itself may be 'lonely,' of course, in the sense that few people
read it. But why bother about that? We know that the few
who do read it really care about it, and who could want the
audience of the cinema novel?" His pique seems to stem from
another cause, however, namely the fact that the congress
conducts its meetings in French. "Why should we be compelled to listen hours at a time to Pierre Emmanuel's rhetorical
frog effusions?" he says, and his anti-batrachian sentiments
continue unabated all evening. "I loathe the frog language,"
he confesses at one point. "How much better Rimbaud, Baudelaire, and Proust would have been if they had written in
English. As for Mallarmé, *chic* rubbish is the most appalling
kind."

He describes how last night when he entered the hall for
our concert with his raincoat over his arm, a "Waltraute"
stopped him and said that all coats had to be checked. "I protested—*Krieg* is the one language the Krauts understand—and
told her that keeping one's coat on one's lap cannot be legally
verboten even in Deutschland. At this an *ober*-Waltraute
intervened and, fearing a scuffle, said I could take it with me
but I would have to wear it, which I did. I must say it was a
very hot concert."

He tells us about a film of his life in Austria which the

Austrian government has just completed, saying there is a scene in church—"not terribly appropriate, perhaps; I mean, a naughty bar might have been better, but you *can* hear me singing. And, oh my, how the priest loved being photographed —got all dolled up for it, too. You can also hear me speaking chatty but ungrammatical Kraut—though I do get in some *echt* expressions."

Chatting about poets, he declares his admiration for Robert Frost, "in spite of his mean character; he was jealous of every other and especially younger poet. So was Yeats a jealous old man, and he behaved abominably to younger poets. But Yeats was untruthful, too, which is why I have come more and more to dislike his poetry. Why can't people grow dotty gracefully? Robert Graves is aging well, incidentally, though he has become terribly boastful, implying he's the oldest poet still fucking. Now, obviously it is normal to think of oneself as younger than one is, but it is fatal to want to *be* younger." Switching to the nineteenth century, he condemns Shelley, "an uninviting character," because of his shareholding in cotton mills, but I think he is seeing the poet in the light of Dickens's "Merdle," as he condones the similar investments by Wordsworth in railroad stocks "because, you see, I'm fond of trains." Byron was "no master of language," he tells us, "but a great master of speed," and "if Goethe had been able to understand him in English he wouldn't have liked him at all." With characteristic misogyny he confesses that Goethe's love-life shocks and bores him. "He seems to be going along so smoothly, and then comes one of those awful outbursts of '*mein Liebchen.*'" Of his own work plans he mentions a desire to translate the *Römische Elegien*, but says he has found the task impossible so far. "I also want to do a poem showing that photography isn't an art," he says, and he quickly adds: "Any claim for the cinema as an art is rubbish." He says, "A medieval anthem is in the works, too; the latter-half-a-mirror-of-the-first-half, and that sort of thing. I promised it to Willie Walton at a party when I was in my cups."

Is he in his cups now? (Before dinner he chews out a waiter for bringing him a glass of water—"I haven't had any of that for thirty years and I don't propose to start now"—but when Stephen Spender joins us later and I.S. asks him what *he* would like to drink, Auden whispers to me, "Cocoa, I should think.") There is no fuzziness, in any case (though I.S. complains that pronunciation becomes less distinct and that "Wystan's dentals don't have enough bite"), and in fact the only way of telling is that with the ebb and flow of *alcools*, as the "frogs" call them, conversation becomes less and less of a systole-diastole exchange and more and more of a one-way street. His memory continues to serve him amazingly well, and he spouts quotations as though struck by the hoof of Pegasus. As he talks, his right hand seems to be stirring an unseen pancake batter, and while rummaging for a date or name, the facial integument (burin-burned lines crossed as in twill weaving, and a wiggly wen) contracts; but these are the only outward signs of the throes of thought.

Talking about Wagner, he says that we must admit that "Mrs. Hunding didn't keep a very proper hearth for the old dear. . . . Incidentally, quite the worst example of stage timing I have ever seen occurred the other day in a performance of *Siegfried;* the anvil broke in half just as the gentleman was raising the sword to strike it." And talking about the U.S.A., he compares the reception of "the Beatles" there with that of Oscar Wilde. On the subject of the forthcoming American election, he thinks we should remember that "it is better to be ruled by a crook than a fool." As he plans to visit East Berlin tomorrow, I describe the lawn-mower-shaped reflector— like the mirror dentists use when working on the upper teeth —which the border police wheel under every car. At this

point Stephen Spender suggests that the Iron Curtain countries are becoming "genteel prisons," to which Auden replies:
"All one can say about a genteel prison is that it would appear
to be better than a non-genteel one." I.S. remarks later that
"One always finds Auden and Spender together like 'the beautiful' and 'the good' in Plato."

Fresh abuse of "the frogs" is mixed with the standard
words of departure. "Their famous *clarté* is thicker than the
worst Wiener treacle," he says, and he foresees tomorrow's
conference as "a day among the Laestrygones. Well, my
dear, the French are hardly white." Finally, he threatens to
bolt "if anybody brings up the subject of literary criticism.
After all, we were put on earth to *make* things."

1965

May 12

Paris. A visit to Giacometti. He is thinner than last year, but otherwise looks the same, or in other words like an unmade bed. Rumpled clothes and disheveling apart, his skin is as cariaceous as old luggage, his hair has never been violated by a comb, his tartared teeth alternate yellow, black, and absentees like an old harpsichord keyboard, and his long fingernails are permanently darkened with what must be paleozoic dirt. In the street where he comes to greet us, however, his appearance is less extraordinary, and he even seems to blend with the *quartier*, like any of the *blousiers* who pass by carrying bread under their arms and talking about (or so I imagine) food.

His studio is no tidier, but the clutter gives the impression of spareness, like the art itself. We enter through an alley, a wall of which has been fitted with Assyrian and other intarsia low-reliefs. The room is small but has a high skylight. In it, one is aware first of the graffiti, the paintings and sketches and scribbles on the walls, which are like those of a cave or catacomb. Next one notices the sculptured figures, a hundred or more of them, some as small as lead soldiers, some larger than life. Some of them seem to walk about the room, as though in another dimension, but most of them are gathered in a corner where, because of their thin and dark or gray trunks, they look like part of a forest after a fire. Two sculptures, bust-shaped, are wrapped in canvas and tied with rope, and from time to time Giacometti sprinkles them from a watering can as if he were tending some very delicate flowers.

We sit on a cot, after clearing it of papers, books, bottles, sketches, canvases, palettes. (It is odd that the palettes contain many blobs of bright colors, whereas the paintings themselves are all dark gray.) The only other furniture is a battered stove, a ditto table, and a small tree which grows up green through the dirty floor like a medieval miracle. All of the paintings are in need of dusting, and, characteristically, the faces of all of them are turned to the wall. Showing them to us, needless to say reluctantly, he supplies a running commentary on the degree of failure in each one: "*Je n'ai pas réussi . . . je dois travailler . . . c'est mauvais, ça . . . toujours la même chose, chaque fois la même.*" And he almost succeeds in convincing us of the latter; the portraits of seated people and the sculptures of walking men do seem to suffer from uniformity. But the shrug of failure in his every phrase is arrested for a moment when we examine a portfolio of his pencil portraits of Matisse done in 1954; he almost owns that one or two of them might actually be good. "Matisse was a difficult subject," he says. "He hated to pose and he never gave me more than two minutes for a drawing. He would tell me as I worked that nobody knew how to draw any more: '*I* can't draw, Giacometti, and certainly *you* can't,' he would say, and of course he was right. He also said that he knew he was dying but that he needed twenty more years in which to complete his work." A dozen times during the conversation about Matisse, Giacometti interrupts himself to remark "*C'est curieux, ça*" about something which is not curious in the least. Just before we leave he pours us a drink from a bottle which in spite of a label reading "whisky" tastes to me like turpentine.

May 14

Henri Michaux for lunch, and a treat of two hours of his marvelous intelligence. His eyes are so striking—a little high on the brow, a little close together, a little exophthalmic, a little oriental (like two jewels in a Chinese statue)—that one hardly remembers the other features, and, in fact, as I.S. says, it seems that *"il n'y a que des yeux dans ce visage."* But I also remember the light-red and dandelion-fluffy brows, probably because the cranium is so entirely moulted; and I remember something rodent-like in the forehead and mouth. Yes! That's it! Michaux is a polymath mouse dropped in from *Alice*, a mouse that sits on its hind legs clasping the table with long, white, and very clean paws, and a mouse with an intellect superior to ours by species as well as experience. Then every once in a while this Lewis Carroll character emits an extraordinary laugh (also incidentally offering a dental survey of gold nuggets in the lower jaw), the most serious, in fact the most *thoughtful* laugh I have ever heard.

His gray flannels and blue sports jacket seem to express the wish for a life that his shyness and claustrophobia ("I look at my watch all the time in airplanes and wonder when my head is going to explode") will not allow him to lead. But he displays a very different and not at all shy character while unfolding an idea, as though he were taking the machinery off of automatic controls. This occurs for the first time when someone mentions mescaline; at once his phrasemaking is more prolific. One of the wonders of mescaline is that "while the thing outside you, the thing you have made, becomes greater, you yourself grow more detached from it; and as the lines in

your drawing begin to seem important to you, you forget
about your own importance, which makes you feel *royale-
ment bien.*" I.S. is caught up by this point, but he does not
like the idea of detachment and he has no wish to leave himself outside or behind. When he has said so, Michaux gra-
ciously supplies him with an argument for abstinence, which
is that, "After all, life contains difficulties enough without
adding new ones. That was Balzac's stand, and it may be preferred to Baudelaire's who, I suspect, rehearsed his drug-
taking for literary exploitation." I.S. interrupts to question the
meaning of "understanding" during mescaline intoxication,
and he says that he prefers thinking to understanding, "for to
think is active and continuous, like composing, and to understand is to bring to an end."

Talking about a type of "enjoyable literary boredom,"
Michaux remarks that "the ennui of Proust's letters is master-
fully composed"; but his only other literary comments are
concerned with Lou Andreas-Salomé who "could wiggle her
shoulder in a way to imply that Nietzsche" (which he cannot pronounce and which comes out to rhyme with "pizza")
"was hiding somewhere within. She used geniuses like make-
up, showing off Rilke as if he were a new kind of lipstick,
and wearing Freud like a face powder. She was a flaming red-
head, and when I first saw her she was stoking a blaze in her
fireplace that exactly matched the color of her hair. She began
to talk about Rilke, I remember, and after half an hour or
so it suddenly occurred to her to inquire about my own profession. I will never forget the shattering look of disbelief
she showed me when I said I was a poet. But what a temperament that woman had! *Une femme ravagée, mais ardente,
ardente!*" And as he goes on to make a point about her Russian accent in French, I wonder if his hypersensitivity to
accents in general can have any connection with the fact that
he is Belgian himself; in any case, he does not gargle his "r's"
quite as the Parisians do.

His greatest enthusiasm is aroused by a conversation about Tibet, and a recent trip of his to Katmandu. "How primitive and empty the Russians and Americans are in comparison to these people, but then, by the side of the *montaignards* the Hindus themselves seem hysterical. What a *maîtrise* of psychology and philosophy they have attained, and not only in their tantras, but in their lives. You feel with them that they are waiting for us to grow up to their height."

As Michaux leaves, Giacometti, come to draw I.S., compliments him on his newest paintings. They are the work of an amateur, Michaux says, and Giacometti does not dispute the word. But then Giacometti confesses that he can see no difference between the paintings done under the influence of mescaline and the others, and this earns him the silent study of those terribly penetrating and intelligent oriental jewels.

Coming so immediately after the neatness and certainty of Michaux, Giacometti is almost too strong a contrast. He seems to be obsessed with his failure, or the idea of his failure, and I suspect that this has become the necessary goad for each new work. Most of his conversation is reduced to a patter of nervous questionings, too: *"Eh?"* *"N'est-ce-pas?"* *"Non?"* *"Vous croyez?"* *"Ce n'est pas vrai?"* And all the while his nicotinized fingers tap restlessly on the tablecloth and his light-brown eyes search from face to face. *"J'ai beaucoup travaillé mais la sculpture est là, et je reste toujours là,"* he says, tracing two "categories" on a napkin to show how he cannot bring them together. Preparing to draw, he peels his jacket, rolls up his sleeves, and with the blade of a small pocket knife whittles a half-dozen hard lead pencils to fine points; his belt has missed five out of eight loops, and his underpants cling to the back of his soiled blue shirt several inches above the belt line. He wishes to practice on me before trying I.S., he says, explaining that he must find the right distance—to which, indeed, he is as sensitive as some pianists are to the height of a piano stool. He works very close to me, in fact, but shifts positions twice. When I ask whether he would like more light, he answers, "That would be different but not easier or better," and anyway, "*La lumière n'a pas d'importance.*" He takes a sheet of slightly rough paper, adjusts his horn-rims, folds the right leg over the left, and begins to study my face. "*Je suis complètement incapable,*" he says, and "*je suis maintenant à zéro . . . je dois recommencer . . . je me trouve toujours avant le même difficulté et je ne peux rien faire. . . .*" Then, finally deciding to take the plunge, he begins to draw, looking rapidly back and forth from my face to his paper about three dozen times. He talks the whole while in dialogue with me, like a loquacious dentist to a gagged patient, for if I talk or budge he will throw the drawing away. He works with great speed and makes only a few erasures, but as soon as he finishes, exclamations of failure pour out in a torrent: "*Mais c'est mauvais, ça . . . j'ai mal fait. . . .*" When not actually drawing he chain-smokes (Camels), the ashes falling where they may, and his cigarette cough could be studied by even the most accomplished Mimìs and Violettas for extra realistic effect. After two drawings of me he starts on I.S., who steers him to the subject of Picasso. Though Giacometti will not answer the question whether or not he "likes" Picasso, he repeats that "*Il m'étonne, il m'étonne . . . comme un monstre . . . et je crois qu'il connait aussi bien que nous qu'il est monstre,*" and two very beautiful drawings are achieved during this one-way conversation.

May 17

Vevey. I.S. directs a supposed "search" for the house in Clarens in which *Le Sacre du printemps* was composed, though Les Tilleuls, as the residence is called, was already tracked down yesterday in a rehearsal excursion, and is, in any case, well-known locally; but the point today is that I.S. must lead CBS Television there "on camera." The experience yesterday was deeply affecting to him, I think, and judging by the way his usually amazing memory became fuddled, so that he directed the driver to turn this way and that like blindman's buff, and with no sense of distance or location, or even the realization that we had not even left Vevey. Today, however, he is unexcited entering his old home, and apparently unafraid of whatever peeps into the past the visit might hold in store. (But has he entirely forgotten that he had pointed out the house to me on a drive from Geneva to Fribourg in 1951?)

In spite of the plural name, only one linden shades the entrance, which is number 51 rue Gambetta at the intersection of the avenue des Châtelards. Entering the building, I.S. climbs one floor too high, but CBS men direct him back to the *premier étage* where thanks to their field work he is admitted to his old apartment after a single buzz of the bell. Inside, he goes from room to room looking for his quondam studio, but soon disappointedly announces that it is not and was not here, and that he thinks this is the wrong apartment. At this point the CBS men spring their *coup*, a red-nosed and frumpish little lady, Madame Louise Rambert, who actually lived in the building at the same time as I.S. and who has never since changed her address. Madame Rambert fusses her way in and is momentarily confounded by the cameras, powerful lights, and sound equipment of the CBS crew, who are standing by for a Stanley/Livingstone scene, and who, in full gear, *do* look something like a nightmare of a Martian invasion. The old lady's voice chokes when she sees I.S., and she seems about to burst into tears, but the explosion takes the form of an uncontrolled volubility instead, a cascade from which there is no immediate prospect of shelter. But I can see that I.S., who is usually contemptuous of anyone who allows past attachments to interfere with the present, is deeply interested in the old lady's memories, no matter how little emotion he himself betrays.

They sit in an alcove with a view of Lac Leman, while the old lady recalls the Stravinsky family of 1911, how Madame Stravinsky did her hair in a bun, how the Stravinsky children were sickly, how I.S. would spend all day in his studio, which she says was on the *rez de chaussée*, though I.S. maintains that it was on the same floor as the apartment. In her role of historian of the house, Madame Rambert describes I.S.'s fellow tenants, a German ex-admiral, an Austrian countess, and others who, as soon as they are mentioned, I.S. remembers as well, sometimes adding a detail or two of his own. (Madame Rambert clearly wishes us to know that the address had *cachet* once, with aristocratic and artistic tenants, this by way of apology for its present lodgers, a family of migratory workers from Spain.) "The other pensioners used to complain that 'Monsieur Stravinsky plays only wrong notes,'" she says, and at this I.S., unamused and returning in a heat to the charge of 1911, replies, "They were the wrong notes for them but the right ones for me." She points down the hill to La Pervenche, another of I.S.'s residences, and beyond that and below the railroad tracks, to the site of yet another of his homes, the former Hôtel du Châtelard. I.S. recalls how the train used to interrupt his work on *Le Sacre*, and how he used to wait for it with baited nerves as he now waits for trains to tear through his summer rehearsals at Ravinia. (Here, doubtless, CBS will insert a New York Central whistle.)

Madame Rambert then leads a disbelieving I.S. downstairs to what she assures him was his studio. This time recognition is immediate and I.S.'s face floods with pleasure, for no matter how upsetting to be reminded of long-dead families and friends, to recall the creation of a masterpiece is evidently something else. He goes to a couch in the amazingly tiny and constricting room and, sitting there exactly as he said he used to do fifty-four years ago, tells us he was fully aware that he was "writing something important" and that he inscribed a sentence to the effect that *Le Sacre* was composed here on the inside door of the closet—nicked it out with a knife, like a declaration of love on a tree, he has said on other occasions, when, too, the verb has been active ("I am composing"). He looks for this autograph, but the incumbent of the apartment, a Madame Carrel, tells us that the door was relined a decade ago and that she knows of no one who could now say whether the palimpsest had been discovered on the former surface.

(And it seems wondrous that *Le Sacre* could have been born here, that such power—I see I.S. at the piano with his hands full of volts—could have been unleashed and contained in this dingy cubbyhole, which probably resembled his childhood bedchamber in St. Petersburg and in any case is exactly the sort of, to me, claustrophobia-inducing room I.S. loves, and not only loves but compulsively needs, to crowd still further with objects and artifices of order. But the wonder is not only in the size of the room, but also in the neighborhood, and in the company of, or, at least, rubbing elbows with, these townsmen—though saying that, one immediately tries to imagine the pensioners of fifty-five years ago, the admiral, the countess, Madame Rambert herself, and, down the street, Ravel and his Basque-speaking mother. How did he, or the powers that mediate, manage to keep the fuse to his taproot so directly and perfectly open here? But then, one must remember that part of Schoenberg's *Moses* was composed at Territet, hardly more than a few blocks away, and that not so many kilometers to the east that most un-Swiss flood of passion, *Tristan und Isolde*, was brought forth.)

When I.S. leaves, the old lady, now in a high state of emotion, gives him an ink-press cliché of Les Tilleuls—and she starts to weep; the moment has come and gone, the witness has been recognized, the content of waiting has been emptied. But for I.S. the confrontations of the morning have run a more complex course. He has had to watch a commerce in curiosity (TV) trying to rub his nose in former power and former emotion, in the hope that he would be able to say what they are like, though, of course, he cannot say but can only repeat conditioned answers a little differently, changing a bead here and there in the mosaic of semi-fictions out of which true history is composed. And ultimately, ghosts or souvenirs, or even the opening of tombs, are probably not so terrible for him as the realization that his *magnum opus* was composed here, and that the yield of fifty-five years has contained nothing to equal it. This, at any rate, is the weight of opinion behind the promiscuous lens that has been prying down on him all morning like a Last Judgment, claiming *Le Sacre* of all his life work.

May 23

Paris to Warsaw in a Caravelle, which we board through the rear door like stuffing going into a turkey. Three hours later, Poland is a glimpse of lettuce-colored fields, thin strips of land newly broken by spring plows, a highway with no traffic, which must have looked the same forty years ago. The closer the view, the more skeptical we are of the blowsy air stewardess's promise that Warsaw is "a gay city"—though it could easily be that with her along. (Did she notice an effect on us of the spectacle of returning Polish fellow passengers, every face an advertisement of how grim life in Poland must be?)

The Warsaw porters seem to find me worthy of sustained curiosity, but this is regrettably not the case with the pretty girl from the PAGART agency sent to nursemaid me through customs and currency control. A veritable Berlin Wall of indifference and *sangfroid*, she selects one or two of my questions to answer, but shoves the others aside as though they had not even been asked. The view en route to the city consists mainly of empty or rubble-filled lots, with a few brick and tile-roof prewar buildings and many barrack-style postwar ones. The Warsaw skyline is dominated by the tower of the Palace of Science and Culture, which so resembles one of the towers of Moscow University that we are misled to expect a city with Russian-style architectural features.

The Europejsky Hotel—the name seems to suggest that Europe is somewhere else—is modern with respect to date, as well as in the intention of some of its conveniences, but it is so bleak and institutional that one expects to hear the clank of a lock or chain after crossing the threshold. While Miss Permafrost enrolls me at Reception (and probably with SMERSH as well), I wait in a restaurant as large as a city block in Peoria and as square. Some potted palmettos have been placed at lonely intervals around the room, but they conjure no atmospheric benefits of southern seas and seem to serve no decorative purpose. (Are they perhaps bugged?) The menu *is* exotic, though, but linguistically, rather than in the actual content of the culinary delights, of which "gravy soup" is one. None of the waiters speaks more than a word or two of any foreign language, a surprising fact, at first, in view of the wartime diaspora, but as the hotel room staff is also, and crampingly, monolingual, the reason must be attributed to policy. The foreigner may order by reading descriptions in any of four languages and pointing to the Polish equivalents. Aside from the natural defect of this system, which is in the lack of allowance for variable detail ("Can you bring mine without the sauce?") a more basic difficulty

is soon encountered in that most of the dishes described do
not exist. No fruit of any kind is to be had, not only no Viet
Cong pineapple or Cuban cantaloupe (lots of Cuban crystal
sugar, though, or is it ground glass?), but even no Polish
cherries or grapes. Every dish is priced by weight, like caviar
in Western restaurants; thus so and so many *zlotis* will buy
38.08 *ogs* (grams) of beans, or 15.29 *ogs* of jello. Miss P.
recommends ham, and indeed it proves to be so good that I
will probably continue on a Gadarene diet for the duration.
The wine, a Bulgarian off-white with the consistency of
mineral oil, is served with a towel tied around the neck of the
bottle like a flapper's scarf in the twenties. The dessert is a
plate of almonds buried in a dune of hot salt.

The I.S.'s suite, which is being readied for their arrival
Tuesday, and through which I accompany Miss P. on a tour
of inspection, must be at other times a meeting room of the
Presidium. The only furnishings in the cavernous main room
are a round table with six straight-back chairs, and a painting
of a naval disaster. When I reckon aloud that the ceiling might
be forty feet high, Miss P. gives precise information. "The
entire apartment is above a hundred square meters," she says
in a special tone of achievement, and as if all that empty
space were useful to us and we intended to spend our spare
time flying toy aeroplanes. But in fact, rentals *are* determined
by spatial volume, just as foods are priced by weight. "This
is because of the inspectors," Miss P. adds, but she does not
explain who these mysterious people are or otherwise develop
this promisingly Gogolian—or is it Scotland Yard?—theme.

But I must stop saying "Miss P."; she has a beautiful name,
Jolanta (pronounced as a "Y," the other way around from
the Spenserian "His sports were faire, his ioyance innocent"),
and she is herself by very evident and potent attractions deserving of better, in fact full-scale, attention. First of all, her
manners are pre-proletarian and lady-like, which sets her

apart. Then, she is tall, has a very white complexion, and strawberry-blonde hair—when at last she removes an absurd hat squatting on her head like an Andean Indian woman's bowler. Her fingers are nervous and bitten like a pianist's, and in fact they seem to be practicing piano exercises wherever they alight. Her luminous brown eyes are afflicted with a slight strabismus of which she is overly conscious, always trying to find an angle to conceal it when she talks, which twisting and curling enhances her feline attractiveness. I suspect a deep romantic temperament lies beneath the capping of *froideur* she is showing me, and I am certain that the de-brainwashing necessary to prove it could develop into an agreeable assignment, but I am bothered by one small incongruity, which is her quickness and openness to express dislike of many things Russian. Is this to draw me out, a part of the East-West game? Probably, but no great matter; if she is a stooge, she is certainly a pretty one; if only she would lose that damned New Year's-party hat.

My room is a different matter. It might have been chosen by a status-conscious capitalist, and the mascot-sized spatial measurements could best be expressed in *ogs*. After sqeezing inside, one sees that to stay flat in bed would be an impossibility, though a heavy comforter has been folded over the middle of the mattress to disguise the fact. There are lights, one on the ceiling with a hum at "E" above "middle C" almost loud enough to cushion the explosions of the passing tram cars; and a reading lamp of the strength of one aged lightning bug, not near the bed but connected to it with a strangling length of wire, if it should come to that.

Walking on the Nowy Swiat in the late afternoon I enter the Church of the Order of the Visitation, attracted by the Venetian façade (at a glance, Warsaw by its church architecture is an Italianate city even now). It is crowded, even overcrowded, and I discover the same situation in two other

churches, full and fervent houses with a large sprinkling of
young men in cassocks and calottes. But the strength of the
Church is underestimated in the West, and one forgets that
even the radical agrarian reform program of the National
Liberation Committee of 1944 did not apply to estates owned
by the Church. The clerical habit is more common in the
streets here than in any European city except Rome. Compared with Russia, the political parent, sidewalk traffic is
much less drab and much more bountiful in good-looking
women, but there is a type of trench-coated, beret-wearing,
portmanteau-carrying pedestrian which is almost the same
here as in Moscow. In the window of a bookstore, also on
the Nowy Swiat, is a display of photographs of death and
devastation, the result of U.S. air raids in North Vietnam, but
they are mild and inconspicuous—after the thousands of
protestations to the same purpose currently decorating the
walls of Paris—and they may be less damaging to the United
States than some of its own propaganda pictures of the happy
apple-pie-eating spouses and baseball-playing infants of the
latest cosmonauts.

Two young Americans, scholarship exchange students
studying Polish cinematography, take me to dinner in the
Club for Film Artists and Writers, a pre-war building, I think,
though it is nearly impossible to distinguish the restored from
the genuinely old. In any case, and far more important, is the
fact that there are a dozen or so remarkably handsome women
present, and not only the film stars, but the waitresses with
auburn hair, very white skins, high bosoms, the dark eyes
of Maria Walewska. The American students confirm the report of the French air-hostess: Warsaw *is* a gay city, and
the "loosest" in Europe. (The question, then, is how does
one get at *it*, or at *them*?)

May 24

Jolanta, this morning, is unable to conceal her exasperation because of my unchaperoned sortie to the Film Club, and she goes so far as to request particulars of other places visited and of people met. I ask if she is required to fill out a report, but with that she changes her approach, and back we go to the superior nursemaid of yesterday. It is clear that we must act out the charade now, she as Ninotchka, and myself as the American, and the rule of the game will be that the more serious she, the more will I have to laugh. But the plot is also resembling the *Ninotchka* play, which is to say that I am beginning to flirt with her, and that this could easily become involuntary.

Arriving at the rehearsal in the Concert Hall on Henryka Sienkiewicza Street, I am shown to a dressing-room furnished with a portrait of Artur Rubinstein's father-in-law (Emil Mlynarski, who founded the Warsaw Philharmonic), and a clock with a heavily premonitory tick and a minute hand that jerks like a taxi meter. The conductor Witold Rowicki presents me to the orchestra, then delivers me over to the "Inspector," a panjandrum who announces the order of the pieces to be rehearsed and calls the intermissions during which we drink tea, Russian style, from a glass. I address the musicians in English which the concertmaster translates, prefacing each of my remarks, before relaying it, with the word "colleagues." Once a question is voiced in German, and when I attempt to answer it in that language, a commotion results, not, as I suppose, of protestation but, on the contrary, to beg me to continue in German, as more than half of the orchestra understands it whereas no one knows more than a word or two of English or French; and from then on we communicate in the language of the wartime master, a fact that few of them seem to feel as an ugly irony. The players are willing, good-humored, patient, slow, but I myself am slow to adjust to their radically different time-scale, which is simply that they are not going anywhere and have lots of it and that I have a date in Paris next week and am therefore in a hurry. They play with energy and passion, but the quality of their instruments is poor, the mode of attack is not well or uniformly defined, and there is no discipline of intonation. (I.S. has often said that hardly any attention was paid to the accuracy of orchestral intonation in the Russia of his youth, and that at that time concern about it was negligible even in Western Europe.) But how callous and pointless these criticisms sound. In view of what took place here, it is a wonder that an orchestra exists at all, and a miracle that there could be such a good one.

In spite of a light rain I walk with Jolanta in Lazienki Park (which is still surrounded by the kind of wrought-iron fences that were melted into the war effort everywhere else; were the Germans never short of scrap metal?). The park preserves a semi-wild beauty contradicted only by red squirrels very professional at begging nuts. But the romantic trappings, the tall larches, poplars, beeches, firs, the lake of swans, the ghostly palace swaddled in mist, have no effect on Ninotchka, whose only emotion, so far as I can see, is patriotism, the colors of which show as bright as a flag when she takes me to see the Park's monument to Chopin. The visit is official, she seems to say, and though I have been given rein to wander where I will, I must not ask her to exceed her office by a whit or a word.

Taxis are not plentiful in Warsaw, and most of the few of them would have been declared unfit for General Gallieni's trip to the Marne, even in 1914. Any automobile owner is therefore legally licensed to sell taxi service, and one of the beret-and-portmanteau types sells us a return ride to the hotel.

In the evening we go to a rehearsal of *Le Sacre du printempts* by the National Ballet, in the new and not yet finished (there are still no seats) Teatr Wielki. This is the largest opera house in the world, though the less said about its other qualities (especially of architectural imagination, which gave out somewhere near the level of the basement) the better. The choreography is of the so-called kinesthetic variety, but with peculiarly alien touches; thus, the "adolescents" appear to be imitating ponies, and their scene alternately suggests a riding academy and a "western," except that the Indians do not actually whoop; and in the *Rondes printanières* hands tremble over heads, I think to suggest spring sprouts on the way up. Apart from the fact that this sort of thing reduces a masterpiece to gag music, tying the music to something not essentially musical and never leaving it to its own description, the difficulty with these exterior associations is their inevitable triviality; and, in fact, any visual complement or commentary to a piece like the *Danse de la terre* is absurd. But the *Danse sacrale* saves *my* evening, if not *Le Sacre du printemps;* not so much the dance, though, as the dancer, one of the tender shoots, a petite blonde who falls on her back just before the end and in that position squirms, grinds, and bounces, exactly as the male audience would want her to do in bed.

May 25

I have been trying to picture the ruins of Warsaw at the end of the War, but a book which Jolanta gives me today, Ciborowski's *Warsaw, Its Destruction and Reconstruction*, does the job horribly well. On opposite pages photographs of the rubble heaps of 1945 are faced with photographs from exactly the same angles of the same sites today, and from these comparisons it is apparent that the feat of reconstruction here far surpasses that of any other city, German, Dutch, and Russian included. But to look at this book is to lose the power of criticism, and to come away feeling that it is cruel and heinous to ridicule not only the new architecture but anything whatever.

No photograph of the prewar Ghetto is included (though "prewar Ghetto" is tautological: a postwar Ghetto does not exist). But if the enormity of the crime is unimaginable, one nevertheless has a sense of it here simply because nothing has replaced the center of the old quarter. The site is now an empty square formed by slab-style apartment houses, but of the largest home of the Jews in Europe no trace is to be found. A monument has been erected, a prismoid pile of black granite placed on a plinth and flanked by black marble Menorahs which, to remind the world that the Jews of Warsaw chose to die fighting, are sustained by pairs of rampant Maccabean lions. In the center of the monument an attempt has been made to depict the murder of the Ghetto in sculptured reliefs of resisting figures, all of them impossibly heroic and even more impossibly husky—as if anything so monstrous could be suggested in a vignette tableau, even a good one; an eternal flame should be lighted here, or rather, seven flames on a candelabrum. On the stone there is a faint chalk mark of the figure 6,000,000, and as I stand looking at it, an old woman wrapped in black and leaning on a small boy walks slowly up to it and spreads a handful of posies under the six zeros.

Later I try to question Jolanta about the Jewish population of Poland today—one sees announcements in Hebrew on the kiosks in Nowy Swiat, a play by Isaac Babel is currently on the local boards, and a few dishes on the hotel menu are described as Jewish, though one wonders whether there are Jews to eat them. But I learn nothing beyond a statement that "we make no distinctions," and her pretty poker face belongs entirely to the professional Ninotchka side. Then suddenly she volunteers the information that "nowadays Polish youth have no sense of belief that such things as Oswiecim really happened"—which is no doubt true; what else is the failure of history? (V. says that in her childhood, the Poles never used the word "Hebrew," but only the contemptuous "*Zhid*," and she recalls how her father took her through the Warsaw Ghetto, which was famous for beautiful women.)

But Jolanta is changing, nevertheless, and I am certain now that the Ninotchka carapace can be crumbled entirely, and in no very great time. The first crack in the wall, though still hardly visible on the outer edifice, is that she has begun to show feelings, and no matter that they are feelings purely of national pride. I see now that at least she is no mercenary, and if a bureaucrat, then one with a soul for the job. What she wishes to achieve above all, and is working for even through me, is the cultural autonomy of Poland and a new *Regnum Poloniae* of the arts; and I offend her most, I now realize, when I fail to distinguish the Polish from the Russian in that to me gray area where the two seem to shade into each other. I have blanketed the Slav under the Russian, in remark after remark, and have consistently failed to distinguish the very Poland that is for her so vividly individual; and I am aware of this even now only because in this area she is so quick to correct me. But that I could have mistaken her ingenuous Polish sentiments for a simulated animadversion to Russia and a political ploy, is more embarrassing. Big Brother *is* listening, of course—we may be swallowing detector capsules with every meal, and everybody from the chauffeur to the waiter may be a gumshoe—but not through Jolanta's attractive antennae, at least not in the way I suspected at first. But patriotism and the suppression of feelings in favor of duties exact their price in a woman, a price, usually, of femininity—

though it may also be a rule of the job to keep the man at bay; in any case, Jolanta needs an eye-do and a hair-do for a start. But what, I wonder, has she been told about me, the me she now addresses as "yourthelf," her lips opening flower-like and farther outward to pronounce English than Polish, forming at the same time a graceless but tempting pucker.

CBS has asked the Ministry of Culture to "lay on a gay crowd if possible in regional costume" for I.S.'s arrival this afternoon, but the request is turned down with the excuse that "Poles are not a gay people." "What about the Polonaise and the Mazurka?" CBS answers, but the Ministry will not be drawn into a definition of its people's temperament, which, after all, is an ideological question nowadays. (Whether "gay" is the word, though, and "Poles" apart, the people of Warsaw seem to me to be remarkably cheerful and light-humored.) At the airport, there is a crackle of cameras like a pine-woods fire as I.S. leaves the plane, and some evidence, as he steps down, of a bibulous lunch. But soggy with Polish vodka as in fact he proves to be (he seems to mistake the TV men poking their light-meters in his face for traffic police testing for drink), he manages to say the right things in a speech.

Already at the airport the I.S.'s begin to react to the Poles as Russians of fifty years ago, and a few minutes of conversation suffice to revert them to the national prejudices of their youth. These amount to something like the so-called natural Russian anti-Semitism of which Dostoevsky is full of examples (though if I remember correctly, the most charac-teristic anti-Polish sentiments are also found in Dostoevsky; doesn't Dmitri Karamazov denounce someone as a *typical* "Mister Cheating Pole"?). I.S. begins to recall Russian phrases that mock Polish pomposity and Polish servility and obse-quiousness (which V. describes as especially dripping: "I am already on my knees" or "already prostrate before you"—

"*Padom do nog ooshe lezhoo*"); and both I.S. and V. aver that the hypocrisy of the Poles exceeds that of the Viennese, whose failings (or successes) in this field are so famous. (No doubt they are right, too: why should the character not develop in these directions with a thousand years of that geo-political background?) The I.S.'s ask Jolanta about changes in the language, which before the war still employed the polite form of the second person and was otherwise well suited to affect the fawning and the niceties the I.S.'s have been condemning; and her answer, which is that the language of speech has become very vulgar, puts her, linguistically speaking, firmly on the side of the *ancien régime*. "To Russian ears," says I.S., "the Polish language sounds like a comical argot, full of somehow related but strangely inappropriate words, like saying of a good perfume that it stinks." The I.S.'s laugh at the transliterations when they read the dinner menu, but when they speak Russian to the room waiter (who looks like another Pole, Vaslav Nijinsky, except for his Boris Karloff bangs), he laughs, too, so perhaps the exchange works both ways; and in any case, laughter at this point is welcome for whatever reason, V., after a walk through the lobby, having declared her intention of "going to bed until the plane to Paris."

May 26

When I.S. appears at the rehearsal this morning, the orchestra does not know how to greet him. Some of the players applaud, some stand, some remain seated, but all hesitate until Maestro Rowicki gives them a signal, at which they leap to their feet and give forth with a genuine though too-late-to-be-spontane-

ous ovation. This uncertainty followed by late but fervent
action is interpreted by V. as an example of the effects on the
Polish character of their historical habits of palliation. And
she claims that I.S. shares this character, that it is a mark of—
as she says with no great fondness for it—"his Polish side.
When I ask him whether he would prefer to do this or that
and he replies with 'I don't know, what would *you* like?' I
hear the voice of his Polish ancestors." (But I myself, seeing
I.S. here, think that his manners—a little sweet, a little over-
polite—are more Polish than Russian and that this is what
marked him out in Moscow two years ago.)

In fact, we soon *do* hear some of those voices, in the form
of relatives, cousins german they pretend, and though it is the
first day, people calling themselves Strawinsky are already
swarming to him, like a gathering of the clans. (The name is
legion here, so we are told, and though telephone books do
not exist, the letters and name cards piling up at the concierge
are proof of it.) A distant female cousin, heavily armed with
photograph albums, calls on him during lunch, but though
I.S. recognizes some of the faces in her files, when she pulls
him out of earshot we deduce, and correctly, that genealogical
research is less the object of her visit than *zlotis*. Another
apparently *bona fide* relative is a Doctor Konstanty Strawinski, the Director of the Zoological Institute of the University
Marie-Curie Sklodowska in Lublin; fortunately, he has contented himself with a letter. Another, though no-kin, correspondent is a poet, Anatol Stern, who encloses a reprint of his
interview with I.S. in the Warsaw Bristol Hotel in 1925. In it,
V. is indiscreetly identified as a "Russian lady-friend," and
the ill humor of both I.S. and V. with Warsaw, the hotel, and
the interviewer himself comes through saliently and characteristically though not, I think, to Mr. Stern. But the most
interesting of all the letters is from the daughter of I.S.'s family doctor at the turn of the century in Ustilug, Russia. This

Dr. Backnitsky was a friend of the Marxist Plekhanov, from whom he used to receive letters which I.S. also read, "as they were written in an unusually intelligible German; that was my first knowledge of Marxism." I.S. has been sending money to Madame Backnitsky regularly since the war. She remembers playing with his children in Ustilug in her youth.

A drive with Jolanta to Chopin's birthplace at Zelazowa Wola. The road is an old brick pavement for about half the distance, and better suited to vehicles of the time of its construction than to the heavy trucks which are now its principal motor traffic. There are many trough-shaped carts, too, horse-drawn but with large rubber tires, as if the mechanization process had broken down after the first step. The farm houses are low-lying, with thatched roofs and TV aerials. Jolanta says that most farms in the area are still privately owned, and she says that there are a few privately owned restaurants, too, the only good ones, in fact, though it appears that the Government is gradually taxing these mavericks out of existence. The farmers work with hand machinery only, but the land and the life on the land seem to be rich.

The relics at Zelazowa Wola—a plaster cast of the composer's small left hand, some nursery chairs and other petite furniture, some manuscripts of juvenilia—are nothing remarkable, but the grand piano stenciled STEINWAY in large white letters (Chopin's choice?) *is* slightly surprising in this land of no advertising. The attractions of the place are the sylvan walks and the willow-washed stream, a Romantic Nature that, alas, works no spell on Jolanta, who, indeed, is doubly careful today to treat me like an assignment. In any case, though, we are soon running from heavier—after four days of merely heavy—rains; Poland, it seems, has a pluvial climate. I note that the Poles do not greatly like having their national composer idol made a Frenchman.

A reception in the evening by the Union of Composers at

their home in the Rynek Starego Miasta, which is the heart of the old city; or, rather, of the rebuilt old city, for every edifice was reduced to rubble during the insurrection of 1944, and every one has since been reproduced in replica, so that the "Rynek" (market), can again be recognized from Canaletto. But as much as one is compelled to admire the feat of this rebuilding, or at any rate the spirit of it, these five-year-old medieval houses in which even the creak of the ancient floorboards has been added, are a little eerie, like movie sets, and I prefer the new city no matter how ugly.

The composers are shy, hospitable, well informed, as people *are* who stay home and read books. They are patriotically proud, too, in the same way as Jolanta. One of them tells me that "though Moszkowski may not have been a very great composer" (no argument) "he *was* Polish"; and I.S. is questioned again and again about his friendship with Szymanowski, whose *Stabat Mater*, written in the shadow of the *Symphony of Psalms*, is here thought to compare not extremely unfavorably with it. Even before coming to Poland, I.S. has feared that he would be kidnapped by, as he says, "the Beckmessers of the older and reactionary generation," and, in fact, this must have happened to some extent (though whether they are "Beckmessers" or not I cannot say), as none of the younger "progressives" is present, not Baird, Gorecki, Penderecki, Serocki, or Lutoslawski (whose *Three Poems by Henri Michaux* has become the display masterpiece of all postwar Polish music). But then, officialdom is always conservative, and for a guest of I.S.'s stature it cannot be escaped. What I regret is that we fail to see in this group those signs of the really remarkable musical renaissance which, since the war, not only has brought the country world prestige but also has enriched it with so many gifted composers, conductors, instrumentalists, and—yes—entrepreneurs, which is a strangely un-Marxist term, but however much the Polish movement came into being as a showcase protest against the Stalinist East, it is the West the Poles have sought to impress. For myself, I would like to talk to someone about music in the Jagiellonian Dynasty, above all about the influence of Marenzio in Cracow; and I would like to hear from unabashed living lips (though they could only be abashed ones), the Marxist interpretation of Renaissance culture propounded in the State Publisher's luxuriously embellished volumes of early Polish music. In *Music of the Polish Renaissance*, for instance, "ideological progress" is equated with "the democratic current of homeophonic structure," and "the abandonment of forms for the select few in favor of simpler but more expressive types"; and in *A Thousand Years of Polish History*, published in 1964, "social and ideological fermentation" is given as the reason for "the flourishing of Romanesque art." But no one, abashed or otherwise, will tangle with these subjects.

As we depart, toasts are given (in French, the language of most of the conversation), each one ending with a *"vive Stra-vin-ski."* I.S., very much in his element, replies to them, castigating Russia for the largest share of Poland's miseries— he seems to assume that these Poles are anti-Russian, as Poles generally were in his youth—and referring twice to the "Iron Curtain," at which times one can fairly hear the creak of those new-old floorboards.

May 27

There is a rehearsal this morning, just before ours, by the Cleveland Orchestra, now returning from a Russian tour. What a contrast to the Warsaw Phil.! The ensemble of the Americans is so perfect, and the playing so polished and refined and beautifully in tune—every note sits squarely in the center of the pitch, whereas with the Warsaw Phil. the notes fly around the pitches as though on trapezes. Nevertheless, we have now adjusted somewhat to the Poles, and the effect of the Clevelanders' efficiency and finesse is momentarily working some inverse returns, even to the extent that we have come to value just that crudity, or call it the vulgar guts, of the Warsaw Orchestra, which the Cleveland has been at pains to iron out.

We learn today that permission for I.S. to visit his old home in Ustilug will not be forthcoming, this after appeals to the Russian embassies in Washington and Warsaw, and even directly to the Kremlin. Ustilug is in a pink zone and therefore automatically off-limits to foreigners, but we had hoped for permission anyway because the reasons for the zoning are not military or strategic, say the Poles, but economic: the neighborhood is reputed to be poor and squalid (mule carts, poorly clothed and shod peasants), and the Russians prefer to keep such places swept under the carpet—or, at least, not advertised on American television. The Ustilug village was some hundred miles within Polish territory from 1919 to 1939, during which period, in the mid-1930's, Grigory Beliankin, the husband of I.S.'s sister-in-law, visited I.S.'s estate there and managed to sell some of the land to the Polish government. When the Soviet Union annexed Eastern Poland up to, approximately, the Curzon Line, and in effect moved the whole country a hundred miles to the west, Ustilug came out on the Soviet side of the frontier, by the margin of the Bug River. Since the war, I.S. has received letters from Russians who have visited the village, and photographs of his home there have appeared in Russian and German magazines. But Warsaw is as close as he will ever come again.

In a conversation with a young Polish writer this afternoon I learn that Joseph Conrad is widely read and that Polish translations of him are, as he claims, "well redacted." Interest in Conrad's father, Apollo Korzeniowski, has revived, too, and his play *For the Love of Money* was produced in Warsaw last year with success. Like his son, Korzeniowski was attracted to English and French literature, from which he was an expert translator; two of Shakespeare's comedies are still known here in the versions by Conrad *père*. But when the talk accidentally vaults from the Conrads to political theory my young acquaintance reveals himself as a neo-orthodox Marxist. History is a kind of Gulf Stream to him, a steady current flowing in a fixed direction. Travel time to any point in this current, or to any point in the past or from the past to the present, is equal and involves no awkward apparatus of cultural comparisons. The evolution of the Marxist concept is the only factor, and it applies everywhere unmodified. Westerners, he argues, are overconcerned with the pattern in history, or the pattern of change, and this leads them to the discovery of parallels which are not really parallel, and rhymes which do not work. "Thus, many capitalists still fear a cyclical repetition of the stock market crash, and some of them actually expect the socialist revolution to be overthrown and, as a result, to return to their old innings." The young man is exceptionally convincing on the subject of "corrupt individualism" in the West, and the picture he draws of us, each in his "existential void," is quite powerfully, through unintentionally, attractive.

Jolanta, on the other hand, as I discover in a late-night conversation—our most personal so far—conceives of history entirely in cultural terms. To begin with, she draws a firm line between "Slav" and "German" cultural watersheds. Then, too, she subscribes to the idea that the Soviet Union is merely the contemporary manifestation of *Russian* history, as Nazism was of *German* history. And she thinks that though nationalism may have declined at the end of the war because of the larger, late-Roman Empire type of division of East and West, "in the socialist countries it is again more important than ever." But *is* the East-West fracture so very sharp in Poland? I ask, and for answer am instructed to study her country from the point of view of a middle ground, an Eastern language with a Western alphabet, an Eastern people with a Western church. But what does "the West" mean to her? "Ideas of liberty and democracy, never much cultivated here," she says, very readily. "Nevertheless, we believe that our socialism is more profoundly democratic in its aims than yours."

But if Jolanta is changing, so am I; and if we are acting as correctives to each other, that action is bringing us together. In my case, the worm has turned so far that I am becoming almost overly respectful of her Ninotchka seriousness and correspondingly ashamed of my native habit of laughter, with its detestable implication of superiority. And how embarrassing it is now to recall my bumptious manner on arrival, the tactless references to the West and the specious analyses and superficial comments on everything I have seen. But Jolanta, at the same time, has become infected with my former laughter, which would be unregrettable except that she doesn't know how to laugh and the attempt is definitely unattractive. Worst of all, she now laughs, and excessively, at my silliest remarks only. Thus, when I question her as to what one does for pleasure in this "gay" city at night, the Ninotchka guise tells me to "go to the Palace of Science and Culture" (that Stalinoid monster-building) "and look at the Book Fair." But when I underline the problem—"I mean, what does one do between one A.M. and four A.M.?"—the point is seen, at length, the funnybone greatly tickled, and the night air shattered with her reaction. How far, how far will this dangerous transformation go?—for she is also becoming a little impish and a little coy, as when, at parting, she permits me a cold peck of *amitié* on each check, Slav style, but lets me see at the same time that she is well aware of how much more I would prefer the sunflower in the middle. If she continues to concede at this rate it will be difficult in a day or two to recognize the truly adamant from the false.

May 28

A shopping tour, to look for a rug for V. and wine for I.S. All store clerks are women, it seems, and it appears that another qualification for this employment is the ability to maintain a total indifference to customers. Wares are displayed reluctantly and only on request, with no effort thereafter to engage interest; and oddly, this absence of the commercial spirit has a depressing effect—though considering the merchandise, one fails to see how either party in a transaction could be expected to show much exhilaration. In one grocery, fifty or more people have queued before a clump of what I fear will prove to be too few sausages (*kilbassa*) to go around; and in another, a still longer line has formed to buy tins of peanuts from Hanoi, as the label advertises, rather too pointedly, in English. After long search, we find one lone bottle of Beaujolais, luckily in a store licensed to accept our *zlotis*, for most stores are off-limits to us or else designated "for foreign currency only," hard money being avidly coveted by the government. The dollar is worth six times more *zlotis* unofficially than officially, and prices are pegged to the international index at the official rate. The Government is said to be so dollar-hungry that the black-market speculators who parade like prostitutes between the two "American" hotels are generally thought to be Treasury Department employees.

The audience at the concert tonight has come more to see

a famous "live animal" than to listen to the music, but I.S. receives a standing ovation, as well as, after each piece, bouquets of carnations in the national colors of red and white. We go to another concert afterward—a kind of jazz *jeunesse musicale*, say the two American film students who have helped to sponsor it, though they neglect to add that the jazz is not very groovy. At about midnight we enter a club where a young saxophonist is playing with his back to the audience and with one foot on the bandstand and one on the floor; when he eventually turns around he turns out to look like Alexander Nevsky in the film. Good as he is, though, the audience interests me more. It is remarkably good-looking, well-dressed, well-mannered, with no air of the beatnik about it—no Beatle forelocks, no quiffs, and even no beards. During intermission, a slightly older woman (chaperon?) tells me that she "grew up under Stalinism and therefore did not dream that I would ever see Stravinsky"; and a moment later the only political utterance of the sort on the whole trip is made by a twenty-year-old girl: "Things were going so well under Khrushchev, but now we are all very frightened again." Oh you poor stomped-upon Janus-headed Poles—though not even Januses either, for as real estate you belong to the East (that watchtower of the "Palace of Science and Culture" standing over your town), however ardently you pursue the *ignis fatuus* of a middle ground.

May 29

There is an unexpected twist in Jolanta this morning, and from her first words we are aware that she is not being frank. We have hired a car to go to Malbork on Monday, but from the very variety of excuses proposed for the impossibility of the trip, it is clear that her superiors have countermanded the plan; the simple truth, as it later appears, is that they themselves wish to have I.S. at a luncheon on that date. The effect of all this on me is disappointment, not, of course, at the content of a small lie of misprision, but because the fact of it could destroy a relationship in which I now realize I have put my trust. Later I reflect that she is a political employee, after all, and one with considerable responsibilities. From the beginning of our stay, her orders must have contained a sizable list of things we were not to know or must be made to do or be prevented from doing. In effect, we have been steered by her from the moment of arrival; and as we are by no means the first of her charges, each stage of our adjustment must have been coolly observed by a professionally complacent eye—which realization makes me feel not only naïve, but nakedly transparent. Is she also aware, as the psychoanalyst is aware when the same thing happens to his patient, that I am caught in the throes of calf-love? And how many times has that happened to her before?

May 30

As today is the first without rain, we drive through the Praga to Wilanow, and walk there under crystalline skies. It is National Election Day, too, and though we see no signs of election fever (how could there be any with a choice of Gomulka or Gomulka?), every factory on the way is draped with banners and flags, the red flag of the Revolution together with the red-and-white Polish flag. The view of the city from the Praga is a popular angle in old prints (*Urbs*

Warsowia with, in the Praga foreground, plumed riders on prancing horses and noble ladies in fur-lined pelisses, like Watteau's *La Femme Polonaise*). It was also the Red Army's view of the city in 1944 when they failed to cross and raise the siege of the insurgents, standing by for political reasons, as is now generally thought, while a quarter of a million people died. But the Vistula from here seems to play no vital part in the life of the city, as the Danube does in Budapest or Vienna.

May 31

After a morning employed in packing, paying bills, and spending leftover *zlotis*, we go to Jablonna for the composers' luncheon, which is in the rebuilt Poniatowski Château. The trans-Vistula landscape—brown wooden houses, pigeons sitting in mud pools, fields of broken corn stooks, farm lands covered with mulch—reminds the I.S.'s of Russia, and so does Jablonna itself, with its circular saloon and veneered-birch furniture.

The cuisine, amazingly, is of a quality to match the surroundings. The chef, who is now eighty-six and looks like Bruckner's death mask, had been chief cook to the tsar. He is sent for at the end of the meal and introduced to I.S., whose hands he kisses like a peasant of a century ago, but though everyone applauds him and admits that his *service royale* is the only good cooking in Poland, no one draws any deductions from the fact, at least not out loud. At table I am seated between, and try to make Ger-French conversation with, Stefan Sledzinski, the president of the society, who chairs the proceedings, and the writer Tomaszewski (a face like

that of the Polish hero Lelewel, but with slightly blunter
features like those of someone out of Wit Stwosz). Toasting
comes to the rescue, except that I fail to recognize myself in
one to "Robertowi Craftowi" because of the tail ornaments,
and have to be nudged. At the heady high point of the fête,
the composers stand, face I.S., and chant an old Polish song
in unison (not very good unison for composers): "May he
live to be a hundred." And then a remarkable linguistic
event occurs. I.S. suddenly switches from French to Russian
—wholly unconsciously, I think; he is very moved—and in
a trice the whole company follows him, as though all along
they had only been waiting, out of politeness, for his permission. And whereas only moments before some of them had
been dropping mildly denigratory digs about the Russians
("They have not played as much modern music as we have"
—which is true—"and therefore their orchestras are not as
quick as ours"—which is false), all of them now seem perfectly at home speaking the Russian language.

After this, I escape with Jolanta to the Château park and
follow its meanders to the roiling river, where there is a bilious
sound of frogs and a dovelike wind. Here are the walks, the
tall trees and lush meadows with dandelion and buttercup, of
my first daydreams of Russian novels, Tolstoy above all. And
here at last and in farewell it is the turn of the sunflower.
It is given slowly, silently, seriously, devotedly, persistently,
and with no outwardly escaping sign of pleasure.

❋ ❋ ❋

Back in Warsaw, I attempt to collect the impressions of a
week in the hope of finding two or three that have survived
the mass reversals. But none has; and the subject of my Polish
peroration must therefore be the reasons for the impossibility
of composing it. Some of them—the brevity of the experience

and the lack of language and even of "common" knowledge of the country—are obvious; and at least one difficulty must be the same, or nearly the same, for every foreigner: the fact that not only is Warsaw not Poland, but that it is hardly even a continuation of the city it was (having been clinically murdered, as doctors say, and left alive only biologically). Still, to me the greatest obstacle of all is in the fact that the visitor becomes a victim of the ambivalence of the Poles themselves (that nonplussing switch to Russian at the lunch today), though to explain the statement I can only recall and compare my own feelings in Russia where, because the attitude to the Westerner is so comparatively clear, being substantiated with power, the psychological discharges of the people are all positive. But what about the psychological strategies of a people whose map has changed with every power shift and who during the whole of the nineteenth century were deprived of their very existence politically and territorially (though admittedly the ethnological problems of the territory are virtually insoluble, or soluble only by transplanting the minority populations to their demographic gravity centers)? And what of a people who, when finally reconstituted at Versailles, found themselves a full century behind the West (whereas before the partition, in the time of Stanislaus Leczinski and others, they had been in the vanguard of the Enlightenment), and who were therefore an easy prey at first to corruption and at last to fascism? And finally, what are the feelings of a nation which after a terrible war of "liberation" is now more than ever before the instrument of another power?

To read even a little in the history of Poland is to be astonished by the survival of a Polish culture at all. The explanation must lie in the integrity of the people. They were a heroic people during the Occupation, when, in spite of the suffering, no Quisling appeared and collaboration was almost unknown. And the heroism has continued, for in many ways life is harder now. There was a mitigating hope under the Nazis in their overthrow and final defeat, but what hope for change is there now? I have no answer, but I know that every reference to the West and "the line" (the Iron Curtain) that I have heard from the Poles seems to contain a choke of emotion. And I know that living conditions *are* grim, and not merely economically. The censorship is the worst in the world. It is a prison offense for us to carry a letter out, and money sent from relatives in the West, as well as much mail both ways, is sometimes confiscated or fails to arrive. Naturally the Poles are suspicious. It is a condition of survival in the underground where, swallowed but not eaten, they still live.

1 9 6 6

January 16

New York. Wystan Auden for dinner, wearing a dark brown flannel shirt, black necktie, wicker beach shoes, dark glasses (pocketed until departure, just before midnight, at which time he looks like a jazz musician), the glittering jewels of his genius. After confounding the waiters by ordering mushrooms as a "savory" and by using "quite" for "yes" ("More wine sir?"—"Quite"), he talks about "anti-opera," beginning with two somewhat out-of-the-way examples ("the *great* anti-operas are *Fidelio, Boris, Pelléas*), Janáček's *House of the Dead*, which "has no characters and no tunes," and Godard's *Dante*, pronounced 'Dant'. "Whereas Act One of 'Dant' merely sets the Florentine scene, the subject of Act Two is the entire *commedia*. In the third act 'Dant' and Beatrice are united in, of all places, 'a nunnery, near Ravenna.' " But he is more at home with the Germans. "Elektra is so definitely a non-U character," he says, "that a singer who does the part to perfection shouldn't attempt Isolde." This leads to a statement that "The first act of *Tristan* offers the greatest of lessons to a librettist: nothing happens on stage, but it is drama, not oratorio, and the drama is achieved entirely by exits and entrances." Telling I.S. of the numerous excisions in the new production of *The Rake's Progress* in Vienna, he proposes to make cutting illegal in future by publishers' contracts. "And, after all, *The Rake* isn't exactly like *Götterdämmerung*, where the stage director can always claim that he has to give people a chance to pee."

On the subject of certain more recent operas he is concerned (not unduly) "lest the Britten pendulum swing so far the other way that people begin to say they are *all* bad." And "though Verdi saw that *Cleopatra* wouldn't do—but perhaps it *would* have done in Boïto's Italian—I understand that it is being tried out here nevertheless. Now, the only Shakespeare that could be turned into English-language opera is *Love's Labour's Lost*, and that would take a great deal of adapting."

Gently teasing I.S. about medicines and money (to me: "Has he scads now?"), he suggests that *millionen* would be a beautiful word for him to set to music. "Think how you could aspirate the final syllable, Igor, and keep it going page after page like the compounding of interest."

Obviously homesick for his house in Austria, he says that the only excuse for buying a newspaper is "to see what the weather is doing there—I don't need to be told what it is like here—though having bought a paper, I always peek at the obits and now and then at the leader and the books." He seems to regret his comfortable Ford Foundation year in Berlin, too, though all we hear of it is the story of a brush with the law one Saturday night on suspicion of inebriety. "The police, who pay people to inform on pedestrians when they seem to be 'tight,' would not believe I was a 'professor.' I had no trouble with their mental and coordination tests" (who *would* have, under any conditions, with *that* intellect?), "but evidently there was too much alcohol in my blood" (as well there might be after, say, a demijohn of chianti). He is immaculately, totally abstinent when driving his Volkswagen at home in Kirchstetten, he adds virtuously, and was always so in "motor cars" since he first drove one in 1925. The date reminds I.S. that he began to drive in the same year but soon gave it up because the gendarmes of Nice stopped him so often and because he was habitually burning up the brakes—which, says Wystan, *sotto voce*, is "another manifestation in the pattern of the pills and the salting away of securities in Helvetia."

Turning to "literature," he complains about "scholars who simply will not believe that Shakespeare could have made a mistake" and about the "you who's" in the new translation of the Bible. (There is, conspicuously, no theological or ecclesiastical talk tonight, and only one reference to the Pope —"publicity mad"—but we hear a variant of Phocion in a remark that "God Himself, when He said 'Let There be Light,' must have realized He was saying something extraordinarily pretentious.") He says that T. S. Eliot wrote "excellent ribald verse that will undoubtedly *not* be collected. Some verses I submitted to him many years ago for *The Criterion* included a then unprintable word, which he circuited by suggesting the more decorous: '. . . like a June bride/. . . sore but satisfied.' "

Books mentioned are Auerbach's *Literary Language;* Tolkien's forthcoming *Silmarillion* ("J.B.B. is no longer the property of dotty schoolteachers and elderly cranks, you know; he's 'in' with the teen-age set"); *Markings* ("my translation was in lieu of the hagiography that was really wanted"); the new David Jones (he apologizes for his place on the subscribers' list: "It's only because of 'A.,' you see, which I can't help, but which makes it appear as though I were somehow next in rank to the Queen Mum"); *In Cold Blood* (can he *really* have read *that*, or did he merely sink a few trial shafts?);

The Ambidextrous Universe ("One knew all along that it wasn't symmetrical, of course," though most of us were brought up thinking of God as someone like Christian Morgenstern's Zäzilie, the symmetry-loving housemaid). He praises the Capote, albeit dismissing as nonsense "the advertisement about a new form" and adding that he hears "the author is remarkably changed and now looks like a banker, which, indeed, he is." The question of capital punishment arises, and England, "where at least they don't keep them waiting about for five or ten years" (though in the Christie case they should have), is brought in for comparison. We ask whether he thinks the death sentence is ever justifiable. "Of course, there *have* been people on whom I can imagine it being carried out. Brecht, for instance. In fact, I can picture doing it to him myself. It might actually have been rather enjoyable, when the moment came, to have been able to say to him, 'Now let's step outside.' I'd have given him a very good last meal, too. Still, you must admire the logic of a man who lives in a Communist country but takes out Austrian citizenship, keeps his money in Switzerland, and even sends for the Pastor at the end, in case there might be something in that, too."

As the I.S.'s slip into Russian, he exclaims on the beauty of the language, which raises the alarming thought, since he has never said anything even remotely pro-Russian before, that his German period may be running out. But he is mellower, in general, than I have ever known him. The deaths of Noah Greenberg and Randall Jarrell have shocked him, I think, though Jarrell had "spent some time in the bin; and then, it's not very nice for the driver whose truck you leap in front of." Suddenly, as if reflecting on his own mortality, he tells the story of a schoolgirl quoting one of his poems in a class recently and "astonishing her teacher with the information that 'Auden is still alive.' In fact, some time ago a newspaper in the Midwest *had* announced that I was dead: I saw the correction saying 'Auden *not*—repeat, *not*—dead,' after which I tried to inquire what it was thought I had died of."

He says in parting: "We all need someone to tell us when we have written rubbish, and we must listen to him and throw it out." Henceforth (it is too late *this* time) I promise to obey.

INDEX I

Aba, Eban, 224
Acnello, Baron, 286
acoustics, and architecture, 6
Adeste Fidelis (setting, Alkan), 16
Afanasiev, Aleksandre, 28
A.F. of M., 6 n.
Afonsky Choir, Paris, 31
Akhmatova, Anna, 66, 75
Albert Hall (London), 126, 252–3
Alcools (Apollinaire), 130
Alexander II of Russia, 32
Alkan, Charles-Henri, 16
Amahl and the Night Visitors
     (Menotti), 101
A.M.A., 6 n.
The Ambidextrous Universe, 351
Amelia Goes to the Ball (Menotti),
     10
American Ballet Company, 35
Ameriques (Varèse), 88
Andreas-Salomé, Lou, 316
Anathemata (Jones), 259
Angel of Fire (contemp. opera), 99
*Animal Dispersion in Relation to
     Social Behaviour* (Edwards), 20
Ann Arbor, Michigan, 19
Annunciation (Jones), 257
Ansermet, Ernest, 150, 153

Antic Hay (Huxley), 170
The Anxious Object (Rosenberg),
     9 n.
Apollinaire, Guillaume, 130
April in Paris (Menotti), 90–92
Arcana (Varèse), 87
Archilochus, quoted, 239
Archipenko, A., 255
Arco (non-composed music), 19
Arendt, Hannah, 308
Aristotle, 251
Arlecchine (Busoni), 99
Arnold Schoenberg: Letters (ed.
     Stein), 132, 143
art centers, London, 9
Athens, 5th century, 8
Auden, W. H., 51, 52, 63, 94–7, 108,
     quoted, 246, 291, 306–7 308–12,
     348–52; collaborated on *Elegy
     for J. F. K.,* 57–9; essay on
     Shakespeare's Sonnets, 306; Fore-
     word to *Markings* 307; librettist,
     96, 97
automation, uses of, 4–8
Aviz Hotel, Lisbon, 182

Babitz, Sol, 47
Baby Doe, 10

Bacci, Baccio, 67
Bach, J. S., 8, 21, 40, 60, 86, 102, 142, 148, 149, 302
Backnitsky, Dr. and Mrs., 334
Bacon, Francis, 8
Baedekers, old collection of, 65
Bagatelles (Webern), 118
Balanchine, Georges, 7, 24, 25, 37, 38, 45, 46, 47, 270
Balzac, Honoré de, 316
Barnes, 'Argyrol', 196
Bartlett *(Familiar Quotations)*, 162
Bartók, Béla, 91
Bassarids (Henzle), 99
Baudelaire, Charles, 144, 161
Bayreuth, 189
The "Beatles," 311, 342
Beckett (Tennyson), 254
Beecham, Sir Thomas, 155
Beethoven, Ludwig van, 3, 14, 42, 70, 79, 117, 118, 140–1, 148, 152, 242, 248, 302, 306
Symphony No. 1, 147; No. 5, 279; No. 6, 56, 140–1; No. 9, 140–1
Behan, Brendan, 260
Beliankin, Grigory, 338
Beliankin, Ludmilla: death of sister-in-law, 38; Requiem for, 31
Bell Laboratory, 4
Ben-Gurion, 221
Ben-Ziv, 228–9
Béranger, Victor, 245
Bérard, Christian, 67
Berceuse (Godard), 15
Berg, Alban, 13, 36, 48, 49, 120 n., 137, 179, 188, 232
Bergen: see travel diary, Norway
Bergson, Henri, 160
Berlin, Germany, 43, 99, 148, 149; Opera House, 308; East Sector, 311
Berman, Eugene, 45, 67, 255
Bernstein, Leonard, 162, 228
Bertillon, Alphonse, 108
Beverly, California, 65, 74, 177, 179

Biarritz, France, 152, 154
Biber, Heinrich, J., 149
The Bible, 55, 222, 350
Biennial of Contemporary Music: Zagreb, 1963, 243
Björnson, B., 249
Blake, William, 12, 257
Blanche, J. E., 36
Blasting and Bombardiering (Lewis), 127
Bliss, Mr. and Mrs. Robert Woods, 39
Blitzstein, Marc, 98
Bloch, Ernest, 153
Blok, Alexander, 66
The Blue Angel (film), 302
Boito, Arrigo, 96, 349; *see also* Verdi
The Book of Armagh, 261
Booth, John Wilkes, 243
Boris Godunov (Moussorgsky), 348
Boston Symphony Orchestra, 54
Bortniansky, Dimitri, 31
Bott, Francis, 67
Boulanger, Nadia, 14, 51
Boulez, Pierre, 16, 17, 108, 118, 140 n.; *see also* Notes, Part II
Bradley, F. H., 127
Brahms, Johannes, 102, 116, 149; Symphony No. 1, 146 n.
Brancusi, Constantin, 10, 256
Brandt, Willy (Mayor of Berlin), 221
Braque, Georges, 18, 244
Brave New World (Huxley), 164
British Broadcasting Company (BBC), 126
Brecht, Bertolt, 75, 232
Britten, Benjamin, 13, 101, 349
Broadway, New York, 45
Bruch, Max, 307
Büchner, Georg, 179
Buddenbrooks (Mann), 221
Buffet, Bernard, 106
Bugaku (Japanese ballet), 25
Burney, Dr. Charles, 190

Bury, J. B., 178
Busch, Wilhelm, 170
Busoni, F. B., 99
Butor, Michel, 247
Byron, George Gordon, 59, 176, 310

The Cabinet of Dr. Caligari (film), 266
Cage, John, 19, 104, 244
California, 43
Camus, Albert, 179, 180
Canadian Broadcasting Company, 30
Canaletto, 190
Cannes, France, 106
Caravaggio, Michel de, 284, 298
Cardew, Cornelius, 18
Cardillac (contemporary opera), 99
Carnaval, (Schumann), 45
Carnegie Hall, 5, 154, 156
Carrée (Stockhausen), 11, 12, 13
Carter, Elliott, 105
Casals, Pablo, 69, 101, 102
CBS television and radio, 319–20, 332
Celeste (cat), 74
Cézanne, Paul, 163, 303 n.
Chagall, Marc, 67, 255
Chanel, Mme Gabrielle, 30
Chanson de Roland (11th century), 285
Chardin, Teilhard de, 250
Charlie Chan in Indochina (film), 15
Chateau de Montoux, Annemasse, 39
Chekhov, Anton, 74
Cheops pyramid, 200
Chernigov, Russia, 129
Chicago Symphony Orchestra, first performance of *Symphony in C,* 43; 148
Chirico, Georgio di, 195–6
Chopin, waltzes, 45, 328, 334
churches and cathedrals:
    Agrigento, 295
    Alexander Nevsky, Paris, 31, 32
    Canterbury, England, 253
    Certosa di Pavia, Milan, 264–5
    Church of the Order of the Visitation, Warsaw, 325
    Outerio da Gloria, Rio de Janeiro, 272
    The Paraclesion of Kariye Camii, Istanbul, 187
    St. Ambrose, Milan, 263
    S. Francesco della Vigna, Venice, 190
    San Lorenzo, Venice, 190
    S. Maria Maggiore, Venice, 190
    St. Sergius, Cairo, 213
    San Bento, Rio de Janeiro, 272
    San Pietro in Castello, Venice, 190
    São Braz, Portugal, 183
    Seville, Spain, 184
Churchill, Sir Winston, 218
Cingria, Charles-Alvert, 40
Clark, Edward, 155
Clarke, Sir Kenneth, 9, 10, 253, 255; lectures, 9, 10; Lady Clark, 253–5
Clarens, Switzerland, 150, 318
Cleopatra, 208
Cleopatra (opera), 349
Cleveland Symphony Orchestra, 337–8; orchestra tour, 58
church music (Russian) in Kiev, 31
The Cocktail Party (Eliot), 178
Cocteau, Jean, 36, 244–6, 247
Coleridge, Samuel T., 126
Collins, Helium Cryostat, 19 n.
Como, Villa d'Este, 149
computers: *see* automation
Congdon, Bill, 67
Connolly, Cyril, 295
Conrad, Joseph, 129, 338–9
Copland, Aaron, 45
Coptic art, 66
Cornberg, Carrel, recording equipment, 6
Couperin, François, 302
Covent Garden, London, 106, 252

Craft, Robert, 30, 72; and Part II, *passim*
Cratylus, 112
SS *Cristoforo Columbo*, 198
Criterion (periodical), 125, 350
Critics and Criticism (interview), 102–8
Crowds and Power (Canetti), 146 n.
cubism, 18
Cuenod, H., 53
The Curse of the Copts (White), 214
Cuticchio, Giacomo, puppets, 284–6
Cymbeline (Shakespeare), 125
Czerny, Karl, 48

da Silva, Vieira, 67
da Venosa, Gesualdo, 302
Dahl, Ingolf, 167
Dahomey, Africa: tribal dances, 308
Darmstadt, Germany, 10
Dante (Godard), 348
Darwin, Charles, 136, 276
Das Liebesverbot (Wagner), 143
Das Rheingold (Wagner), 12, 144
Daudet, Alphonse, 72
Dead Sea scrolls, 229
Death of Santa Lucia (Caravaggio), 298
Decoration Day (Ives), 15, 16
Degas, Hilaire, 256
Degenerate Music, 36
Delia (libretto, Auden), 23
The Derby (English horserace), 126
Der Rosenkavalier (Strauss), 237
Deserts (Varèse), 87, 89
Deutches Schauspielhaus, Hamburg, 232
The Devil and Daniel Webster (film), 53
Diaghilev, Sergei, 30, 78, 90, 155, 192, 195 n., 244
Dialogues and a Diary (Stravinsky), 245

Die Geschichte als Sinngebung des Sinnlosen (Lessing), 11 n.
Die glückliche Hand (Schoenberg), 176
Die Meistersinger (Wagner), 119
Die Reihe (periodical), 7, 18
Dietrich, Marlene, 302
Divine, Father, 278–81
Dmitri, Stepanitch (gardener), 74
Dokter Faust (Busoni), 99
Dr. Faustus "Tagebuch" (Mann), 75
Dolce, Danilo, 291
Dollar, William, 38
Domaine Musical (group), 116
Donaueschingen: *see* travel diary, Germany
Don Carlos (Verdi), 236
Don Giovanni (Mozart), 83, 148
Dostoevsky, Fëdor, 332
Dresden, Germany, 35
Droscher, Vitus, 19 n.
Dryden, J: *see* Purcell, H.
Dublin, Eire: *see* travel diary, Eire
Dufy, Raoul, 67
Duke of Edinburgh (Prince Philip), 214
Dumbarton Oaks, D.C., 39
Duparc, Henri, 153
Durrell, Lawrence, 211

Edel, Max (physician), 66
Edison, Thomas, 163
Eichmann (Arendt), 308
1812 Overture (Tchaikovsky), 6 n.
Einstein, Albert, 106
Eisler, Hans, 75, 136
Elektra (R. Strauss), 348
Elgar, Edward, 307
Eliot, T. S., 94, 124–6, 127–31, 161, 178–9, 350; Hon. Deputy Sheriff, Dallas, 131; Mrs. T. S. Eliot (1), 178; (2), 126, 128
Elizabeth, Queen Mother (England), 252–3, 255, 350
Ellis, William Ashton, 139

Empress Elisabeth of Austria, 132
Encyclopedia of Pacifism (Huxley),
72
The End of the Tether (Conrad),
338–9
Entartete Musik, 36
Epstein, Jacob, 126
Erwartung (Schoenberg), 99
España (Ravel), 88
Este, Isabella d' (portrait, Romano),
128
Eugenio de Bourbon, Prince, 185
Europe, concert halls of, 5
Euryanthe (Weber), 142, 143
Evaporations (Kagel), 19
Evenings in the Orchestra (Berlioz),
142
Evtushenko, Y., 126, 246, 308

Falstaff (Verdi), 3, 101, 176, 302, 307
Falla, Manuel de, 193
The Family Reunion (T. S. Eliot),
179
Fanfare (R. Strauss), 105
Ferrara, Italy, 128
Festa Romane (Respighi), 105
Ficino, Marcello, 172
Fidelio (Beethoven), 152, 348
Finlandia (Sibelius), 88
Finnegans Wake (Joyce), 259
Fischer-Dieskau, Dietrich, 99
Flaubert, Gustav, 72
Florence, Italy (15th century), 8
Fluctuations (Sigurdjörnsson), 19
The Flying Dutchman (Wagner),
270
Ford, Glenn, 303
Ford, Ford Maddox, 178
For the Love of Money (play, Kor-
zeniowski), 339
4'33" (Cage), 19
Franco, Generalissimo, 102
François-Poncet, André, 36
Fränkischer Kurier (newspaper), 35
Franz Liszt Hall, Budapest, 6, 240

Freud, Sigmund, 316
Frisch, Max, quoted, 6
Frost, Robert, 310
Fuleihan, Anis, 18
Fulgentius, Fabius, P., 172
Fuller, George, 11
Furtwängler, Wilhelm, 149
Fux, Johann, J., 146

Galileo (Brecht), 75
Galitzin, Prince (physician), 74
Galuppi, Baldassare, 31
Garches, France, 30
Gate, Mrs. (Evegenia Petrovna), 72,
74, 76
Gattopardo: see The Leopard
Gaulle, General de, 239, 346–7
Gauthier, Judith, 140
Gazette de Lausanne, 129 n.
Geneva, Switzerland, 39, 69, 153, 319
Genet, Jean, 245
Genoa: *see* travel diary, Italy
Gesualdo, Don Carlo, 244
Gewandhaus, Leipzig, 6
Giacometti, Alberto, 67, 256, 313–14,
317–18
Gibbon, Edward, quoted, 250
Gill, Eric, 258
Giotto, 195
Giuliano, Salvatore, 290–1
Glazunov, Alexander, 93
Gluck, Cristoph, W., 48, 49, 93
Godard, Benjamin, 15, 348
"God Save the Queen," 14
Goethe, 86, 121, 287 quoted, 288 n;
lecture on by T. S. Eliot, 127,
310
Goetz, Hermann, 14; Symphony in
F, 14
Gogol, Nickolai, 179, 246
Goldberg Variations (J. S. Bach), 60
"Golden Coaches of Belem", 182
Golden Fleece (Krenek), 99
Gomes, Antonio, 275
Goncourts, E. and J. quoted, 72

Goossens, Eugene, 155
Gorky, Maxim, 51
Götterdämmerung (Wagner), 349
Graham, Billy, 279-80
Grainger, Percy, 155
Grand Hotel, Budapest, 238
Graves, Robert, 310
Greece, ancient, 6
Greenberg, Noah, 351
Grieg, concert in Oslo, 249
Gris, Juan, 18
Gropius, Walter, 10
Gruppen (Stockhausen), 12, 13
Guggenheim Foundation, 137
Guggenheim museum, 11
Gulbenkian, Calouste, 82

Haaretz glass museum, 230-1
Hakluyt, Richard, 140
Hamburg: *see* travel diary, Germany
   production of *The Flood*, 268-70
Hamlet (Schlegel), 233-5; Hamburg
   production criticized by Stravin-
   sky, 235
Hamlet's Wissen, program notes by
   Karl Jaspers, 235
Hammarskjöld, Dag, 307
Hampton Court, England, 128
Happenings (Ligeti), 19
Hare, Augustus, 162
Hauer, J. M., 136
Haydn, Joseph, 42, 148, 304; "Clock"
   Symphony, 151; "London" Sym-
   phony, 303
The Heart of Midlothian (Scott),
   127
Hebrew, Stravinsky's interest in, 70
Hegel, George, 198
Heidegger, Martin, quoted, 17
Hemholz, Ludwig F., 6
Henie, Sonja, 248
Henzle, Hans, W., 18, 99, 101
Herbert, George, 197
Hermogenes, 112
Herzgewachse (Schoenberg), 19

Hindemith, Paul, 36
Hilter, Adolf, 134, 307
Hofmannsthal, Hugo von, 96, 133
Hollywood Bowl, 156
Honegger, Arthur, 14
Hotel du Chatelard, Vevey, 320
Hotson, Leslie, 306
House of the Dead (Janáček), 348
Houston, Walter, 53
Hungarian National Ballet, 240
Hungarian National Radio Orches-
   tra, 240
Huntingdon Library, 302
Huxley, Aldous, 159, 160-5, 169-72,
   177-9, 209, 298, 300-1, 302, 305;
   personal recollections of Robert
   Craft, 299-304
Huxley, Mrs. (1) Laura, 299; (2)
   Maria, 159, 160-5, 169, 170, 171,
   299, 300-1

Ibn Saud of Arabia, 218
Ibsen, Henrik, 176
Igreja da Candelaria, Rio, 273
Il Guarany (Gomes), 275
Im Sommerwind (Webern)
In Cold Blood (Capote), 350
In Parenthesis (Jones), 259
International Congress on Tropical
   Medicine (1963), 276
Ionesco, Eugène, 245-7
ISCM festivals, 19
Istanbul: *see* travel diary, Turkey
Ives, Charles, 15, 16, 48, 106; Sym-
   phony No. 4, 154

Janáček, Leos, 99, 348
Jannings, Emil, 302
Janssen, Werner, 46
Jarrell, Randall, 351
Jerusalem, 227
Jews in Music (pamphlet), 141
Joan of Arc, 12
Johnson, Philip, 5
Johnson, Samuel, quoted, 50

Joie du Sang des Etoiles (Messiaen), 15
Jolanta (guide in Warsaw), 323, *passim*
Jones, David, 256–9, 350
Josephus, Flavius, 224
Journal (Renard), 80
Joyce, James, 127, 161, 259, 261
James Joyce Tower, Dublin, 260

Kafka, Franz, quoted, 258; 276
Kagel, Mauricio, 19
Kallman, Chester, 51
Kandinsky, Vasily, 67, 133, 134, 255
Kaparcona (steamship), 35
Kassner, Rudolph ("On Vanity"), 125
Kennedy, President John F., 56, 94, 130–1, 298–9, 306
Kennedy, Mrs. J. F., 299
Kierkegaard, Sören, 172
King Lear (Shakespeare), 8
Kirstein, Lincoln, 38, 47
Klee, Paul, 67
Klemperer, Otto, 150–1
The Knights of Malta, 284
Kodály, Zoltán, 102, 240
Kokoschka, Oscar, 165
Kolisch Quartet, 121
Kollek, Theodore, 229
The Koran, quoted, 89; 90, 188
Korzeniowski, Apolla, 338–9
Koussevitzky, S. A., 149, 152
Koussevitzky, Mrs. Natalie, 152
Kursaal Orchestra, Montreux, 153

Lacerda, Carlos (Governor of Rio), 276
La Dolce Vita (film), 270
La Femme Polonaise (Watteau), 344
La Fenice, Venice (theatre), 52
La Fontaine, quoted, 39
Lampedusa, G., Prince Salina, 293–4
Lampedusa, Principessa (wife), 292–4
La Mer (Debussy), 147

La Nausée (Sartre), 42
La Petite Messe Solonelle, 306
Larionov, Mikahail, 255
La Scala, Milan, 39, 265–6
The Last Savage (Menotti), 97–9, 100, 101
Laughton, Charles, 75
L'Avventura (film), 287
Lawrence, D. H., 164, 280, 284, 290
Lawrence, T. E., 307
League of Composers concert, 151
Lear (Britten), 99
Lear, Edward, 126, 127, 192
Lecky (historian), 178
Leczinski, Stanislaus, 346
Lafanu, Sheridan, 260
Lehar, Franz, 15
Léger, Fernand, 67
Leipzig, Germany, 149, 150
Leong, Jimmy, 67
The Leopard (Giuseppe Tommasi, Prince of Lampedusa), 293–4
Lessing, Theodore, 11 n.
Les Tilleuls (house in Clarens, Switzerland), 318–9
Lévi-Strauss, Claude, quoted, 115, 132
Lewis, C. Day, 172
Lewis, Wyndham, 126
Leysin, Switzerland, 33
Lieberson, Brigitta, 247–8
Lieder, opus 22 (Schoenberg), 167
Lincoln, Abraham (photograph of), 66–7
Lincoln Center, New York, 156
Lippmann, Walter, quoted, 19
Lisbon, Portugal, 182; *see also* travel diary, Portugal
Literary Language (Auerbach), 350
Livre pour quatuor (Boulez), 118
Livy, 10
Lolita (film), 229
London, England, 9, 78, 120, 124, 246
Long Island, wooden ducks from, 66
Los Angeles, California, 58, 62, 84, 88, 106

Music Center, 105, 106; Monday Evening Concerts, 30; *Times*, correspondence with, 82–7

Love's Labour's Lost (Shakespeare), 349

Loti, Pierre, 186

Lulu (Berg), 99, 132

Maazel, Lorin, 148

McCarthyism, 300

Machado de Assis, family of, 276

Mackenzie, Compton, 307

MacNeice, Louis, 51, 130

Macumba religious ceremony, 277–81

Mad (periodical), 7

Madame Tussaud's, London, 198

Magnificat (J. S. Bach), 86

Mahagonny (Weill), 99, 232

Mahler, Gustav, 134, 146 n., 155

Mahler, Frau Alma, 67

Malevich, Kazimir, 255

Mallarmé, Stephane, 127, 308

Malzel (inventor of metronome), 150

Mandelstam, Yuri (Stravinsky's son-in-law), 39

Mann auditorium, Tel Aviv, 220–1

Mann, Thomas, 75, 142

Manzù, Giacomo, 256

Marenzio, Luca, 337

Marie-Curie University, 334

Marini, Marino, 256

Marion, André (Stravinsky's son-in-law and secretary), 72

Markings (Hammarskjöld), 307, 350

The Marriage of Figaro (Mozart), 148, 252

Mascagni, Pietro, 100

Masson, Antoine (engraver), 67

Mathis der Maler (Hindemith), 99

Matisse, Henri, 256, 314

Ma Vlast (Smetana), 228

Melville, Herman, 179

Mendelssohn, Felix, 14, 142

Mengelberg, Willem, 150

Menotti, Gian Carlo, 97, 100–1

Mirdle (Dickens character), 310

Merleau-Ponty, Maurice, 250–1

Messager, André, 35

Messiaen, Oliver, 14, 15, 47, 199

"Met" the, Metropolitan Opera House, 5, 99; audience, 98, 99, 148

Meyer Collection (Schoenberg), 143

Mexico City, 30

Michaux, André, 315–18, 336

Microtonalist sects, 18

Middlemarch (George Eliot), 127

A Midsummer Night's Dream (Britten), 307

Miró, Joan, 67

Mirza, President of Pakistan, 186

Mississippi, River, 131

Missouri, boyhood of T. S. Eliot, 131

Mitropoulos, Dimitri, 155–6

Mlynarski, Emil, 327

A Model of the Brain (Young), 22 n.

Mondrian, Pieter, 303 n.

Monet, Claude, 303

Montaperts, attorneys, 72

Monterey, California, 66

Monteverdi, Claudio, 48, 93, 302

Monteux, Pierre, 54, 152, 153, 253

Monumentum, Gesualdo, 244

Moore, Henry, 67, 126, 255

Morris, William, 254

Morton, Lawrence, 30

Moses und Aron (Schoenberg), 99, 137, 321

Mostel, Zero, 246

Moussorgsky, M. P., 66, 336

Mozart, W. A., 14, 50, 91, 138, 140, 142, 117, 237, 252

Munch, Charles, 54

Munch, Edward, 249

Munich, Germany, 44, 75

Murai, Jurica, 244

Murano, Italian objects of art from, 66

museums: of archaeology, Sicily, 295; Cluny, 254; Egyptian art, 204; Guggenheim, 11; Haaretz glass, 230–1; Islamic art, Cairo, 215–6; Munch, Olso, 249; National, Dublin, 261; Palazzo Reale, Milan, 263; San Marco, Venice, 189, 190
Musical America (periodical), 86
Music of the Polish Resistance, 337
Mussolini, Benito, 298
"Muszici" Orchestra, Zagreb, 243
Mysterious Senses (Droscher), 19 n.

Nabokov, Nicolas, 72
Naples, Italy, 52, 246; *see also* travel diary, Italy
Nasser (Egypt), 208–9, 217
Nativity (Caravaggio), 284
Nazareth, 225–6; *see also* travel diary, Israel
"Nearer, my God to Thee" (Alkan), 16
Neri, St Philip, 163
Neturi Karta sect, 228
New Orleans, Louisiana, 296
Newton, Isaac, calculus, 26
New York Philharmonic, 105
New York Times, 87–9, 146 n.
Nice, France, Russian Church, 31
Nicolas Priuli (Tintoretto), 213
Nielsen, Carl: Symphony No. 5, 45
Nietzsche, F. W., 141, 143, 144, 316
Nijinsky, Vaslav, 333
Nilsson, Bo, 18
Nixon, Miss Marni, 122
Nobel Prize, 131
Noguchi, Isamu, 47
non-composed music, 19
N. Carolina, festival in, 54
Norton Lectures, Harvard, 42
Nostromo (Conrad), 129
Observer (London newspaper), 146 n.

Offrandes (Varèse), 88
Olaf, H. M. King of Norway, 247–8
Onieda experiment, 161
Onnou, Alphonse, 47
Oppenheimer, Dr., 112
Ormandy, Eugene, 148
Ortega Y Gasset, 185
Ostrovsky, A. N., 74
Otello (Verdi), 176
Ottawa, Canada, 7 n.
Ovid: *see Orpheus*, Index of Stravinsky's compositions
Oxford, England: *see travel diary*, England

Palermo, Sicily: *see travel diary*, Sicily
Palestine, 137
Pandemonium X (Cardew), 18
Papageno (*Marriage of Figaro*), 202
parametric artificial talking device, 8
Parennin Quartet, 118
Paris, France, 38, 39, 75, 78, 119, 120, 151, 152, 167, 179, 246, 328
Paris Conservatoire, 36
Parsifal (Wagner), 143, 189
Passacaglia, opus 1 (Webern), 122
The Passion of Jonathan Wade, 10
Pierce, C. S., 106
Pelléas et Mélisande (Schoenberg), 143; (Debussy), 348
Pergolesi, Giovanni, 21
Perotin, 12
Perse, St John, 130
Peshkov, General Z., 51
Petrov, Vladimir I: *see Stravinsky*, Vera, letters from
Philadelphia, Pennsylvania, 111; Symphony Orchestra, 148
Philebus, quoted, 115
Philharmonic Hall, 5
Picasso, Pablo, 18, 67, 106, 244, 250, 318
Pierné, Gabriel, 153

Pierrot lunaire (Schoenberg), 167-8, 176

Pique Dame (Tchaikovsky), 151

Plekhanov (Marxist), 334

Point Counterpoint (Huxley), 171

Polish Academy of Sciences, 214

Pope John (photograph of), 67

Pound, Ezra, 94, 161

Prague, Czechoslovakia: *see* travel diary, Czechoslovakia

Prévost, Germany (violist), 47 n.

Princeton University, 106

Prokofiev, Serge, 93
Third Piano Concerto, opus 26, 156

Propes, Ahron, 221

Proust, Marcel, 309, 316

Puccini, Giacomo, 92

Purcell, Henry, and Dryden John, collaborator, 96

Pushkin, Aleksander, 66, 246

Qualtinger (German poet), 308

Quantz, Johann, quoted, 146

Quarles, Philip (Huxley character), 171

Quebec Province, 7 n.

Rachmaninoff, S. V., 93, 112

Ramases II (statue), 203

Rambert, Mme Louise, 319-22

Rasputin (opera), 307

Ravel, Maurice, 38, 88, 184, 321

Reiner, Fritz, 148

Renard, Jules, 80

Rennert, Dr., Hamburg State Opera, 265-7

Renoir, Pierre Auguste, 4

Respigihi, O., 105, 106, 150

Rhinoceros (Ionesco), 246

Ricercar (Webern), 122

Rienzi (Wagner), 84

Rigoletto (Verdi), 50, 100

Rilke, Rainer Maria, 181, 307, 316

Rimbaud, Arthur, 309

Rimsky Academy, 153

The Ring (Wagner), 139, 143

Rio de Janeiro: *see* travel diary, Brazil

River Club, N.Y., 128

Rodin, François, 256

Rohe, Miles van der, 10

Romana, Giulio, 128

Roland-Manuel, 42

Rome, Italy, 6, 41; *see also* travel diary, Italy

Römische Elegien (Klebe), 310

Roncalli, Cardinal, later Pope John, 190-2

Roosevelt, President F. D. R., 276

Rorschach tests, 12

Rosbaud, Hans, 105, 148-9

Rosenberg, Harold, 9 n.

Rossini, Gioacchino, 35, 138, 143; cartoon, 66

Rounseville, Robert, 53

Roussel, Raymond, 287

Rowicki, Witold, 227, 333

Rowse, A. L., 306

Ruskin, John, 126

Ryle, Professor G., 249-50

Sacco and Vanzetti (Blitzstein), 98

St. Francis of Assisi, 199

St. Jerome, 204

St. Petersburg, Russia, 42

Salvan, Switzerland, 33

Salzburg, Austria, 151

Sancellemoz (sanitarium), 41, 42
Symphony in C and *Dumbarton Oaks Concerto* completed there, 40-2

Sanskrit, and Indian speech, 127

Santa Fe, New Mexico, 62

Sappho, 308

Sarapheem, Fares, 207-8, 214

Sartoris (painter), 67

Sartre, Jean-Paul, 42, 135

Savoy Hotel, London, 124

Scherchen, Hermann, 148

Schlegel, August, 233
Schoenberg, Arnold, 36, 87, 88, 106,
  115–16, 132–8, 166–8, 175–6, 301;
  Quintet, 136; Trio for Strings,
  176; Violin Concerto, 175–6; *see
  also* under names of separate
  compositions
Schonberg, Harold, 87, 88
Schopenhauer, Arthur, 143
Schubert, Franz, 14
Schumann, William(copyist), 38
Schütz, Heinrich, 302
Schwarzkopf, Elizabeth, 53
Schweitzer, Albert, 69
Searle, Humphrey, 18
Second Regiment March (Alkan), 16
Septet Suite, opus 29 (Schoenberg),
  167
Serenade (Schoenberg), 136, 176
Sex Life of Lobsters (film), 301
Shakespeare, W., 8, 65, 79, 306, 339
  349, 350; quoted, 23, 52
Shaw, G. B., 13, 168, 260
Shelley, Percy B., 310
Sibelius Prize, 182–3
Siegfried (Wagner), 311
Sigurdjörnsson, Thorkell, 19
Silmarillion (Tolkien), 350
Simaika, Victor, 214
Sinfoniae Sacrae (Schütz), 302
Sledzinski, Stefan, 344
Smit, Leo (rehearsal pianist), 38
Socrates, 112
Sommerfelt, Arnold, 21
"Song of Solomon," 191
Sorenson, Ted, 94
Sotherby's (London), 4
Sousa, John P., 13
Soutine, Chaim, 255
Soviet Union, 93, 126, 224, 239, 246,
  250, 255, 338
Sovremenniyaa Zapiski (Russian
  newspaper published in Paris),
  39
Spenser, Herbert, quoted, 324

Staatsoper, Hamburg, 232, 236–7,
  268–9
Stabat Mater (Szymanowski), 336
Steinberg, Saul (cartoonist), 66
Steiner, Rudolph, 151–2
Stern, Anatol, 334
Stevens, Wallace, 106
Stickney, Trumble, 162
Stockhausen, Karlheinz, 11, 12, 18,
  24, 108
Stockholm, Sweden, 54
Stokowski, Leopold, 154
Strauss, Johann, 35
Strauss, Josef:*Alpine Symphony*, 155
Strauss, Richard, 35, 92, 105, 133,
  146 n., 184, 237, 348; collaborated
  with Hofmannsthal, 96, 133
Stravinsky, Catherine (first wife),
  40–1; Mika and Milena (daugh-
  ters), 39, 40, 41; Vera (2nd
  wife), 51–4, 65; letters to Petrov
  (quoted) 65–76, 77; *see also*
  travel diary *passim*
Stravinsky, Igor: on his music, 27–
  51, 54; recollections of by V.
  S., 67 *passim*
A Streetcar Named Desire (Wil-
  liams), in Haifa, 225
Strindberg, August, 176
Stuckenschmidt, 18
Sudwestfunk Orchestra, 105
Sunless (Moussorgsky), 66
Suvchinsky, Pierre, 42
Strawinski, Dr. Konstanty, 334
Syzmanowski, 336
Szell, George, 148

Tales from Shakespeare (Lamb), 233
The Taming of the Shrew (Goetz),
  14
Tanguy (artist), 67
Taps (Alkan), 16, 48
Tchaikovsky, P. I., 21, 42, 101, 105,
  151; Symphony No. 1, 42; Sym-

phony No. 4, 54; Symphony No. 7, 148

Tchelichev, Pavel, 67, 255

Teato Municipal, Rio, 275

Teatr Wielkl, Warsaw, 329

Teatro Colón, Buenos Aires, 6

Teatro San Carlo, Naples, 6

Telefunken, Germany, 35

Tenebrae (Couperin), 302

Tennyson, Alfred Lord, 254

terminology, new, 20, 21

Territet, Switzerland, 321

Theatre des Champs-Elysees, Paris, 179

Theodora, Empress, 188

Thoreau, Henry David, 106

A Thousand Years of Polish History, 337

Three Poems by Henri Michaux (Lutoslawski), 336

Tibetan Book of the Dead (Evans-Wentz), 171

Tiepolo, Giovanni, 67

Time magazine, 104

The Times (London), quoted, 13

Tintoretto, 213

Titian, Vecelli, 128

Titus Andronicus (Shakespeare), 8

Tolkien, J. R., 350

Tolstoy, Leo N., 72, 161, 345

Tomaszewski (writer), 344

Toronto, Canada, 30

Tosca (Puccini), 188, 263

Tourel, Jennie, 53

Trakl, George, 122

Trakl Songs (Webern), 122

travel diary 173–347; Brazil, 270, 282; Czechoslovakia, 237 *passim*; Egypt, 200–19; England, 249–53, 256–9; France, 179–81, 313–18; Germany, 199, 232–7; Hungary, 237 *passim*; Ireland, 260–3; Israel, 219–31; Italy, 188–98, 283; Norway, 247–9; Poland, 322–47; Portugal, 182–3; Sicily, 282; Spain, 183–5; Switzerland, 318; Turkey, 186–8; Yugoslavia, 237 *passim*

Trinity College, Dublin, 261, 131

Trionfo della Morte (fresco), 289

Tristan and Isolde (Wagner), 125, 138, 139, 155, 189, 321, 348

Turangalila (Messiaen), 14, 15

Turgenev, I. S., 72

Turner, Joseph (painter), 126

The Turn of the Screw (Britten), 101

Twain, Mark, Russian translation of, 131

12-tone fundamentalists, 18

Ulysses (Dallapiccola), 99

Ulysses (Joyce), 259–60

Umbrage for Eleven Instruments (Searle), 18

Un Ballo in Maschera (Verdi), 50

Union of Composers, Hungary, 240, 335

Union of Soviet Composers, 240

The Uniqueness of the Individual (Medawar), 22 *n.*

United Nations, 128, 276

The Unknown Answer (Ives), 16 *n.*

Valen, Fartein, 18

Varèse, Edgard, 87–9, 253

Vedova (painter), 67

Venice, Italy, 31, 51, 78, 118–93, 195, 246; *see also* travel diary, Italy

Verdi, Guiseppe, 96, 149, 236, 349

Verklärte Nacht (Schoenberg), 135

Versailles, Treaty of, 346

Vespers (Monteverdi), 302

Vevey, Switzerland, 318–19

Victoria, Queen, 187

Victorian philosophers, 170

Vienna, Austria, 117, 137, 220, 344, 349

Vienna Philharmonic Orchestra, 151

Vier Jahrezeiten Hotel, Hamburg, 233
Villon, Jacques, 67
Vinland, map, 112
Vishnu, Hindu God, 161
Vitruvius, Pollio, 6
Volf, Dr. C. A., 6 n.
Voltaire, quoted, 102
Von Heute auf Morgan (Schoenberg), 168

Wagner, Richard, 49, 93, 125, 138, 139–44, 236, 303, 308
Wagner on Music and Drama (ed. Goldman and Sprinchorn), 138–44
Walewska, Maria, 326
Wallace: see Darwin, Charles
Walter, Bruno, 147, 151–2
Walton, William, 311
War and Peace (Tolstoy), 127
War Requiem (Britten), 13, 15
Warsaw, Its Destruction and Reconstruction (Giborowski), 329 –31; see also travel diary, Poland
Warsaw: Europejsky Hotel, 323–9; Palace of Science and Culture, 323, 340, 342; Opera House, 66; Philharmonic, 327, 337–8
Warshaw (painter), 67
Water Lilies (Monet), 303
Watteau, Jean, 67, 344
Weber, Carl-Maria von, 142, 143
Webern, Anton von, 93, 115–23, 137, "complete" works of (Columbia), 121; "Anton-olatry", 115 Concerto, opus 24, 119; First Cantata, Second Cantata, 119–20; Five Canons for Voices and Three Clarinets, opus 16, 122; Six Pieces for Orchestra, 120; String quartets, 118, 119, 120–1; Symphony, opus 21, 93, 121, 122, 123; Trio for Strings, 122; Variations for Orchestra, 122
Weill, Kurt, 36, 232
Weimar, German, 8
Weingartner, Felix, 147
Weisgall, Dr., 223
Weizmann Institute, Israel, 223
Wesendonk, Frau Mathilde, 140
White House, Washington, 131
Whitman, Walt, quoted, 8
Wiener, Jean, 120
Wilde, Oscar, father of, 260, 211
Wolf, Hugo, 118
Wolpe, Stefan, 105; Symphony No. 1, 105
Wolpe, Thomas, 94
Wordsworth, William, 310
Wotruba (sculptor), 256
Wozzeck (Berg), 99, 106, 179, 180, 181
Wynne-Edwards, Professor, 20 n.

Yeats, W. B., 260, 310
Yevtushenko: see Evtushenko
Youth (Conrad), 130

Zamora Club, Madrid, 185
Zeitlin, Zvi (violinist), 225
Zéphyre et Flore, 90
Zelenka, Johann D., 149
Zemlinsky, A. von, 148
Zola, Emil, 72

INDEX II

Compositions by Stravinsky mentioned in the text

Abraham and Isaac, 55, 107
Apollo, 25
Ave Maria, 31

Berceuses du Chat, 29, 59

Canticrum Sacrum, 191
Capriccio, for piano and orchestra,
   149, 150
Concerto in D, for strings, 58, 101
Credo, 31

Danse Concertantes, 45, 46
Dumbarton Oaks, 39, 40, 42

Ebony Concerto, 40   z
Eight Easy Pieces for piano duet, 30
Elegy for J. F. K., 56–8, 59, 306
Etude for pianolo, 15

The Firebird, 153
The Flood, 94, 266–8
Four Etudes, 32, 33

Greetings Prelude, 54

Histoire du soldat, 27, 155, 266

Introitus, 62, 63, 306

Jue de Cartes, 34–8, 153

Miniatures, 30
Movements, 23, 25, 244

The Nightingale, 27, 33, 27 *n.*
Les Noces, 27, 58

Octuor, 152
Ode, 152
Oedipus Rex, 23, 56, 66, 245, 265, 269
Orpheus, 46–8

Pater Noster, 31
Perséphone, 66, 154
Petrushka, 15, 92, 150, 155, 242
Piano Rag Music, 29
Pribaoutki, 28, 29, 120 *n.*
Princeton Requiem, 23

The Rake's Progress, 23, 42, 48, 49,
   50, 52–4, 82–4, 96, 97, 199, 349
Renard, 27, 28, 88, 266

Le Sacre du Printemps, 36, 37, 80,
   90, 155, 240–1, 253, 318, 320,
   329; composed in Vevey, Switzerland, 320–2.

Septet, Gigue, 30

Sleeping Beauty Ballet (arranged), 46

Symphony in C, 40, 41, 43, 33, 154

Symphony in E flat, 35

Symphony of Psalms, 23, 44, 92, 156, 336

Symphonies of Wind Instruments, 29, 152

Variations, 17, 108, 60, 61, 62

Vom Himmel Hoch (Variations), 294

A NOTE ABOUT THE AUTHORS

IGOR STRAVINSKY

(born at Oranienbaum, Russia, June 18, 1882) has been recognized for more than fifty years as one of the great composers. His compositions form an important part of the repertoires of instrumental and vocal performers throughout the world. Stravinsky also is renowned for his extraordinary erudition and wit, both of which illuminate his published writings. He now lives in Hollywood, California.

ROBERT CRAFT

(born at Kingston, New York, October 20, 1923) is a conductor well known for his specialized attention, in both concert and recording, to such composers as Carlo Gesualdo, Stravinsky, Arnold Schoenberg, and Anton von Webern. He has collaborated with Stravinsky on four earlier books: CONVERSATIONS WITH IGOR STRAVINSKY *(1959),* MEMORIES AND COMMENTARIES *(1960),* EXPOSITIONS AND DEVELOPMENTS *(1962), and* DIALOGUES AND A DIARY *(1963).*

A NOTE ON THE TYPE

The text of this book was set on the Linotype in Janson, a recutting made direct from type cast from matrices long thought to have been made by the Dutchman Anton Janson, who was a practicing type founder in Leipzig during the years 1668-87. However it has been conclusively demonstrated that these types are actually the work of Nicholas Kis (1650-1702), a Hungarian who most probably learned his trade from the master Dutch type founder Kirk Voskens. The type is an excellent example of the influential and sturdy Dutch types that prevailed in England up to the time William Caslon developed his own incomparable designs from these Dutch faces.

The book was designed by Betty Anderson and was composed, printed, and bound by The Haddon Craftsmen, Inc., Scranton, Pennsylvania.